LIBYA SINCE INDEPENDENCE

OIL AND STATE-BUILDING

Dirk Vandewalle

CORNELL UNIVERSITY PRESS

ITHACA AND LONDON

First published 1998 by Cornell University Press

Printed in the United States of America

Library of Congress Cataloging-in-Publication Data

Vandewalle, Dirk J.
Libya since independence : oil and state-building / Dirk Vandewalle
p. cm.
Includes bibliographical references (p.) and index.
ISBN 0-8014-3472-6 (cloth : alk. paper). — ISBN 0-8014-8535-5 (pbk. : alk. paper)
1. Libya—Politics and government—1951–1969. 2. Libya—Politics and government—1969– 3. Petroleum industry and trade—Political aspects—Libya. 4. Petroleum industry and trade—Government policy—Libya. I. Title.
DT235.5.V36 1998
961.204′1—dc21 98-3461
CIP

Cornell University Press strives to use environmentally responsible suppliers and materials to the fullest extent possible in the publishing of its books. Such materials include vegetable-based, low-VOC inks and acid-free papers that are also recycled, totally chlorine-free, or partly composed of nonwood fibers.

Cloth printing 10 9 8 7 6 5 4 3 2 1
Paperback printing 10 9 8 7 6 5 4 3 2 1

كان فرغ جيبك يكثر عيبك

If your pocket gets empty, your faults will be many.

—Libyan proverb

For Joan,
and
for my parents,
Georges Vandewalle
and Maria Gryspeerd.

Contents

PART II: LIBYA SINCE INDEPENDENCE

PART III: CONCLUSION

List of Acronyms

AAN	*Annuaire de l'Afrique du Nord*
ASU	*Arab Socialist Union*
BPC	*Basic People's Congress*
BPCO	*Basic People's Committee*
EIU	*Economist Intelligence Unit*
FBIS	*Foreign Broadcast Information Service (Near East and South Asia)*
GPC	*General People's Congress*
GPCO	*General People's Committee*
GPSCO	*General People's Specialized Committee*
JR	*Al-Jarida Ar-Rasmiyya*
MEED	*Middle East Economic Digest*
MPC	*Municipal People's Congresses*
MPCO	*Municipal People's Committees*
MBPC	*Municipal Branch People's Congresses*
MBPCO	*Municipal Branch People's Committees*
RCC	*Revolutionary Command Council*
SA	*Statistical Abstract (Census and Statistical Department, Tripoli)*
SQ	*As-Sijil Al-Qawmi bayanat wa ahadith al-aqid Mu'ammar al-Qadhafi*
ZA	*Al-Zahf Al-Akhdar*

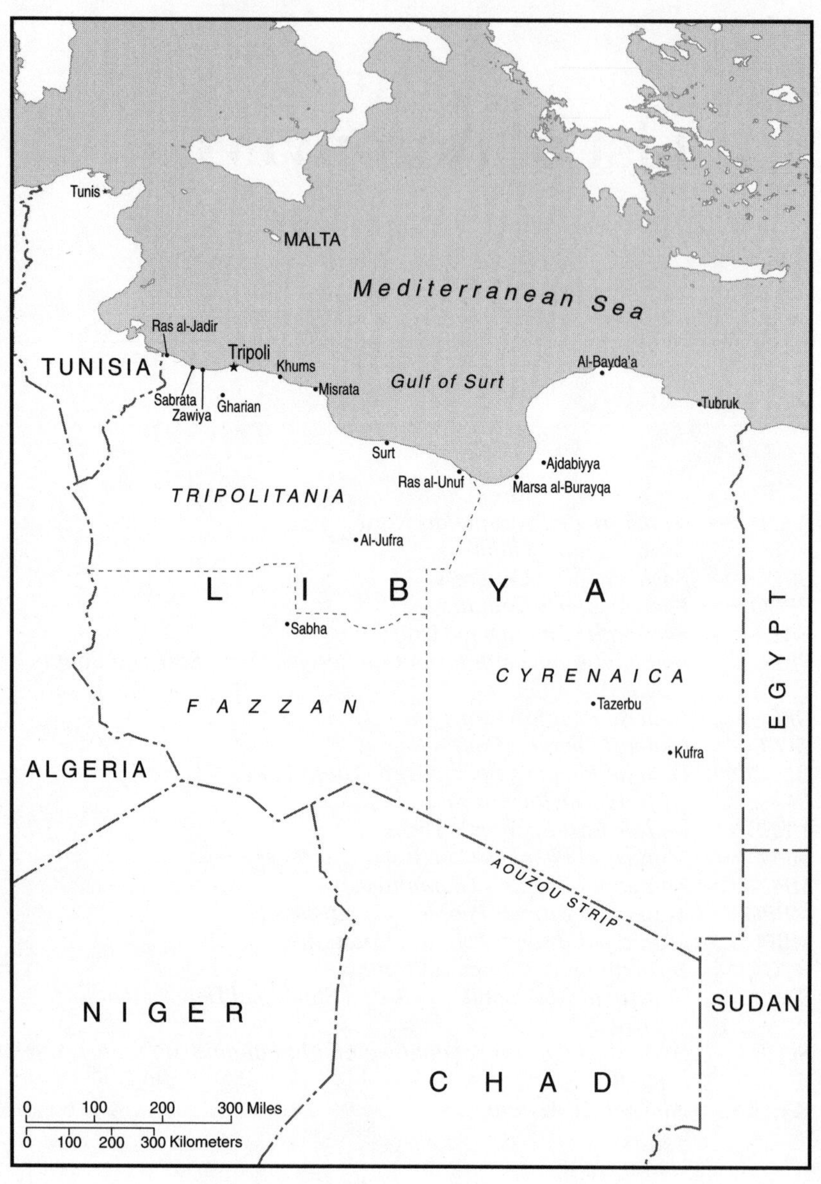

Tunis
MALTA
Mediterranean Sea
Ras al-Jadir
Tripoli
Khums
Misrata
Gulf of Surt
Al-Bayda'a
Tubruk
TUNISIA
Sabrata
Zawiya
Gharian
Surt
Ras al-Unuf
Ajdabiyya
Marsa al-Burayqa
TRIPOLITANIA
Al-Jufra
L I B Y A
Sabha
CYRENAICA
Tazerbu
Kufra
FAZZAN
EGYPT
ALGERIA
AOUZOU STRIP
SUDAN
NIGER
CHAD
0 100 200 300 Miles
0 100 200 300 Kilometers

Preface

Libya since Independence is about the impact of massive and sudden capital inflows on state-building in the Libyan Jamahiriyya—a country that, since its creation in 1951, has relied almost exclusively on capital inflows for its existence. It analyzes how the simultaneous inflows of external capital and initial attempts at state-building affected that state's economic and political institutions and how those institutions in turn influenced the state's ability to promote or halt political and economic development. *Libya since Independence* is a historically and theoretically informed study that investigates state-building under conditions where local rulers do not have to extract state revenues from their own citizens. Although its evidence is drawn from a single case, its arguments are more broadly comparative. Indeed, one of its conclusions is that, although idiosyncratic factors are important, late developers in the region, with open economies and an extreme reliance on capital inflows, demonstrate similar patterns of state-building.

I therefore make occasional comparisons to other oil exporters in the Middle East. I owe a great intellectual debt to those who made such comparisons possible, a debt I detail in the bibliographical note at the end of this book. The small but important political science literature by Jill Crystal, Kiren Chaudhry, Gregory Gause, and a few others on rentier-type development and state formation in Kuwait, Qatar, Saudi Arabia, and the remainder of the Gulf states has been a treasure trove and a constant touchstone for my own writing. Earlier work on Libya by Lisa Anderson, John Anthony Allan, John Davis, and Jacques Roumani inspired me to study in greater depth the anomalies and problems of state formation, institutional and economic development they discerned in late developers in North Africa. Terry Karl's dissertation on Venezuela, and literature by economists such as Ian Little and Richard Cooper on commodity booms and Dutch Disease, provided entry to different cultural contexts.

Although my primary focus is on Libya, I value the insights provided by these and other broad-based regional and cross-cultural comparisons. Indeed, Peter Gourevitch's account of the differential impact of and reaction to the oil crises in the West prompted my initial interest in the legacy of oil revenues on the more politically and economically fragile producing states in the Middle East and North Africa. Finally, although I was able only to glance through Nazih Ayubi's masterful *Over-stating the Arab State* (1995) before finishing the manuscript, his insights concerning Arab politics and society have been truly illuminating to me. I have borrowed from his concluding chapter the two key words that are contained in the title of Chapter Five, in tribute to an intellectual whose untimely death has deprived us of his further contributions to the discipline.

Libya since Independence is based on roughly fourteen months of intermittent fieldwork in Libya. Research in the Jamahiriyya presents daunting and formidable obstacles that can be overcome only through enormous patience, persistence, and long-term contacts and friendships. The lack of diplomatic relations between the United States and the Jamahiriyya, the absence of scholarly exchanges or accommodations, and an international ban on direct airline flights into the country are a few of the difficulties the researcher encounters. They are exacerbated by a legacy of internal turmoil that destroyed or left undocumented many of those aspects of economic and political development researchers are interested in.

This helps to explain why, despite the countless books and articles about Libya under the Qadhafi regime, only a handful were written by authors who enjoyed long-term access to the country. This book relies in part on primary materials, on archival research in Tripoli and Benghazi, on personal interviews, and on secondary sources. In researching and writing it, I have incurred large intellectual and personal debts to many individuals, particularly to Libyan friends and acquaintances who arranged interviews with several of the country's economic managers and political leaders. As one of a few western academics to visit Libya over an extended period of time, I observed firsthand the impact of Qadhafi's revolution on ordinary Libyans, collected data unavailable in the West, and traveled throughout the country. Access to documents and people in Libya remains a matter of perseverance: it depends crucially on friends and colleagues both willing to help and to facilitate access to people in power and to necessary documents.

I must, however, emphasize two points concerning sources and my use of standard economic indicators, as both practical and methodological problems arise when studying distributive states. The first point is availability and reliability. Even available primary source materials in the Jamahiriyya are far from ideal; they often reflect officially approved and selected data. In a fashion that reflects general concerns about the reliability of national accounting data in other developing countries, Libya's officially published reports must be approached with caution (World Bank 1981). A second point is methodology. Many of the standard economic criteria may have little interpretive value in distributive states, because such criteria are normally "production linked" concepts, inappropriate where much of the state's economic function is distributive (Chatelus and Schemeil 1984).

As under all authoritarian regimes, information in the Jamahiriyya is highly guarded and compartmentalized, for political, economic, and security reasons. The lack of clear data also results from one of the peculiar patterns of state-building I note in this book: the lack of distinction between formal and informal state administrative practices. In Libya, this trend has been exacerbated by the very process I analyze: the immense state-controlled inflow of capital allowed the government to alter or ignore the information-gathering tasks that bureaucratic structures typically perform in productive economies, where those structures partly form the basis for further economic and financial decisions. Several of Libya's already weak bureaucratic institutions lost their coherence as the revolution unfolded after 1969, assumed narrow and limited functions, and either were not invigorated when regulation was needed in the 1980s or (as was the case with several ministries) were simply abolished.

The result was a bureaucratic, political, and economic chaos few countries have witnessed. Both by inclination and as a result of its policies, the Libyan government has made documentation very difficult for academic observers and international financial institutions alike. The only real exceptions were data the government would have difficulty tampering with: reports of the country's Central Bank and data pertaining to the petroleum industry—both of which, incidentally, were always kept outside the popular management that all other economic activity fell under. Even revolutions as ambitious as Qadhafi's, however, eventually need to gather more reliable facts, particularly in times of financial crises; thus by the mid-1980s better organized, more abundant, and less ideologically tinted information became available. Nevertheless, colleagues at local universities and research centers would often dispute and amend official statistics in the privacy of their offices or homes. I have attempted to cross-check whatever data were available, but this was not always possible: for example, there are, to my knowledge, no government evaluations of the country's development plans available. Military expenditures also were carefully concealed across categories and sectors, making accurate estimates almost impossible, and figures on employment are notoriously unreliable. The economic data therefore should be interpreted as reflecting trends rather than actual figures.

The same caveat applies to materials gathered through interviews. Despite unprecedented access to the country's political elite, to its economic managers, and to ordinary citizens, I have used interview materials sparingly and with great caution—even though virtually all interviews were conducted without the presence of the official intermediary normally assigned to foreign researchers. For reasons ranging from fear to genuine admiration, virtually no one I encountered in the Jamahiriyya speaks dispassionately about Qadhafi's revolution or about Libya as a political community. Furthermore, rhetoric is part and parcel of all real and self-proclaimed revolutions. In the Libyan case, it became an indispensable element both of the regime's strategy to legitimize its historical role and of the strategies and tactics by which the revolution attempted to consolidate itself. Particularly at the highest level of government, I observed that official rhetoric by the late 1980s had often become a self-reinforcing belief system. Interviews, including those with Qadhafi himself, more often than not became recitations of long-held beliefs codified in the Libyan leader's ideological primer, the Green Book.

Finally, during my stays in the Jamahiriyya I saw that very few of the country's technocrats and middle and upper-middle managers had at their disposal the documentation and data that would allow for the comprehensive and interpretive answers I was seeking. Here also the compartmentalizing of information was all too evident. In several instances, the data the managers shared consisted of recycled figures and projections generated by the (often incomplete) figures the state supplied to international agencies and consulting bureaus. For all those reasons, I have treated my research data with great caution, relying often on careful personal interpretations—particularly of information conveyed to me during interviews dealing with political issues—that relied on multiple sources. I have minimized my reliance on interviews unless the speaker's insight added something new to my own understanding.

While many individuals requested anonymity, there are some I can thank publicly. I owe, first of all, a large debt to colleagues at the Libyan Studies Center in Tripoli, whose director, Muhammad Jerary, facilitated my stay on numerous occasions and arranged several interviews with key advisers and top government leaders. My thanks also extend to Habib al-Hisnawi, Salah al-Din Hasan, and in particular to Miriam Shirkazi at the center, who unfailingly worked on my behalf to set up appointments and to clear my path of seemingly insurmountable obstacles.

Many thanks also to Muhammad Shirkazi, formerly of the Libyan Central Bank, who provided access to Central Bank documents; to Ibrahim Ibjad of the Green Book Center; and to Ambassador Ali al-Hudairi. My gratitude also to academic colleagues, friends, and other Libyans who facilitated my research in the Jamahiriyya: Aghil Barbar of al-Fatih University, Khalid Kadiki of the Libyan Human Rights Commission, Ali Farfar at Bab al-Azaziyya, Ibrahim al-Ghawil and Ibrahim Rabu of the Islamic Call Society, Sassi Salem al-Hajj of the Libyan Supreme Court, Mr. and Mrs. Navet of the Belgian Embassy, Ali Fahmi Khushaim, Rawhia Kara, Ramadan Imteres, al-Madani Abu Twirat Ramadan, Abd al-Wahhab al-Zintani, Muhammad Falugi, Muhammad al-Malhuf, Abu Bakr al-Fituri, Salma abd al-Jabbar, and Mahlul al-Yagubi, dean of Faculty of Sciences at al-Fatih. My gratitude also to people who generously gave interviews when it was not always convenient for them to do so: Ibrahim Abu Khzam, former assistant general secretary of the General People's Congress; Abd al-Ati al-'Ubaydi, former prime minister of Libya; and Mu'ammar al-Qadhafi. A special thanks also to Tariq Yousef, who arranged for an invitation to the national conference of the National Front for the Salvation of Libya in Atlanta in April 1995, where I interviewed several of the country's main opponents to the Qadhafi regime.

My personal and warmest thanks go to Mahmoud al-Fighia (a pseudonym), who first functioned as my unofficial go-between and, as my stay lengthened into several months on one occasion, became a close personal friend and interlocutor. Within the safe confines of their home, he and his family answered privately many questions that could not be asked publicly. A special thanks also to Mrs. Suad al-Ghazali and her husband, who provided lodging for several weeks in one of Tripoli's suburbs when all accommodations had been commandeered for anniversary celebrations during one of my visits. My stay in their home provided me a unique window on contemporary Libya few outsiders have peered through. Their daily struggle to make sense of their leader's revolution was both poignant and insightful, but my analysis and interpretation of developments inside the Jamahiriyya should not be attributed to any of them. My gratitude also to the staff and to colleagues at the Institut de Recherches et d'Études sur le Monde Arabe et Musulman in Aix-en-Provence, who provided expert access and guidance to an enviable collection of Libyan documents. Many thanks as well to Moncef Khaddar, longtime friend and travel companion extraordinaire, whose sense of humor, as always, sustained us on that moonlit, all-night drive to Tubruk.

I thank in particular the contributors to my earlier edited volume, *Qadhafi's Libya 1969–1994:* Lisa Anderson, François Burgat, Taoufik Monastiri, Moncef Djaziri, Monte Palmer and Omar al-Fathaly, Ann Mayer, and George Joffé. These colleagues challenged my own ideas and analyses about Libya. In addition, their own long-term observations of the country proved immeasurably helpful in conceptualizing and measuring some of the arguments I develop in this book.

Funds provided by the Walter Burke Research Initiation Award for junior faculty at Dartmouth College made a final research trip to the Jamahiriyya possible and facilitated the book's creation. Most of the writing took place while I was a visiting scholar at the Center for Middle Eastern Studies at Harvard University and was made possible by a sabbatical leave quarter and a faculty fellowship provided by Dartmouth. For intellectual support, I am indebted to several people at both institutions, to the members of the seminar on the methodology of the social sciences, and to those of my Harvard study group on the political economy of development in rentier states.

Libya since Independence is primarily a book on state-building in Libya. Because of its peculiar focus—meant to investigate a larger, more theoretical debate—readers will not find in it all the descriptive details that have formed the basis of numerous other accounts of the Jamahiriyya that are discussed in the bibliographical note. This book represents a more abstract exercise at revealing the underlying processes and structures of state-building in Libya. A first and condensed version of the main argument of this book was published as "The Failure of Liberalization in the Jamahiriyya" in my edited volume *Qadhafi's Libya 1969–1994* and as "Qadhafi's Failed Economic Reforms: Markets, Institutions and Development in a Rentier State" in my edited volume *North Africa: Development and Reform in a Changing Global Economy.* An earlier draft of the penultimate chapter appeared as "Qadhafi's 'Perestroika': Economic and Political Liberalization in Libya" in *The Middle East Journal*. I thank all publishers for permission to incorporate segments into the present book.

The research for this book, including an initial extended stay in the Jamahiriyya, would not have been possible without funding from the Institute of Current World Affairs (ICWA). I am particularly grateful to ICWA for funding a three-year fellowship in the Arab world that allowed me to pursue my own intellectual interests while immersing myself in the region as few other fellowships permit. Because normal sources of funding for research in Libya disappeared as relations between the United States and the Jamahiriyya deteriorated, this book could not have been written but for ICWA's largesse and for the kind attention lavished upon its fellows by the institute's trustees and by its current director, Peter Martin, who followed my progress with a seemingly detached but critical eye. Six reports for ICWA on Libya were published as part of its fellows' newsletters series.

For obvious reasons, Libyans will likely not be able to evaluate the impact of Qadhafi's experiments with popular rule and statelessness until the Libyan leader has departed from the scene. Until that time arrives, I hope this book provides a tempered explanation of a political experiment that, despite its seeming incoherence and excesses, has been an unrivaled and utterly fascinating experiment in the building—or perhaps, more accurately, the attempts to avoid the construction or elaboration—of a political community and of a modern state in a late developer.

DIRK VANDEWALLE
Hanover, New Hampshire

Note on Transliteration

In transliterating from the Arabic, I have used the classical Arabic spelling except where any attempt to do so would render names unintelligible to some readers—hence *Tripoli* rather than *Tarabulus, Gamal Abdul Nasser* rather than *Gamal abd al-Nasir.* I relied extensively on standard place names as adopted by the United States Board on Geographic Names in its Gazetteer No. 41 of Libya (June 1958), except that the *ta marbuta,* when not in construct state, is rendered *a* and not *ah* as in the Gazetteer: hence *Zuwara* rather than *Zuwarah.* In all except a few familiar cases, I maintained the definite article *al* with the so-called moon letters but assimilated it with the sun letters: *sult ash-sha'ab.* Arabic words familiar to a western audience—such as *ulama* and *sharia*—are written without diacritical marks.

Reliance on the classical spelling eliminates a number of problems peculiar to Libyan arabic: local pronunciation that, for example, reduces *Qadhafi* to *Gaddafi* or *Qar Yunis* to *Gar Yunis,* with the *g* pronounced as in "good"; the use of Berber words and arcane French transliterations of settlements in southern Libya; and Italian usage that transliterates Jaghbub, among other versions, as Giarbub in colonial documents.

A further problem concerns personal names. Particularly after 1969, references to individuals in official documents are often to his or her middle name rather than to the first name. For example, Abd as-Salam Ahmad Jalud—one of the original members of the Revolutionary Command Council—is seldom referred to as Abd as-Salam Jalud by Libyans. Rather, he is often called Ahmad Jalud or simply "Brother Ahmad." I have consistently tried to use the full name to avoid unnecessary confusion.

Finally, Qadhafi has invented, with an almost Kantian devotion, a number of neologisms meant to express the uniqueness of his political and economic experiments. Many of these neologisms are reduced to almost equally incomprehensible acronyms. For simplicity's sake, I have retained the conventional names rather than the elaborate ones the Qadhafi government assigned to its ministries and ministers from the mid-1970s onward. The general secretariat of the People's Bureau for Planning is simply the Ministry of Planning. The secretary of the General People's Committee of the People's Bureau for Foreign Liaison and International Cooperation remains the foreign minister.

Chronology 1951–1996

The dates included in this chronology generally reflect those officially recorded in *Al-Jarida Ar-Rasmiyya,* the country's official gazette. A slight discrepancy may occur on occasion between the announcement and official recording of certain events.

The Libyan Monarchy

24 December 1951	The United Kingdom of Libya proclaims its independence and is headed by King Idris al-Sanusi.
Spring 1952	Political parties are banned throughout the kingdom.
26 July 1953	Libya signs a twenty-year military agreement with Great Britain.
9 September 1954	Libyan–United States military agreement.
January 1963	Re-establishment of Sanusi *zuwaya* [religious lodges].
Summer 1963	The federal arrangement is abandoned in favor of a unitary state.
1963–1968	First development plan.

The Qadhafi Period

1 September 1969	A military coup, headed by Mu'ammar al-Qadhafi, overthrows the monarchy.

29 October	The Libyan government demands the withdrawal of all British troops and the liquidation of its military bases.
30 October	The government requests the evacuation of Wheelus Airbase, operated by the United States.
14 November	The first foreign banks and hospitals in Libya are nationalized.
28 November	First major speech by Qadhafi on why representative democracy is unsuited to Libya.
11 December	Proclamation of the new Constitutional Declaration.
5 May 1970	First colloquium of Libyan intellectuals and revolutionaries to debate the revolutionary orientations of the country.
16 June	The last U.S. troops evacuate Wheelus Airbase.
21 June	Confiscation of Italian properties.
5 July	First major laws on the nationalization of the oil industry, initially limited to the nationalization of the internal distribution networks of Shell and Esso.
1 August	The internal distribution networks of the remaining oil companies are nationalized.
14 November	Administrative reorganization: creation of governorates [*muhafadhat*] and municipalities [*baladiyyat*] or districts [*mudiriyyat*] to break down traditional tribal administrative boundaries.
December	Nationalization of all banks.
14 January 1971	At Zawiya, Qadhafi announces the creation of popular congresses.
15 January	Libyan Producers' Agreements announced.
5 June	All foreign cultural centers, except that of France, are closed.
12 June	Creation of the Arab Socialist Union (ASU).
15 October	All Libyan insurance companies are nationalized.
28 October	Creation of a commission by the Revolutionary Command Council to revise the country's legal system in conformity with Islamic law.
7 December	British Petroleum nationalized.
28 March–7 April 1972	First national ASU congress in Tripoli.
12 April	Abolition of the right to strike.

30 May	The ASU adopts a law making all political activities outside the single party punishable by death.
4 August	The United States reduces its embassy staff in Tripoli to fifteen members at Libya's request. The U.S. ambassador in Tripoli resigns.
November	Qadhafi for the first time specifically proclaims sovereignty over the Gulf of Surt.
16 April 1973	Qadhafi issues his Third Universal Theory and announces the popular revolution in a speech at Zuwara.
18 April	Creation of the first popular committees.
2 June	Popular committees take over the country's television and radio stations.
8 June	Libya accuses the United States of infringing its one-hundred-mile "restricted air zone" off the Mediterranean coast. Tripoli expels a U.S. diplomat for not having an Arabic passport.
11 June	The popular committees take over education, agriculture, and culture in the country.
11 August	The Libyan government nationalizes 51 percent of Occidental Petroleum.
1 September	Fifty-one percent of all remaining foreign oil companies nationalized.
6 October	Start of the Ramadan/Yom Kippur war, leading to the end of Qadhafi's unity plans with Egypt.
18 October	The average price of Libyan crude oil jumps from $4.604 to $8.925 per barrel.
26 October	Libya embargoes oil exports to the United States for its support of Israel.
1 January 1974	The price of Libyan crude jumps from roughly $9 per barrel to $18.769 per barrel.
11 February	Libya nationalizes three U.S. oil companies: Texaco, the Libyan American Oil Company, and California Asiatic.
7 April	Qadhafi resigns to devote himself to revolutionary activities, becoming the *qa'id ath-thawra* [Leader of the Revolution] but remains head of the armed forces. Abdessalam Ahmad Jalud becomes head of state.
May	Jalud visits the Soviet Union and concludes the first major Soviet-Libyan arms agreement.

6 September	Reinvigoration of the popular revolution.
2 March 1975	Students demonstrate against the Qadhafi government in Benghazi.
27 April	New statutes of the ASU announced.
13 August	First major abortive coup against the Qadhafi regime, led by two RCC members.
26 August	Creation of Revolutionary Courts.
3 September	Three major "socialist" laws are announced, restricting real estate speculation and imports of certain goods.
12 September	The United States announces restrictions on strategic equipment purchased by Libya and restrictions on training of Libyans in the use of certain types of aircraft.
17 September	Publication of the first of several essays in *al-Fajr al-Jadid,* which will eventually become the Green Book.
November	First Basic People's Congresses created.
5–18 January 1976	The first General People's Congress (GPC) convenes; the ASU is abolished.
7 April	The government puts down student demonstrations.
25 May	Qadhafi announces the creation of special committees that will intensify the revolution. They will eventually become the Revolutionary Committees.
17 September	Official publication of *Democracy,* the first volume of the Green Book.
13–24 November	Second meeting of the General People's Congress.
4 February 1977	Libya is added to the U.S. Defense Department's list of potential enemies of the United States.
28 February	Extraordinary GPC meeting at Sabha to ratify the declaration of People's Power.
2 March	Sabha Declaration: The GPC special congress declares Libya a Jamahiriyya—a state managed directly by its citizens.
3 July	Major debate between Qadhafi and the *ulama* at Tripoli's Moulay Muhammad mosque regarding the political and economic role of Islam in modern societies.
21–24 July	Egyptian-Libyan border clashes.
November	Third GPC meeting; the second volume of the Green Book—*The Solution of the Economic Problem*—is published.

6 November	Establishment of the first revolutionary committee in Tripoli.
March 1978	Announcement of the elimination of private property.
6 May	Promulgation of the *bayt li sakinihi* policy [the house belongs to those who live in it].
1 September	First calls for the separation of "the instruments of the revolution" and "the instruments of governing."
19 December	Qadhafi resigns as Secretary General of the General People's Congress to dedicate himself to the intensification of the revolution.
December	Intensification of the campaign to abolish all retail and private trading.
2 March 1979	Remaining Revolutionary Command Council members are relieved of their duties. The "instruments of the revolution" and the "instruments of government" are officially separated.
1 June	Publication of *Social Problems,* the third part of the Green Book.
1 September	Libyan embassies are converted into People's Bureaus. Announcement of the creation of revolutionary committees within the Libyan army.
2 December	Attack on the U.S. embassy in Tripoli; the embassy is set on fire.
3 February 1980	Qadhafi calls for the physical liquidation of Libyan dissidents living abroad.
15 February 1980	The U.S. embassy in Tripoli closes.
Spring through Fall	First campaign against "stray dogs" (Libyan dissidents) overseas.
March	Elimination of private savings accounts.
16 May	Twenty-six U.S. citizens expelled from Libya; the United States withdraws its two remaining diplomats.
2 September	Libyan-Syrian union announced; Libya opens itself up to all Arabs and creates Arab passports.
12 May	The right to maintain private practices for all professional occupations is abolished.
19 August	Two Libyan aircraft downed by the United States over the Gulf of Surt.
7 October 1981	Creation of the National Front for the Salvation of Libya, an opposition movement to Qadhafi.

10 March 1982	The United States bans all exports except food and medicine to Libya; the import of Libyan oil into the United States is prohibited.
13 December	Qadhafi announces the replacement of the country's armed forces by a popular army.
June 1983	Second major Libyan invasion of Chad.
Spring 1984	New campaign against "stray dogs"; creation of state supermarkets.
July/September 1985	Libya expels large numbers of foreign laborers in an effort to help balance the country's budget in the wake of lowered oil revenues.
7 January 1986	The United States halts imports of all goods and services of Libyan origin. U.S. companies are prohibited from engaging in industrial or commercial contracts with Libya.
15 April	United States aerial attack on Tripoli and Benghazi.
1 January 1987	Qadhafi declares Jufra Libya's new capital.
February 1987	At the General People's Congress meeting, open criticism of the country's economic hardships pave the way for an attempted economic and political liberalization.
26 March	Announcement of Libya's *infitah* [economic liberalization].
23 May	Qadhafi speech on industrial and agricultural reform.
1 September	Qadhafi speech at the anniversary celebrations of the revolution, allowing the reintroduction of a private sector.
22 November	The revolutionary committees are severely criticized at the thirteenth General People's Congress.
March 1988	Creation of the Ministry of Mass Mobilization and Revolutionary Orientation to limit and institutionalize the power of the revolutionary committees.
May 1988	Curtailment of the power of the Jamahiriyya's revolutionary courts.
12 June	Adoption of the Great Green Charter of Human Rights.
21 December	Pan Am flight 103 explodes over Lockerbie.
March 1989	Creation of a new Ministry of Justice.
September 1, 1989	Libya agrees to submit the Aouzou dispute to the International Court of Justice.

November 1991	Libya is indicted by the United States and Great Britain in connection with the 1988 Lockerbie bombing of Pan Am 103.
21 January 1992	The U.N. Security Council unanimously approves a resolution requiring Libya to cooperate with investigations made by the United States and Great Britain in the Lockerbie incident by surrendering two of its citizens.
15 April	A boycott of commercial airflights into the Jamahiriyya, approved by the United Nations Security Council, takes effect.
3 February 1994	The International Court of Justice assigns the Aouzou strip to Chad, voiding Libya's claim to the disputed territory.
October	Major rebellion by army units near Misrata are put down by units loyal to Qadhafi.
11 November	The U.N. Security Council further extends its embargo against Libya.
5 August 1996	The United States adopts new legislation that threatens retaliation against foreign companies doing business with Libya.
1 September	Celebration of the twenty-seventh anniversary of the revolution.

I

INTRODUCTION AND THEORY

1

Introduction: Issues and Framework

This poor oil, God knows how much we blame it. We would like it to do everything as if this oil is a magic wand. It is not a magic wand. It is a raw material, and its value is limited. It is being sold for a very low price and you think that it is a magic wand or Moses's staff capable of doing everything. You rely on oil, and you do not rely on your efforts at all.

—Mu'ammar al-Qadhafi, in *FBIS* 2 December 1993

The rulers of later nation-states encountered different challenges and opportunities from those faced by state builders in the original core of the system . . . a state's boundaries and identity were determined not only by its own struggles, but by institutions or dominant powers of the international system . . . [that] dictated certain uniform characteristics of states and enunciated laws and norms for their behavior . . . this change in the international context transformed the process of state building.

—Barnett Rubin, *The Fragmentation of Afghanistan*

Although Iran's revolution remains indelibly etched in our minds as the foremost example of the sudden and wrenching socioeconomic and political changes that international capital inflows and oil wealth can provoke within late developers, oil revenues have provoked equally spectacular but sometimes carefully concealed and long-lasting upheaval in virtually all oil exporters of the Middle East (Parsa 1989; Abrahamian 1982; Bakhash 1984). In this book I study the less readily visible but important structural processes sparked partly by sudden capital inflows: their impact on state-building in the Libyan Jamahiriyya and on the nature of local economic and political institutions that were revealed or destroyed as state-building unfolded. At the book's core are questions meant to increase our knowledge about state-building in oil-exporting countries: what happens when rulers of a late developer find themselves freed from the burden of taxation? How does this seeming luxury affect the process of building the local state? And how do local rulers create economic institutions and political processes that under more conventional circumstances reflect the compromises under which they historically emerge?

For almost half a century Libya has provided fascinating and highly original answers to those questions, answers that expand our knowledge about state-building in late developers and about the deleterious impact of oil revenues on local institutions and subsequent development. Created by the United Nations in 1951 at the behest of the Great Powers, Libya's state-building attempt coincided from infancy with large capital inflows that seemingly freed the Sanusi monarchy, and the Qadhafi revolutionary regime after 1969, from creating a political community that matched the territorial state bequeathed to them—and simultaneously allowed both rulers to use the country's revenues to pursue arduously that vision of statelessness. Much of the current Libyan regime's rhetoric has obscured Qadhafi's and his predecessor's attempts to avoid the burdens of creating a modern state in its multiple dimensions (Tilly 1990; Giddens 1987) and to pursue a vision of statelessness cloaked in nostalgia for times when family and tribe provided solidarity and egalitarianism.

The tension between pursuing an earlier form of political community and meeting the exigencies of a modern oil state provides the leitmotiv in this book, which traces state-building in Libya across almost half a century. Although much of the book covers the post-1969 revolutionary period, a logical progression from the monarchy to its successor regime emerges: the pattern of state-building and institutional development that emerged (or failed to develop) during the monarchy was extended—in a highly dramatic and confrontational fashion—by the revolutionary regime. Institutions created during the early part of state-building generated their own dynamics—their "politics of structural choice" (Moe and Caldwell 1994, 192)—that reverberated in time throughout the political system.

Qadhafi's conviction that oil revenues could be instrumental in accomplishing this extraordinary pursuit of statelessness has not been unique. Leaders of other oil exporters have also thought of the oil riches their countries possessed as assets that would profoundly and irrevocably transform their societies, allowing them to jump several rungs on the ladder of social and economic development. In addition to Qadhafi's insistence that the Great Jamahiriyya is, as the arabic neologism conveys, a unique transformative experiment that would put the Libyan people in charge of their own political and economic destiny, Carlos Andres Perez's vision of *La Gran Venezuela* and the Shah of Iran's earlier references to the creation of a Great Civilization are examples of this tendency. A decade after the 1973–74 oil boom, such transformations had clearly become more elusive than local leaders envisioned, and such growth seldom entailed real development. Wealth, much like scarcity of capital, provoked developmental crises no government could adequately address. Economists began referring routinely to Dutch Disease symptoms as commodity booms unfolded (Mahdavy 1970; Roemer 1983), while other social scientists rediscovered rentier states and rent-seekers (Beblawi and Luciani 1987; Becker 1987; Buchanan 1980a, b, c; Krimly 1993; Skocpol 1982; Vandewalle 1990–91b).[1]

During this boom-and-bust cycle, the state in oil-exporting countries, regardless of its ideological preferences, intervened massively in economic management. It became a pervasive economic presence, a role judged necessary by local rulers who argued—in a fashion that reflected Gerschenkron's argument regarding late developers—that their entrepreneurial classes lacked both the skills and the investment capital necessary for international competition. The central accumulation of revenues made government intervention in planning, financing, and managing economic development unavoidable. It also provided each state and its managers with the "power of the purse" to help create, re-create, or maintain political coalitions to sustain those in power, and, if so inclined,

[1] Dutch Disease is named after the deleterious results the marketing of natural gas in the Netherlands had in the wake of major discoveries following World War II. The symptoms normally include, among others, artificially improved exchange rates, preferential treatment of nontradables over tradables, rapid increases of imports, and a frequent neglect of the agricultural sector (Roemer 1983).

to simultaneously extend the reach of the state. Sustained struggles for power occurred among shifting coalitions as new social, political, and bureaucratic institutions emerged that both devised solutions to each country's economic challenges and lent support to local rulers' political strategies and objectives. Those in charge of the state and its new institutions attempted to create client groups ex nihilo, and the distribution of wealth for that purpose became a normal but deftly handled policy instrument for local regimes.

The impact of oil on the fortunes of local states showed both remarkable similarities and subtle but important variations, which tell us a great deal about their respective state-building experiences. Oil revenues, in countries where they became part of larger, diversified, and productive economies, led to distortions and other ills associated with commodity booms. But such impact remained tempered by the boom's contribution to overall development. In Libya, where oil represented the exclusive income of the local government, its impact on state-building, growth, and development was both more powerful and, as Chapter 6 demonstrates, more detrimental to the state's ability to face a severe fiscal crisis.

Furthermore, in countries where the process of creating the territorial state was substantially completed before oil became the primary source of state revenues, capital inflows were mediated through existing state institutions and were subject to extensive bargaining between the state and local societies. In Libya, where both state-building and national integration were in their infancy when oil revenues started to accrue, the process proved more dramatic and was confined or suspended in favor of complete state management of social, economic, and political relations. *Étatisme* in those cases, I contend in this book, was a shortcut that hid a profound inability to regulate both economic and political life. Under such circumstances, the use of revenues as a strategic commodity to help build the state is as likely as the reverse process that we observe in most other countries.

Situating the Debate

The Distributive State focuses on a number of important debates both in comparative politics and in third world politics. It investigates, first of all, the process of *state-building*—the creation and extension of structures for organizing human political and economic life; that is, the growth of formal government vis-à-vis society—in a so-called rentier state (Spruyt 1994). Throughout the book I use the term *distributive states* to refer to states that do not rely on local extraction of revenues and that spend inflows of capital generated by commodity sales as their primary economic activity.[2] Libya is one of a handful of truly distributive states in the world, and it is the only one led by a military regime. In distributive states, state-building differs in key ways from states found both in the West and in the third world that rely on domestic sources of revenue.[3] I deliberately use the term *state-building,* rather than *state formation,* throughout the book to indicate the peculiar nature of that effort in late developers such as Libya, where the international community bestowed the territorial state upon the state's leaders and where the challenges those rulers faced overwhelmingly exceeded the capabilities of that state. My intention is to emphasize the mechanisms by which the administrative capability of public life is organized, maintained, and extended—or left disorganized—through extractive, regulatory, distributive, and redistributive bureaucratic institutions. I agree with Lustick (1993) and Branthwaite (1993) that state-building also includes an ideological-psychological dimension but have included that dimension as an instrumental aspect of the creation of administrative capability.

Charles Tilly (1990), Douglass North (1981), Margaret Levi (1988), Theda Skocpol (1985) and others have analyzed, in studies on state formation outside the region, how revenue extraction and coalition building are intricately linked and produce particular political and institutional outcomes. They argue that the creation of states, particularly strong states, involves a tax-gathering mechanism and a fiscal apparatus, both of which necessitate the emergence of a coercive monopoly. In the context of European history, extraction, coercion, and bureaucratic institutions to regulate and regularize extraction have played crucial roles in that process.

A distributive state, I argue in this book, is highly unusual in that state and local institutions emerge not to extract wealth but to spend it. In a

[2] I prefer to use the term *distributive state* because it more clearly conveys the overwhelming economic activity the state undertakes in what the literature normally calls rentier states. As I elaborate in Chapter 2, the ambiguities of the concept of rentier states make that term problematic. Other purely distributive states, according to my definition, include Kuwait, Qatar, Saudi Arabia, the United Arab Emirates, Oman, and Brunei.

[3] My definition of *state-building* borrows in part from the work of Spruyt (1994), Korany (1987), and Skowronek (1982).

peculiar fashion, oil revenues allow local rulers to skip the historical extractive process typical of productive economies. Revenues can be gathered without capital accumulation; the growth of the state can proceed without the usual bargaining between the rulers and the ruled. The state does not need to be perfected. Distributive states, therefore, provide an ideal testing ground for evaluating theories of institutional and political response to exogenous shocks.

Part of that response is conditioned by the fact that rulers of distributive states do not have to arrive at social contracts with their citizens against a backdrop of coercion; they can often buy out elites and social coalitions and convince them to trade power for wealth, as events in Kuwait, Saudi Arabia and Qatar have amply demonstrated (Crystal 1990; Chaudhry 1989). In Libya, where state-building and the state's distributive largesse went hand in hand, this buy-out ability extended beyond traditional elites to the country's citizens and—as I argue in Part 2—led to a profound depoliticization of the local population that was encouraged by the country's rulers.

The impact of exogenous shocks on local states' institutions is equally dramatic. *Institutions* are the formal and informal rules, compliance procedures, and standard operating practices that structure the relationship between individuals in the polity and economy.[4] Because the state's institutions in distributive states are often articulated, created, and relied upon purely for economic largesse and distributive purposes, they tend to remain, for regulatory purposes, inefficient and weak. In effect, direct state intervention in economic activities—from employment to price setting and production—substitutes for regulatory and extrac-

[4] My definition of *institutions* here is borrowed from Peter Hall's work (1986), but I include informal rules in my definition, as they are often as determinative as formal ones, particularly in distributive states where informality is an important part of the political process. See also Riker and Weiner's definition, which specifies "complex bundles of formal and informal rules" (1995, 99) and North (1980, 201–202) who includes "moral and ethical behavioral norms designed to constrain the behavior of individuals." Different definitions of *institutions* that all focus on regularity and compliance can be found in Verba 1971, 300 ("generally accepted regular procedures for handling a problem and to normatively sanctioned behavior patterns"); Young 1986, 107 ("recognized practices consisting of easily identifiable roles, coupled with collections of rules or conventions governing relations among occupants of these roles"); and Lustick 1993, 37 ("a framework for social action which elicits from those who act within it expectations of regularity, continuity, and propriety"). My account of institutions in this book is almost purely functionalist: institutions fulfill certain demands put upon them by the environment that develops and nurtures them.

tive capability. As I detail in Part 2, the twin process of weakening institutional capacity and increased state intervention often results in informal arrangements that cannot be mobilized when the state faces a severe crisis.

Superficially, then, distributive states may appear strong and autonomous—at least as these terms are defined in comparative politics literature. An apparent political stability masks the profound transformations that exposure to the international economy inevitably brings. The state's stability and continuity may appear as an indication of a degree of autonomy but not necessarily as state strength or capacity: local states have not yet been forced to flex their institutional capability for systematic coercion, cooptation, or taxation.

Governance of the local political economy depends crucially on the continued flow of external resources to the state's coffers. When those external resources suddenly diminish—a process whose contours and impact I detail in Chapter 6—the state needs to refashion its social contract with entitlement groups within local society. If the state loses its ability to dispense economic largesse, the social contract may be renegotiated under conditions where buying out is no longer possible—a condition that renders the previous exchange of wealth for power inoperable. In Libya, as in other oil exporters bent on *infitah* [economic liberalization] in the 1980s, the composition and organizational strength of social coalitions determined the outcome of that process, in ways distinctly tied to the historically constituted patterns of state-building. Despite the enormous social, political, and economic adjustments that economic liberalization inevitably entails, all regional oil exporters attempting an *infitah* have kept their political regimes in power—albeit at the cost of dwindling reserves, at the risk of great and perhaps irreparable damage to their economies, and in a fashion that subtly suggests a window of opportunity for certain social coalitions to re-emerge and to act upon some form of collective identity.

The inability to implement economic reforms raises important questions about state-building in distributive states and about the impact the economic organization of late developers has on the institutional reach of local states (Polanyi 1944). It reflects not only the unique pattern of state-building that historically develops in distributive states but also highlights the deleterious impact of the relative autonomy local regimes can purchase during their own "institutionalization phase" (Stepan 1978). Strategies of economic liberalization and privatization, or broad-based economic reform in distributive states, are therefore viewed as highly suspect by local rulers. In Libya, they were almost immediately abandoned—in part because of the inability of state institutions to help create internal markets and in part because the Qadhafi government clearly understood their dangerous, destabilizing political implications.

The state-building pattern in all regional oil exporters not only obliterated or prevented adequate institutions that make an *infitah* possible but also prevented their flourishing after long periods of neglect. If the preliminary evidence in Kuwait, Qatar, and Saudi Arabia is correct, the economic retreat of the distributive state demonstrates that even in extreme cases of state dominance, the state cannot obliterate long-standing primordial affiliations. Even in Libya, despite draconian efforts to suppress them, shared social interests can be maintained after long periods of inactivity, although, in contrast to other regional oil exporters, they have not yet resurfaced as a political force. Social groups may prove more resilient than the state anticipates: even highly powerful and autonomous states remain embedded within local societies.[5]

In this book I also explore a core question: how does state-building proceed when a ruler finds himself free of the need to extract internal revenues or does not rely on local elites or other coalitions for extraction? In providing an answer, I engage a lingering debate in comparative politics about the precise role of the state in social transformation, a debate Lisa Anderson (1986a, 1987) and Joel Migdal (1988, 1994), in particular, have promoted among specialists of the region, and Thomas Callaghy (1984), Peter Evans (1985), Alfred Stepan (1978), Susanne Rudolph (1987) and others have analyzed outside the region. A central question of the debate is whether the state takes shape under the interests and pressures of social forces or whether it can be an independent factor in analyzing political outcomes.

In the study of Middle Eastern states and of state-building within the region, the debate has yielded two opposing interpretations that starkly reveal the contradictory hypotheses that underpin them. Paradoxically, the traditional attention paid to the coercive aspects of local states' power—what Ayubi (1995) refers to as their "fierce" character—has produced a literature that simultaneously regards state power as over-

[5] Crystal (1995) notes a process in Kuwait where the fiscal crisis, brought about by declining revenues and the Gulf War, led to the return of the country's merchants who had traditionally traded power for wealth. See also Gause (1994) for a similar argument concerning other Gulf states. My reference to *embeddedness* is to Peter Evans's work (1995).

whelming and pays little attention to its exact nature. As Crystal noted, "The received wisdom on the region has long been that states are strong and societies are weak, indeed that civil society . . . has at best a fetal consciousness" (1995, 197). This assumption in several studies reflected either a tacit acceptance or a genuine ambiguity about its heuristic value in explaining local patterns of politics and, within the area itself, a deeply anti-Western ideology—which is not surprising, considering that the concept of the state was an imported commodity, introduced partly by colonial pressure and partly by the local elites' mimicry of Western ways.

In contrast, the dominant interpretation of the state's role in the region, until recently, has reflected the study within comparative politics of other world regions since World War II: an essentially "society-centered" approach that assigned a weak independent role to local states in shaping local politics. With its emphasis on tribalism, regionalism, sectarianism, or other aspects of primordial affiliation, this literature reflected Lisa Anderson's earlier contention that the state in the Middle East was often viewed as "little more than an arena of socially engendered conflict or an instrument of family, sect, or class domination" (Anderson 1987, 1). Much of the literature on the region has been based on these society-oriented interpretations, which often resulted in highly descriptive case studies that gave little credence to the notion of the state as a distinct actor whose actions had a causal influence in local societies.

In this book I intentionally focus on the institutional aspects of state-building rather than on the state as polity. State-building constitutes the single most important process that provides a powerful focus for investigating these competing claims. The institutional aspects of that process—how the state "builds" itself through its institutions—pit the state and society directly against each other in their attempt to shape the contours of power and to elaborate a vision of what a political community should look like. Most oil exporters, at first glance, make the case for the "state-as-dominating-actor" approach. Indeed, they appear to be at one end of the continuum.

This raises another issue of interest: what precisely does the failure of Libya's *infitah* tell us about the nature of the distributive state's power and, by extension, about the state-building with which it was intertwined? In answering that question, this book selectively borrows conceptual tools from earlier approaches, and from the institutional economics literature, and suggests an alternative to the zero-sum approach to state-society relations that marked earlier studies (Migdal 1988). It provides an antidote both to "over-stating the Arab state" (Ayubi 1995) and to the societal approaches mentioned earlier. In a fashion that borrows selectively from institutional economics and from New Political Economy literature, I argue that the interaction between state and society reveals a shared project in which the crucial keys to understanding the power of the state and state-building in oil exporters (and other late developers) are the precise tasks these states are asked to perform, the power they derive from performing those tasks, and the institutions they create in the process.[6]

In the last decade, many specialists studying the Middle East have abandoned earlier essentialist or reductionist explanations once used to describe both the uniqueness of states in the region and the imperviousness to analyses that yielded insights into state-building and state-society interaction in other regions of the world (al-Arawi 1988; al-Naqib 1989; al-Hirmasi 1987; Salamé 1987a, b; Ibrahim 1987; Davis and Gavrielides 1991; Anderson 1990a; Sharabi 1990). With few exceptions, the state-building processes of oil exporters have escaped this interest. Only in the last few years has a small but growing literature of theoretical interest developed around so-called rentier states (Beblawi and Luciani 1987; Crystal 1990; Chaudhry 1989; Vandewalle, 1991b).

I wrote this book, in part, to extend some of the earlier arguments of that rentier state literature by focusing on a distributive state where state-building and capital inflows coincided and where, as a result, its rulers obtained inordinate power to shape the institutional, economic, and political arenas. One of those arguments concerns timing: if existing social groups have weakly developed collective interests when state-building commences, their common identities can be easily erased through the state's distributive largesse. This power allows rulers to weaken civil society and to create politically expedient coalitions by doling out revenues. This selective depoliticization in Libya, as I demonstrate in Chapter 3, began as a process of relatively benign neglect during the monarchy and, as detailed in subsequent chapters, accelerated and deepened after the 1969 coup.

The distributive state thus becomes the purveyor of economic necessities and privileges that, in productive economies, are normally mediated through social coalitions and social pacts. This fact helps us to un-

[6] For a critique made by a political scientist of the New Political Economy, see Bates (1991).

derstand one of the paradoxes of development in distributive states: rulers seem little inclined to diversify their economies—even when, as in Libya, an economic boycott and a continued reliance on Western markets leaves the local regime vulnerable to an international boycott. Local regimes tolerate this vulnerability to outside pressures precisely because the alternative—diversification and growing reliance on internally generated revenues—threatens to create or revive social groups the local state eviscerated, or prevented from emerging, as a political force. Rulers in distributive states retain independence from local social groups precisely because of the external dependence their peculiar economies create—to break the latter distinctly raises the possibility of affecting the former.

The Libyan Monarchy and Jamahiriyya

Studying a small late developer such as Libya is useful partly for the political anomaly it represents; more importantly, its sociopolitical and institutional development can tell us about state-building in similar oil exporters and late developers. Libya's experience with state-building is worth observing because its dogged pursuit of statelessness—seemingly so antithetical to our own identification with the Jacobin state—is ultimately an achievement of "human constitutional creativity" that deserves our attention (Davis 1987, 258). At a time when, as Evans says, "one of the few universals in the history of the twentieth century is the increasingly pervasive influence of the state as an institution and social actor" (1995, 4), Libya's rulers since its independence have openly questioned its validity and have acted forcefully upon that conviction. The wish to create a stateless society, a *Jamahiriyya,* where direct popular participation and management replace hierarchical structures and where those management structures remain prebureaucratic, may strike most observers as naive and archaic.

I hope to show simultaneously that there is nothing specifically "arab"—in any cultural or ideological sense—that explains state-building and development in the Jamahiriyya. A distributive state such as Libya is not simply an extension of the "tribal origins of these states . . . now confirmed by an *état providence,* distributing favours and benefits to its population" (Beblawi 1987, 53). There is undoubtedly a *grossmotif* that runs through Qadhafi's personal politics: the nefarious impact of the West's intrusions now lingers on in what he views as a neocolonial economic domination; and the West's haphazard creation of territorial states makes Arab unity impossible. He has used those resentments on numerous occasions for his own purposes; but this should not obscure the essence of the process this book describes: rulers in other areas of the world, under similar circumstances of wealth and lack of institutions at independence, and discounting for historical specificities, would likely have moved along the same path. And several have attempted to do so.

As in all Arab countries, formal change in Libya has been checked by social, cultural, and religious constraints that resonate within the body politic—the "pervasiveness of informal constraints" (North 1990)—and I analyze them in some detail in Part 2. But while the political or juridical decisions of the Qadhafi regime introduced sudden and often erratic change, those decisions were embedded within—or superimposed upon—a system of traditions, codes of conduct, and customs that informally resisted more deliberate (but perhaps less formal) government policies. I return to that topic in Chapter 7.

The spectacular and often seemingly bizarre actions of the regime obscured the more profound struggles the Qadhafi government faced in its attempts to create and re-create its social base of support during the boom and bust periods. When viewed and interpreted in light of the difficulties Libya experienced with state-building and with the creation of political community, many idiosyncrasies of both the Sanusi monarchy and the Qadhafi regime become relevant and illuminate those processes. Libya's path as a late developer, with its unique incorporation as an oil exporter into the world economy, led to a pattern of state-building that, although decidedly different in degree, is structurally similar to that found in other oil exporters. This book thus suggests that the concept of the distributive state can not only provide us with a better understanding of state-building and its consequences in oil exporters but it can also do so through a theoretically informed account, fortified by empirical data. My conclusions about institutional development, state strength, autonomy, and political development apply to many countries, both within and outside the Middle East, whose rulers rely on external rent.

Overview

For the purpose of analysis, I divided the book into distinct periods: the Sanusi monarchy that ruled Libya from independence in 1951 until 1969, when the country's first economic boom took place; the time between the 1969 coup and the country's second oil boom in 1973; the long decade after 1973 that included two oil booms in 1973 and 1979 and a recession in the early 1980s; and, finally, the most recent period, during which the state attempted to step back from its distributive role. My approach is both chronological and longitudinal, as the central theme of the book concerns the development and changes within state institutions over time, in response to two types of crises: the rapid increase and the rapid decrease of inflows of market-regulated capital.

Chapter 2 provides the theoretical framework of the book. It contrasts traditional patterns of state formation against those found in late developers that also happen to be oil exporters. It raises questions about institutional development, state strength, and the nature of politics in distributive states that sustain my inquiry throughout the remainder of the study. Which tools did the monarchy have at its disposal to embark upon state-building when Libya was created in 1951? How well did it use those tools in creating the necessary state institutions? Those questions, framed by insights from North, Tilly, and some of the institutionalist literature, are answered in Chapter 3. The state's capacity for action in late developers is formed partly by its insertion into the international economy, partly by its social structure, and partly by the historically created institutions that are in place (or not) when state-building starts in earnest. The chapter details how the legacy of Libya's colonial period, together with the initial attempts at state-building and the simultaneous inflows of capital, set the stage for a distributive state with weak regulatory or extractive institutions.

Chapter 4 details how the Qadhafi government inherited this pattern of politics and economic development from the Sanusi government and, in a more systematic way and with the aid of even greater oil revenues, further weakened the administrative structures of the country in a deliberate pursuit of statelessness. Chapter 5 analyzes the long decade of the country's boom-and-bust cycle that started in 1973 and ended by 1986. Initially, during the boom period, the state took on increasing economic tasks—but simultaneously grew less entrepreneurial and heightened its use of distributive institutions and mechanisms for political purposes. As the economic role of the state grew, political and economic functions clashed, and economic problem-solving yielded to political objectives. Formal economic and political processes and institutions were abandoned and gave way to economic distribution, a proliferation of the state's bureaucracy engaged in such distribution, and informal politics—the so-called revolutionary means of governing at the expense of the formal instruments of governing. After 1982 the curtailment of wealth made the customary distributive largesse of the state more difficult to maintain. The regime attempted, through a flurry of political and economic activities, to outmaneuver (and, paradoxically, to outspend) both a looming economic crisis and a growing crisis of legitimacy. The initial part of the bust period therefore represented an interregnum: although the signs of crisis were looming ominously, Libya retained enough financial reserves to extend its distributive measures a while longer.

By 1987 the situation had changed, and the regime felt economically and politically more constrained. When the distributive state faces a fiscal crisis that truly challenges its ability to continue its distributive policies—described and analyzed in Chapter 6—the link between state-building and economic development is more clearly illuminated. The attempt by the Qadhafi government to reduce its distributive largesse would inevitably have entailed more competitive mechanisms—markets—and greater economic differentiation among the country's citizens. But after a long period of deliberately ignoring markets, their recreation inevitably raised tensions between private and collective interests that the government could not reconcile. It ultimately would have confronted Qadhafi with difficult political choices and struggles—intricately linked to the creation of requisite legal and regulatory institutions that define the way markets work—that he and his predecessor had deliberately circumvented since independence.

It was not surprising, therefore, that the attempt at economic liberalization was so quickly abandoned, and the reader by that time should have a good sense of why the Libyan government responded as it did to the fiscal crisis and why the attempt to move toward a market-oriented economy was both economically and politically beyond the Qadhafi regime's reach.

The concluding chapter recapitulates the theoretical findings, draws lessons from the linked process of state-building and oil-led development in Libya, and revisits the three sets of questions about institutional development, state strength, and the nature of politics in distributive states initially framed in Chapter 2. It concludes with a brief, more speculative section on the future of the Libyan state and is followed by a bibliographic essay that contains references to the literature on state formation and on Libya in English and, for the regional specialist, in Arabic.

2

The Distributive State

> The history of state revenue production is the history of the evolution of the state. . . . One major limitation on rule is revenue, the income of the government. The greater the revenue of the state, the more possible it is to extend rule. Revenue enhances the ability of rulers to elaborate the institutions of the state, to bring more people within the domain of those institutions, and to increase the number and variety of the collective goods provided through the state.
>
> —Margaret Levi, *Of Rule and Revenue*

> [In rent-seeking societies] at the level of individual decisionmakers, the behavior, as such, is not different from that of profit seeking in market interactions. The unintended consequences of individual maximization shift from those that may be classified "good" to those that seem clearly to be "bad," not because individuals become different moral beings and modify their actions accordingly, but because institutional structure changes. The setting within which individual choices are made is transformed.
>
> —James Buchanan, *Rent Seeking and Profit Seeking*

"The revenues of the state" Edmund Burke reminds us in his *Reflections on the Revolution in France,* "are the state" (1955, 26). How revenues are gathered, which compromises rulers must make with their citizens to obtain them, which institutional capabilities the state develops to accomplish this task, and how those institutional arrangements reflect the interests of both ruler and ruled: those questions are at the heart of every political system. They have also been, based on historical processes observed in Europe, at the center of the literature on state formation.

What happens, both to the state-building process and to institutions that the state develops, when the ruler gathers revenues without having to rely on the citizens of the state? This book is about a state whose experience differed significantly from that of most other states: as in all other oil exporters in the region, Libya is a late developer whose rulers did not have to worry about extracting surplus from their subjects, who could limit their role to distributing revenues and who, as a result, could invoke the "no taxation, no representation" principle to exclude citizens from the political process.

State Formation: Revenues and Institutions

Throughout the book I distinguish between *production states* and *distributive states*. The former are states that depend on extraction linked to its citizens' economic activity within its borders; the latter are states that do not depend on extraction of its citizens but derive their income almost exclusively from the sale of a commodity. Both are obviously ideal types, although, as this book will show, Libya comes extremely close to being a purely distributive state.

Whether productive or distributive, modern states need a lot of money, for economic, social, and military objectives (Brewer 1989; Furgeson 1961).[1] How their governments get this money, from whom they take it, and which compromises they must make in return for the revenues they extract has constituted both the most basic and the most difficult issues states have faced since the emergence of the modern state system (North and Weingast 1989). It is, nonetheless, a crucial task for the creation and maintenance of the coercive and administrative institutions the state needs (Schumpeter 1918; Skocpol 1979).

[1] I define *states* here as the administrative and bureaucratic apparatuses by which public life (most notably the management of resources and the coercive capability to maintain law and order) are organized and maintained. Although essentially from Weber (1947), my definition also approximates those of Levi (1988), Taylor (1982), Tilly (1990), and Giddens's (1987) "traditional state."

In modern welfare states, taxation is simultaneously the core task of redistributive efforts and a vital element of state economic and political policy. No wonder therefore that "no other public policy issue has been used so widely for so many purposes or been so consistently at the center of ideological conflict over the proper role, size and functions of the modern state" (Steinmo, 1993, 1). Rulers in production states must set up elaborate tax gates in order to tax goods, services, and capital. As a result, they establish intricate rules to decide when, what, and whom to tax, and their administrative capacities reflect those arrangements. They must attempt to devise impenetrable systems so that no citizen or company can avoid entering the created gates. Without an elaborate system for gathering revenue, those in charge of productive economies get no revenue at all; without persuasion—or, failing that, coercion—they get less than their economies should deliver.

The manner in which revenues are gathered therefore matters greatly, with important ramifications far beyond the often elaborate processes of generating revenues and of redistributing the accumulated wealth of the state (Skocpol 1985). Tax systems reflect a broad and competing range of goals pursued by the state. Through its system of taxation the modern state not only raises revenues and redistributes income but also encourages or discourages secondary goals: it stimulates and channels economic growth into certain sectors, and it may penalize consumption and channel investment into economic activities it considers important to its overall economic and social objectives. Taxation is the prime instrument through which governments attempt to shape domestic economic sectors, particularly the private sector. It becomes a tool that state officials can use to manage efficiently their economies: taxes can be adjusted at both the micro and macro level to regulate the pulse of modern economies (Steinmo 1993). The ability to tax provides rulers with the power selectively to target groups of citizens, and by doing so they can dramatically affect their subjects' economic fortunes.

Historically, the ability to extract revenues has resulted in two complementary developments: the appearance of new institutions in response to the growing complexity of the state's economic organization and its need to extract resources, and the demand for representation in return for taxation (Hoffman and Norberg 1994; North and Weingast 1989; Levi 1988). As elaborated before, by *institutions* I mean those formal and informal rules, compliance procedures, and standard operating practices that structure the relationship between individuals in the polity and economy. In examining state-building in Libya, I am interested primarily in the differential development of the country's extractive, regulatory, distributive, redistributive, and coercive institutions (Ayubi 1995; Chaudhry 1989) and, in particular, the fiscal, legal, and information-gathering mechanisms and institutions that accompany extraction—all of which stand in contrast to patterns found in productive economies.

The state as it evolves into a large-scale social order creates institutions not only to maximize revenues and their collection but to solve problems generated by the intrusive nature of extraction and to forge bureaucratic compromises among those arguing for alternatives. Bureaucratic and institutional development represents an important intervening variable between the revenues that accrue to the state and their wide-ranging effects within local societies. As embodied within institutions, informal constraints in productive economies yield to more formal ones: traditions and customs are replaced by economic, political, and judicial rules codified in official records. Formal rules either complement, increase, or overtake the effectiveness of informal constraints (North 1990; Levi 1990). At the same time, the demand for political participation has historically been a direct response to taxation (Tilly 1975; Anderson 1974). States engage in bargaining with those groups they must rely on for extracting surplus. In return for the revenues, the rulers of the state establish social contracts that specify the duties of ruler and ruled. In "social contracts," the latter trade taxation for collective goods such as protection, justice, and property rights and for services such as enforcement provided by the state.[2]

How a state gets its money thus determines not only the compromises its managers need to make with society but the institutions it creates to regulate the extraction and redistribution of those revenues. In the classic European patterns of state formation described by Tilly, Bendix, and others, the extraction of resources—originally meant to pursue war—together with the encouragement of capital accumulation by the power holders' creditors, inadvertently led to the creation of national states (Tilly 1985; Bendix 1978). The interlocking iron triangle of revenue extraction, institutional development, and representative politics was forged over relatively long periods of time (Tilly 1975; Anderson 1974; Webber and Wildavsky 1986).

State-Building in Distributive States

Reflecting the experience of most third world countries, state-building in Libya was not, as in the European context, linked to in-

[2]Hence Tilly's notion of the state as a racketeer.

ternal processes of war and peace that slowly allowed a central authority to take command over a territory.[3] On the contrary, Libya's sovereignty and independence came at the end of a period of international war and peace and were directly bestowed upon the country by the newly created United Nations. The crucial distinction between those earlier historical patterns of state formation and their more recent varieties among oil exporters such as Saudi Arabia, Kuwait, Qatar, and Libya is that the latter obtain their revenues in a highly anomalous fashion: they accrue directly to those in charge of the state and thus eliminate the need for domestic extraction or taxation. Often described as *rentier states—rent* defined here as "that part of the payment to an owner of resources over and above that which those resources could command in any alternative use . . . receipt in excess of opportunity cost" (Buchanan 1980a, 3)—they rely almost totally on the inflows of market-regulated capital for their revenues.[4]

In order to avoid the definitional problems that persist with the notion of the rentier state, I instead use the term *distributive states,* because the primary internal economic function is to divide among their citizens revenues that accrue directly as rent from the marketing of a natural resource or asset under their control.[5] Distributive states do not engage in

[3] Although war has often been seen as the all-decisive mechanism for the creation (or destruction) of states, Spruyt argues convincingly that it need not be the only one and that success in warfare is "only an indicator which itself needs to be explained." Rather, some states were created and persisted because "their institutional logic gave them an advantage in mobilizing their societies' resources" (Spruyt 1994, 157, 185).

[4] The study of the notion of rent is long-standing and has attracted, among others, the interest of Adam Smith (1884), David Ricardo (1953), and Karl Marx (1972). The application of the concept to so-called "rentier states" of the Middle East is based on Mahdavy (1970) and Mabro (1969). One of the central outstanding issues in the literature remains definitional: how much rent must a country receive, and how much state control over the capital inflows is necessary, before it can properly be called a rentier state? In order to solve the problem, categories have been created in order to separate, for example, *rentier states* (highly dependent on rent) from *rentier economies* (less dependent on rent and engaging in extraction and redistribution; or states where rent falls outside direct state control—remittances, for example) or to distinguish allocative states from rentier states. In all instances the outcome has remained imprecise and confusing.

[5] When exactly does a state become a rentier state? Mahdavy (1970, 428) defines a *rentier state* as one receiving "on a regular basis substantial amounts of external rent." Davis (1987, 263) sets "the dividing line at about 90 percent [of total revenues]; Gause (1994, 43) at "certainly over 50 percent, in the Gulf monarchies usually over 75 percent." Chatelus (1984, 1) distinguishes between rentier states and those that demonstrate "rent-oriented" behavior; Luciani refers to them as allocation states; while Beblawi (1987) distinguishes between rentier and semi-rentier states.

the extraction of resources from their citizens. Their overwhelming share of revenues is derived from external rent rather than from internal rent, which requires a productive domestic economy. The rent furthermore accrues directly as revenue to the state and not—as is the case of remittances, direct foreign investment, or international aid in other rentier states—to a combination of state and private sector groups. Nor does that rent constitute income to domestic labor or capital (Katouzian 1979), and the revenues received by the rulers of distributive states are accumulated through the taxation of third parties. The state needs only a few professionals to negotiate the size of the rent with the producers and technocrats to manage the assets fully owned by the state.

The primary political and administrative characteristic of distributive states is the disarticulation of the integrative process that developed in Europe during its state formation period. In theory, the unique fashion in which revenues accrue in distributive states can break the constraints of the iron triangle of state formation: neither taxation nor institutional development based on economic differentiation nor political accommodation must take place. In productive states the need for taxation provides an incentive to expand the income base on which it can be levied, because economic growth is seen as necessary for the maintenance and expansion of state functions. The state can expand and exercise its allocative function only as much as its extractive capacity allows; as a result, it creates interest groups that try to influence the adoption of fiscal instruments. In distributive states rulers do not have to specify property rights to their citizens in order to maximize income; they do not have to create and monitor internal tax gates in order to maximize the rent they receive; they do not have to worry unduly about transaction costs and only need a few agents, who can be hired or temporarily imported, to help manage the system (North 1981; Davis 1987).

There is little incentive then to develop coherent economic policies in order to expand the income base of the distributive state. Income is generated by selling a commodity; economic "growth" can be bought by increasing the sale of the revenue-generating resource. Increases in income can be accomplished painlessly by increasing production of the commodity, which involves undertaking an activity that is not linked to the domestic economy and that puts no demands on citizens. Rather than show interest in economic policies and taxation that would strengthen the purview of the state, the rulers of the distributive state can remain focused on their distributive policies and use them to shape and constrain their economies. Where the state does not rely—either directly or indirectly—on taxation for its expenditures or for the economic policies it wants to pursue, domestic economic sectors rely directly upon the state for welfare gains through the distribution of oil revenues (Katouzian 1979).

The absence of a need to extract resources from citizens has important results for the long-term functioning of the distributive state. At first glance the state's managers appear to profit from their financial autonomy: they can forego the creation of an extensive administration and its ancillary information gathering and legal bureaucracies and avoid the social tension of taxation regulations and collection procedures. From a state-building perspective these immediate gains and the seeming financial autonomy of the state are amply offset by the long-term implications of not extending the state's extractive capacities, for extractive institutions form the basis of any state's administration and make economic regulation impossible without them. They are instrumental for centralizing the state's fiscal instruments. They provide a clear sign of territorial control and indicate the state's social preferences by targeting certain groups of citizens. They form the basis for establishing fiscal and economic goals. They are instrumental in the codification of legal norms and obligations, and in their wake create supervisory, information-gathering, and regulatory institutions that the state can then use for further discriminating among social and economic policies.

The lack of an efficient bureaucratic apparatus for taxation will likely result in "inefficiency in any field of activity that requires extensive organization inputs" (Mahdavy 1970, 466). Particularly in developing countries, where much economic activity often falls outside state regulation—that is, where parallel markets exist for goods and services—and where monetary policy is limited, the extractive capability of the state remains one of the few mechanisms its government can muster to set guidelines for the local economy and to monitor the private sector. To paraphrase Chaudhry (1989), the ability of the state to tax does not only affect what it knows but also what it can do.

Politics and Development in Distributive States

What kind of political community is created when the primary social contract is not between rulers and citizens but between rulers and the multinational companies that provide the state with revenues? In

productive economies, taxation generally requires an implicit acceptance by those being taxed, which links the process to legitimacy and, ultimately, to some form of political contestation. In distributive states contestation may be avoided on the grounds that when taxation is superfluous, it may be done without formal representation—the reverse of the "no taxation without representation" principle that contributed to state formation dynamics in Europe. In Saudi Arabia, Kuwait, Qatar, and Libya, in a trade-off that has been neither formalized nor agreed upon, a long process of disenfranchisement accompanies state-building experiences. This disenfranchisement did not halt all attempts at altering the internal distribution of power, but it limited and circumscribed them for relatively long periods of time, and it introduced on a national scale a process observed in all distributive states: the trade of relative wealth for formal power (Crystal 1990).

The state's economic role in distributive states encourages the wealth-for-power trade. With the state in charge of licensing and regulating all economic activity, the normal division of labor that creates interdependence in productive economies ceases to exist. As long as external rents can be generated, there is no need for individuals to influence public agencies and shape public policy to material advantage. The more the state intervenes in the market, the more internal rent seeking occurs: as the state creates restrictions and grants privileged groups special access to goods through legal monopolies and licenses, it creates artificial scarcities that individuals attempt to offset at the expense of efficiency (Levi 1988; Buchanan 1980; Tullock 1980; Tollison 1982; Bates 1981, chapter 6).[6] Individuals increasingly become rent takers—a process rulers often encourage for reasons of political manipulation, despite the enormous social and economic waste it engenders.

The state itself may make few demands upon its citizens and may remain minimal beyond some cursory attention to issues of distribution and the necessary coercion to keep rulers in power. It becomes only a superficial arena for bargaining. In distributive states rulers must not, strictly speaking, "offer some return for the revenue extracted." The resulting form of government—in all cases exclusionary—reflects the small percentage of the population that is part of this limited contract

[6]Buchanan (1980, 4) defines *rent seeking* as "behavior in institutional settings where individual efforts to maximize value generate social waste rather than social surplus."

(Levi 1988, 10). The constraints on rulers' behavior are relatively few. They do not need to extract revenue from the population and do not have to adopt particularly coercive or predatory methods vis-à-vis the citizens to obtain revenues: revenues can be maximized, in principle, simply by increasing production. The only constraints are those of the international market through its pricing mechanism, not those imposed over time by the citizens. This is an important consideration I return to in Chapter 6.

At the same time, there is, within distributive states, no need for clearly articulated bureaucracies and state institutions to evolve to capture gains from trade. In this regard, distributive states face peculiar difficulties. The pattern of economic development they are able to adopt removes some of the constraints Levi noticed in productive economies, where "transformations in the state tend to correlate with changes in the relative prices of goods and services and with changes in the specialization and division of labor" (Levi 1988, 5). Whereas in productive economies the adoption and implementation of a development strategy is subject to sociopolitical restraints and to the limitations of the state's organizational capacities, both the collection and the amount of the distributive state's revenues seemingly diminishes these constraints.

As such, the expanded range of resources may also increase the structure of choices distributive states can make, both in the development goals they pursue and the strategies they rely on (Karshenas 1990). But unless deliberate policies to that effect are adopted, distributive states can achieve high rates of growth without any immediate need to make structural adjustments in the domestic economy. Such *perverse growth*—where the growth pattern is not viable in the long run and is subject to sharp cyclical fluctuations in the medium term—is likely to occur when oil income rises quickly (either because of rising oil prices or increased international demand) and is a result of the pursuit of the sociopolitical objectives rulers insist upon (Kalecki 1979). At the same time, rulers of distributive states can simultaneously pursue both growth and equity and thus avoid the classic pattern of widening the gap of inequalities, once thought unavoidable as economic growth takes hold in late developers (Kuznets 1966).

These policies do not necessarily benefit every citizen equally, even though most rulers of distributive states make great efforts to portray them as highly egalitarian. In general, however, the financial rewards furnished to local citizens are such that unequal distribution—unless conspicuously so—is unlikely to lead to the coalescing of political interests or to the demand for changes in political and economic institutions in charge of distribution. One possible outcome—in Saudi Arabia and Kuwait in particular—is that the governmental bureaucracy turns itself into a rentier class whose independent source of income provides it with considerable power over time. Another alternative—primarily in Libya—is that citizens themselves remain rent takers and engage in unproductive economic activities in a process that leads to the "rentier-type development" often commented on in the literature on oil exporters. In such a scenario, manual labor becomes devalued, and expatriates are increasingly imported for manual labor while the country's citizens move into semimanagerial positions or become employers.

There is another, more generalized political outcome to this individual rent-taking: because citizens do not contribute to the creation of wealth, they are hard pressed to argue for a greater share of the state's distributive largesse. Luciani points out the important political result: "[T]o the citizen who feels his [*sic*] benefits are not enough, the solution of manoeuvering for personal advantage within the existing setup is always superior to seeking an alliance with others in similar conditions" (Luciani 1987, 74). Politics in rentier states thus by nature tends to be atomistic and generates personal rather than group interests. An important corollary is that the loyalty of citizens is likely to focus on the system that is in charge of distribution rather than on the individuals who provide it—even though, as particularly in Libya, a careful and deliberate association of the two can yield a high political payoff, especially if it involves a charismatic leader.

There is another important political result: if neither the citizens' relations with the means of production nor their relative earnings provide a clear cause for social stratification, the means of production become a function of relative dependence on the state (Katouzian 1979). Social stratification is likely to result from the distributive and spending patterns of the state, and the state may be able to create entire sectors through its distributional policies (Chaudhry 1989). In distributive states, we find high levels of corporatist policies or *segmentary incorporation*—where certain segments of the population are coopted while others are deliberately left depoliticized—in order to promote and maintain this particular role of the state (Becker 1987). Far from the passive role often ascribed to rulers of distributive states, they tend to be actively trying to promote their clients and to buy off other claimants to the wealth.

The absence of supervisory, information-gathering, and regulatory institutions in distributive states has an important political result: rulers can easily conceal the country's revenues from public scrutiny. They may fail "to distinguish treasury from pocket" without worrying unduly about recriminations. Or they can reward, without public accountability, groups whose support they rely on. Rulers of distributive states therefore "may consider it prudent and efficient to refrain from making explicit rules about the division of spoils among interested parties" (Davis 1987, 18–19) and may not want the state's revenues and spending patterns revealed. Finally, because the state is the only real decision maker concerning economic policies, distribution, investments, and other activities and assigns these decisions to itself rather than to the market, it becomes inevitably the focus of conflict and not simply the arena where conflict is played out.

Politics and development in purely distributive states will thus reflect both the unique historical circumstances under which state-building takes place and the unique way of revenue gathering. In the West, the state's legitimacy—and the concurrent notions of citizenship and clearly specified rights—has been linked intimately to the power of the state to tax and to the resultant political representation and participation among the state's citizens. Where neither exist, legitimacy will not reflect this compromise but more likely the historical, religious, or cultural notions of the rights and duties of ruler and ruled. The rulers of such states will rely on personalized power, either legal or extralegal. They dominate the coercive and suppressive apparatus of the state. Their legitimacy is seldom arrived at formally—in either a constitutional or traditional sense—but is determined by the possession of power.

As a result, the political legitimacy of distributive states often remains quite low and is inextricably bound to the rulers or to their ability to continue the state's welfare functions. Although the political system may be portrayed as representing the interests of citizens—a distinct part of Libya's strategy but unknown in Saudi Arabia or Kuwait—it is unlikely to have much significance beyond window dressing and lip service. True political debate is rare, and representative bodies often are meant to "vent and control some of the resentment that even court politics generates" (Luciani 1987, 14) or to become institutions that help strengthen rulers' chances for political survival (Palmer 1995).

It does not mean, however, that politics is suspended—only that the kind of politics practiced is highly peculiar and follows from the roles both the ruler and the citizens assume in distributive states. Although the ruler could remain passive beyond basic distribution simply by doling out money, continual and careful political monitoring and adjustment still need to take place. The ruler's fortunes are closely tied to distributive ability and to effectiveness in managing support coalitions. Changes in the international economy to which the country is highly vulnerable and in citizens' perception of the ruler's ability to provide continued distribution and to manipulate informal politics must constantly be attended to. In this peculiar form of political management, the objective is not to engage upon political institution-building or to expand the country's capacity to settle political issues through (depoliticized) institutions but rather to expend political energy on keeping the ruler and supporting coalitions in power.

Indeed, because support coalitions are highly dependent on the state—and in some cases are created directly by the state through its financing policies—the pattern of corporatism found in distributive states entangles the state in economic issues that arise between different groups. During periods of both booms and stagnation, the distributive state needs to increasingly intervene, but in a peculiar fashion. In a boom the state faces a snowball effect when the "economic development itself . . . [fosters increasing] actual or potential demands on the system" that force the state to ever increase entitlements "in order to forestall systemic crisis" (Becker 1987, 73). During stagnation, the state must arbitrate among groups for shrinking resources. In all oil exporters, the petroleum bonanza had run its course by 1986, and the state had to face not only economic retrenchment but an incipient fiscal crisis that threatened to turn quickly into a political one as client groups clamored for protection. At that point, as Chapter 6 demonstrates, the predicted barriers to reform in distributive states are institutional and political: it is beyond the state's capacity to create institutions for managing a fiscal crisis after a period of inactivity or, in some cases, atrophy. But the key constraint, more often than not, are the protests made against the proposed austerity measures by the regime's key client groups.

In sum, *institutionalization*—"the tendency of patterns of behavior, norms, or formal structures to persist through time" (Krasner 1989, 77)—found in productive economies to meet the growing complexity of the state's activities does not occur in distributive states beyond those institutions necessary for distribution. Institutionalization can be significantly slowed down; informal constraints will have "great survival tenacity" because they solve basic social, political, and economic exchange problems among citizens (North 1990, 91). Contrary to what Luciani (1987) has argued, we can therefore expect a high degree of persuasion—symbolic politics—to take place within distributive states.

Such persuasion is meant to compensate for the absence of institutionalization or of formally obtained legitimacy, the "generalized consent to rules of conformity enforced by the rulers of the polity" (Levi 1988, 68).

Where formal mechanisms for political energy or economic differentiation are absent, and where state institutions are weak and few, the ruler willy-nilly must either rely on outright coercion or develop considerable skills in generating both support and legitimacy through informal arrangements and symbolic mechanisms. What the ruler cannot—or does not want to—achieve politically, he may accomplish symbolically. In Libya, particularly, we find its leader employing a powerful combination of ideology, charisma, reliance on moral suasion and religious symbols, and invented national myths—the fight against the Italian fascists yesterday; the struggle against the West today—to instill a sense of community and create political allegiance where formal mechanisms are absent or meaningless. This incorporation of traditional references is part of the process of accommodating enormous changes within a tradition that needs to be reinvented.

Although some distributive states have adopted formal constitutions, they do not represent "the fundamental underlying rules designed to specify the basic structure of property rights and control of the state" (North 1981, 203), nor do they reflect the polity's most fundamental rules that define political roles and relationships within it. The split in distributive states between formal (but powerless) political institutions and the real loci of power tends to be so pronounced that citizens give up interest in politics altogether.

In addition, because political parties meant to represent the economic interests of citizens are unlikely to emerge in distributive states, whatever political opposition develops normally possesses, by default, either an ideological or cultural orientation—in the Libyan case an opposition with Islamic ideals—that inevitably brings it into conflict with the ruler's attempts to use the same beliefs. A heightened importance is then given to symbolic expressions and claims, but they mask the real origin of whatever political struggle takes place. Both phenomena—the importance of informal politics and politics based on highly charged symbolic elements—are the result rather than the cause, as more reductionist analyses would have it, of a peculiar form of economic and political development.

In Libya the notion of informal, deinstitutionalized politics has been taken to its logical extreme: both the kingdom and the Qadhafi regime have repeatedly expressed a remarkably similar suspicion of a political community within national boundaries and of the modern state with its clearly articulated and hierarchical institutions and centralized decision-making procedures. The newly created state in 1951 never faced what in European counterparts formed an indispensable rationale for state formation—a common enemy or problem that required coordination among the individuals facing it—although its rulers would occasionally create such obstacles as part of their efforts at political legitimacy. In Libya, particularly after 1969, the country's rulers based their call for statelessness on the ideas that the Arab nation is the only significant and valid historical example of a political community and that modern states in the Middle East are the artificial creation of the West that have no historical validity.

The vision of statelessness as expressed by Libya's rulers is long-standing and has been investigated by political scientists and social and political anthropologists in various settings (Evans-Pritchard 1940; Bates 1983; Colson 1974; Ensminger 1992; Taylor 1982; Davis 1987; Mair 1962).[7] It occurs in societies that do not require the complexities, hierarchy, structured social relationships, and differentiated roles of the modern state, that are assured of economic self-sufficiency, that do not have to hand coercion over to a third party to maintain order, and that have primordial ties and reciprocity both efficient and powerful enough to meet the basic needs of the community. Its long-term pursuance is highly uncommon, however, in a country that is tightly integrated into the world economy and during a historical period when the territorial state is the dominant expression of national political and economic organization.

Although the very notion of a *Jamahiriyya* is for those reasons alone both an anachronism and a utopia (First 1975), Qadhafi has cultivated what he views as indigenous political mechanisms at the expense of national ones. (Indigenous political mechanisms rely on a community with common values that can provide both for social order and for collective action; it is a community that relies on the equality of its members, in which enforcement is decentralized and relies on cooperation rather than on third-party specialists such as state representatives.) As expressed in his Green Book, the community envisioned by Qadhafi relies on consensus rather than majority or dictatorial rule and is guided by informal rather than formal constraints.[8] Obviously, Qadhafi cannot

[7] In reality, although Qadhafi's vision does include a questioning of the state's legitimacy for its monopoly over force, what he really envisions is, to use Colson's language that is based on Mair, a "minimal" or "diffuse" government "when the organization of public affairs is left . . . to the community as a whole" (Colson 1974, 2, 15).

[8] These ideas were expressed at greater length in his Green Book; see Chapter 5.

escape the state and its institutions; even the seemingly simple task of distribution has required institutions, organizations, and administrative practices and regulations that eventually provided employment for most of his citizens. But, through enormous expenditures, he can pursue his notion that the state is irrelevant to its citizens.

Distributive States: Oil and History

Whereas in Europe the protracted process had strictly been one of state formation—the forging of the iron triangle over time that resulted in the territorial state—in late developers such as Libya the process was fundamentally different and disarticulated. The territorial state had been created by outside powers before state-building started. It was up to Libyans after independence to engage in state-building, as some authors have defined it: to extend the reach of the territorial state through administrative, bureaucratic, legal, and strictly coercive instruments and measures and in the process to adopt the symbolic accoutrements of twentieth-century statehood (Gerschenkron 1962; Jackson 1990). As Eric Davis has argued, this allowed a dynamic element to come into the concept of state formation, focusing on how the rulers can increase the state's strength.[9]

At the outset of state-building, some late developers were more privileged, or less disadvantaged, than others. The impact of each state's insertion in the world economy and the differing legacy of colonialism produced a checkered pattern of potential strengths and weaknesses that can only be understood in the historical context of each late developer (Owen 1992; Anderson 1986; Davis and Gavrielides 1991). Of particular

[9]Davis (1991) also distinguishes between state formation and what he calls "statecraft." His notion differs from mine in that it focuses on the "skills whereby political elites or ruling classes promote state formation." Davis is generally less concerned with the institutional, formal forms through which power can be accumulated and expressed and sees politics as equally relevant in state-building. While not disputing that informal politics is important, I argue that it lingers when formal politics remains outside the reach of the rulers of distributive states such as Libya. Contrary to Davis, I do not consider a "strong state . . . one that can exercise this craft [to use and invent symbols] and that continues to forge emotive links with the populace over which it rules." On the contrary, I consider this a sign of lingering weakness and of an inability or unwillingness to move toward institutionalized forms of power. And I fundamentally disagree with his notion that the use of symbols or historical memory "helps create a more favorable environment to exercise more overt, institutionalized forms of power and authority" (1991, 13).

interest here are the legacies of bureaucratic forms and of the forms of control over local societies bequeathed to the new states' rulers at independence; in this regard Libya was extremely weak, virtually a blank slate. The Libyan kingdom's potential for engaging upon successful state-building looked highly problematic: the emerging clientelist ties of the Ottoman period had crumbled and been replaced by a resurgence of kinship networks during the Italian occupation of the country; institutional and administrative development had been halted and reversed. Furthermore, in distributive states where state-building closely coincides with the inflows of capital, the efforts of the state to raise its ambitions were less pressing (Krimly 1994; Chaudhry 1992). Indeed, it was only in 1963 that Libya was unified as an immediate reaction to the exigencies of oil-driven development: the need to create national bureaucracies and administrative structures and to replace existing kinship networks with nationwide patron-client relationships, and the need for clearly defined property rights for the oil companies that provided the rent.

Capital inflows thus became the catalyst for the profound institutional, political, and social transformations that take place within oil exporters, but they cannot fully explain state-building in distributive states. After all, the features of political development in the region that mark distributive states are also found in non–oil states and precede oil development. Secondly, distributive states show a large variety of political forms, indicating once more that there are other contributing factors in state-building (Bromley 1994). Owen (1992) and Anderson (1986) both suggest that a more complete understanding of state-building needs to incorporate, in addition to the impact of oil-led development, the development that occurs within a framework that is historically shaped as the state becomes integrated into the capitalist world economy.

The structures left to the territorial state by its colonial powers determine in part how attractive the newly created state is and the responses it engenders as it attempts the difficult process of expanding, centralizing, and consolidating the state apparatus and its accompanying institutions and organizations. Analyzing the consolidation of the state apparatus in countries such as Libya by focusing on a combination of oil development (the patterns of internal development and the position of the oil state in the international economy) and historical context (the preexisting social formations) yields a more fine-grained interpretation. This interpretation is no longer reductionist or essentialist; it traces state-building patterns not simply to oil, Islam, or other cultural factors but to the internal and external obstacles late developers face. This refractory inheritance for state-building from the colonial period once more forms an important factor in understanding the lack of enthusiasm for a single political community in some of today's distributive states.

State Strength, Autonomy, and Social Setting

As distributive states do not rely on domestic surplus,[10] one would expect their peculiar insertion into the international economy to have as its corollary domestic state autonomy (Anderson 1987), possessing the ability "to define and pursue an agenda not defined for it solely by private societal interests" (Caporaso and Levine 1992, 181). Or, in a developmental sense, it may be able to "make decisions that favor the long-range vision of technocrats over the short-term interests of dominant social groups" (Chaudhry 1989, 111).[11] It seems almost intuitive at first glance that the more the rulers' sources of revenues are external to their domestic constitutents, the greater their bargaining power will be. During the oil booms, the actions of rulers in all distributive states confirmed this (Kiser 1986). In the literature, state autonomy is normally considered a prerequisite for state strength, the ability "to implement official goals, especially over the actual or potential opposition of powerful social groups or in the face of recalcitrant socio-economic circumstances" (Skocpol 1985, 9ff).

Although state autonomy has been a central focus in explaining state capacity in much of the literature that "brings the state back in," one must question the utility of applying the notion of state autonomy to distributive states. Unlike states with productive economies that engage in the redistribution of resources and provide organized groups within society the institutionalized means to prevent certain state policies, income in distributive states accrues directly to the state, which then distributes it among its citizens in patterns that promote its interests. The dual and contradictory nature of the distributive state is that it is in charge of all economic activity that makes it, particularly during the

[10] Keep in mind Skocpol's observation (1985, 17) that the crucial element in gauging the power of the state to "create or strenghten state organizations, to employ personnel, to coopt political support, to subsidize economic enterprises, and to fund social programs" lies in the means the state has to raise and deploy financial resources.

[11] A conclusion Skocpol also reaches in her "Rentier State and Shi'a Islam in the Iranian Revolution" (1982). The important exception to this general analysis can be found in Ikenberry (1986).

boom periods, financially autonomous. But this autonomy allows it to avoid creating institutions and mechanisms that could translate this strength into a long-term power base. The state has the dubious luxury of not expanding its overall capacity to govern effectively: its rulers dole out or, at best, intervene or mediate between those making claims upon the generated revenues—but only if it becomes necessary do to so for political reasons.

Superficially, the distributive states looked in some aspects financially autonomous and strong during the oil booms. They monopolized, in a fashion seldom encountered elsewhere, all coercive, political, and economic resources and were able to shape political relationships in their support.[12] State managers did not seem beholden to any coalition that could impede the implementation of their goals. Contrary to Levi's hypothesis (1988, 10) that "rulers [in productive states] maximize revenue to the state, but not as they please" in distributive states such as Saudi Arabia, Libya, Qatar, and Kuwait, the rulers could do so at their own pleasure during the boom period—the only limitation being their inability to control the price and the market share for oil on the international market. As a general rule, local citizens grew highly reliant on the economic resources and the corresponding distributive largesse the government controlled and once more increased the bargaining power of their rulers.

In reality, however, the institutional and political relationships that developed during the boom period and the state's reliance on distribution mask any real measure of that strength, as events in the bust period would soon demonstrate in all regional oil exporters. Most of the transformations that had taken place had been made possible by massive spending via elaborate distributive mechanisms that had been created when oil revenues started to accrue directly to the state. And while the distributive functions and institutions of the state proliferated, its extractive and regulatory capabilities foundered. Its ability to tax its citizens declined precipitously, as did the functions of the bureaucratic, legal, and information-gathering and information-providing institutions. In distributive states, the institutional response to market-regulated capital remains low and is limited to institutions that deal directly with the international economy. State bureaucracies—particularly in countries such as Libya and Saudi Arabia, where institutional development was

[12] Levi (1988, 19) points out accurately that it "is difficult to imagine a situation in which rulers monopolize all these resources, although the hydraulic societies probably come close."

virtually nonexistent when state-building started—are often a direct response to international economic forces. These bureaucracies closely reflect and are highly vulnerable to changes in the international market and are little prepared to deal with changing conditions when oil booms turn into oil busts. Institutions created during the oil booms have an "institutional obsolescence" that distributive states must face in a recession that leaves them highly inflexible and undifferentiated (Chaudhry 1989, 107).

The notion of strength must thus be disarticulated and analyzed across the institutions and bureaucracies the state creates or chooses to ignore to find out under which circumstances "windfall revenues . . . can render states *both* more autonomous from societal controls and, because social roots and political pacts are weak, more vulnerable in moments of crisis" (Skocpol 1982, 35ff, 44). The issue of autonomy not only must concern the state's ability to escape the demands of domestic accountability but, more importantly, must focus on its ability to promote and implement policies of economic and social transformation. Although during their oil booms all distributive states exhibited all the symptoms of state autonomy, the real measure of strength inevitably arrives when the state encounters a fiscal crisis that threatens the continuity of its distributive policies. This crisis will almost certainly be a fiscal one, prompted by international developments beyond the control of the state's managers.

In the case of all oil exporters, the crisis occurred after 1985, when revenues declined precipitously as a result of changes either in oil prices or in the demand for oil. Adjustment to lower capital inflows can then be accomplished in many ways. But, most importantly for distributive states, the reduction in capital inflows necessitates curtailment of the state's previous distributive largesse. Even if suggested reforms are mild—as they were in Saudi Arabia and Kuwait—the crucial parameters for success are whether the state can force upon the political coalitions it helped to create during its distributive period economic adjustments that affect its fortunes and whether it is institutionally equipped to implement the necessary changes, which may include, for the first time, extraction.

The response to a fiscal crisis thus tells us much about the strength and autonomy of the state and about state-building. In all distributive states that power was sorely lacking after 1985. In Libya, despite Qadhafi's willingness to abandon some of his earlier spectacular populist measures, the country singularly failed to implement an economic reform that would have substituted domestic revenues for the diminishing external capital. But this failure in distributive states to adopt liberalization policies was not due solely to the lack of political will, as several accounts suggest. In all cases the steady evisceration of regulatory and information-gathering institutions and mechanisms over the decades made the transition toward a market economic system impossible.

When states possess financial autonomy during their initial attempts at state-building, they may prematurely curtail their power: state institutions do not develop the capacity to penetrate society and, because of their distributive nature, are prevented from doing so as state-building continues. As a corollary, financial autonomy during this initial phase is likely to harden, and existing social divisions within distributive states will become institutionalized as those groups that control the state attempt to prevent the creation of institutions that could develop into truly national organizations. The state's financial autonomy thus casts a shadow over its potential for centralizing the state, when the creation and building of basic and fundamental bureaucratic institutions is needed. Rather than extend itself through bargaining and through creating dependencies on national institutions that can overcome primordial loyalties, financial autonomy in distributive states leads to the opposite process: the creation of a strong bias against those institutions and bureaucracies that rely on technical qualification, impersonality, and complexity and that are needed for further national integration. Qadhafi's notion of statelessness is thus not simply a regional or cultural phenomenon—the ethos of the tribe or of Islam, as some have argued—but is concretely founded on state-building and the rent-seeking patterns it generated.

The bias against creating bureaucratic state institutions is worrisome in distributive states because they rely on a nonrenewable resource for their revenues and have limited opportunity to make the state relevant to its citizens and to develop economically. The vulnerability of their economies, with their reliance on the vagaries of the international market and on the inflows of market-regulated capital, makes this transition even more urgent. The Libyan *Jamahiriyya* undoubtedly represents an extreme example of rentier development and of a peculiar form of state-building. It presumably could have opted for a path where the state became increasingly relevant for its citizens and where institutions reflected and strengthened that process. That option would have been difficult and undoubtedly imperfect, but not impossible. It would have forced the country's leaders to confront the long-standing notions of statelessness among its citizens; to make the state appealing not only by creating institutions that engage in distribution but also by nurturing those institutions that provide continuity and predictability and that form both a buffer and a locus of interaction between the state and society. That endeavor is much more difficult, and it was, unfortunately, one Libya and other distributive states decided not to fully engage in.

This does not mean that governments of oil-exporting countries are powerless to prevent the unbridled use and waste of their sole natural resource. In other instances where natural resources were crucial to economic development—water resources in Taiwan, for example—some governments have successfully managed to devise political mechanisms that can be used "as implicit market surrogates to generate incentives for efficient resource use."[13] In those cases, the key ingredient seems to be the presence of strong regulatory institutions that allowed South Korea, for example, to garner successfully the remittances of its expatriate labor by offering preferential investment rates.

As I contend later, however, the combination of the structures left by colonialism, the lack of institutional development, and the luxury of oil development allows local rulers not to extend the state. The creation of well-developed, coherent, and relatively independent economic bureaucracies are crucial to long-term economic development, but their creation for anything but distributive purposes is likely to be delayed in distributive states during boom periods. In sum, the large role assumed by the state in distributive economies does not accurately gauge either its strength or its autonomy. On the contrary, state participation is often an indication of weakness. Lacking the means to carefully calibrate their economies, distributive states engage in wholesale economic "management" in order to avoid developing their capabilities to manage effectively their economies. The size and extent of intervention are poor indicators of actual strength and obscure the continuing relevance of powerful political coalitions often created by the state itself to support its original policies.

It is almost a truism by now within the economic reform literature that scaling back the state's role during periods of reform entails, at least temporarily, a more active role for the state's regulatory and institutional capabilities (Bates 1994; Cooper 1995; Grindle 1995). A distributive state—for a combination of historical, economic, institutional, and political events linked specifically to market-oriented capital inflows—faces particular difficulties in doing so. In evaluating development in

[13] See, for example, Mich Moore's discussion of water allocation in Taiwan in his chapter on "Rent-seeking and Market Surrogates," in Colclough and Manor (1991).

the Jamahiriyya it is therefore important to have an integrated understanding of those conditioning factors.

Theories that focus exclusively on so-called rentier development explain only some features of state-building. The notion of the distributive state as an analytical concept is only partially helpful in understanding the impact of market-regulated capital. It needs to be based "in historically shaped institutions and in the actions of real people in various parts of the world" (Becker 1987, 218–219); such an understanding calls for a larger historical and institutional framework in which to explain structural outcomes (Ikenberry et al.). But both of these emphases need to be supplemented by a clear understanding of the features of the state's indigenous society within which historical and oil development take shape and resonate. Studied individually, each provides an inadequate and reductionist answer to the question of state-building in distributive states.

In the following chapters I attempt to provide such a comprehensive understanding. Three questions sustain the inquiry across the different chapters: (1) How does state-building in distributive states such as Libya affect local institutional development, and how does the latter in turn affect economic and political development? (2) How precisely does the peculiar institutional development made possible by large inflows of market-regulated capital affect the state's strength? (3) How does the nature in which revenues are obtained by the distributive state affect political legitimacy and representation, and how do these ways differ significantly from states that rely on extraction from a domestic productive base?

II

LIBYA SINCE INDEPENDENCE

3

Shadow of the Past: The Sanusi Kingdom

History matters. It matters not just because we can learn from the past, but because the present and the future are connected to the past by the continuity of a society's institutions. Today's and tomorrow's choices are shaped by the past. And the past can only be made intelligible as a story of institutional evolution.

—Robert North, *Institutions, Institutional Change and Economic Performance*

The coming years . . . will bring vast and tremendous prosperity emerging from the riches of our territory which God blessed upon us. But the strife from now on will be less difficult than the past years because prosperity carries with it problems which ought to be faced and solved in the best interests and welfare of all sections of the Libyan people.

—King Idris al-Sanusi, Tenth Anniversary of Independence speech 1961, in *The Libyan Review,* March 1966

Libya is an accidental and a reluctant state.[1] It was created in the aftermath of World War II at the behest of the Great Powers and,

[1] John Davis, one of a few westerners to have observed Libya's revolution firsthand, eloquently describes it as "a residual category" (Davis 1987, 25). I have borrowed the terms from Crystal (1990), who describes Qatar and Kuwait in a similar fashion.

since its independence in 1951, has relied almost exclusively on exogenous capital. At independence, the Kingdom of Libya consisted of three provinces—Cyrenaica, Tripolitania, and Fazzan—that had virtually nothing in common economically, socially, or politically. Cyrenaica and Tripolitania had been forcibly joined during the Italian colonial period—reincarnated as "Libia" in 1929—while Fazzan was added as negotiations over the territories' fate took place within the United Nations after World War II. In one of the most brutal exercises at colonial rule in the century, the fascists had destroyed whatever embryonic state institutions the Ottoman Empire had bequeathed to the local population earlier in the century and left most future Libyans with dismal memories of their first exposure to the modern state (Barbar 1980; Dajani 1971; Gaber 1983). Libya at independence, therefore, represented little more than "a geographical expression," as Metternich had said about Italy a century earlier. The political will to turn the three disparate units into a unified state was, even among the country's leadership, extremely weak. The country's economic viability was at best problematic (Four Power Commission 1948).

There was, at independence, no hint yet of the oil riches that would transform the country from a barely self-sustaining agricultural and tribal society into a high-technology hydrocarbon economy with intimate links to the international economy. However, Libya became one of the largest oil producers in the Middle East within a decade after their discovery in the late 1950s. The rapid transition from an isolated and impoverished desert country to an oil exporter—while national integration had barely started, and while state-building was at a primitive stage—prompted the creation of increasingly complex state institutions and economic bureaucracies in order to meet the economic and accompanying sociopolitical challenges. The abandonment of the kingdom's federal system and its subsequent real unification in 1963 took place as a response to the demands of an oil economy that required unified legal structures and central control instead of administratively autonomous regions.

Large numbers of state institutions were created to employ growing numbers of urbanized citizens and to distribute the newfound largesse. Intricate patterns of rent-seeking behavior emerged, and the state deftly used its power to ascertain that rent-seeking was matched by political exclusion: in a process that went far beyond that observed in other oil exporters, virtually everyone in the kingdom was forced to trade power for wealth. By 1969, a combination of factors—traditional distrust of the hierarchical structures of modern statehood (exacerbated during the turbulent Italian colonial period), rapid international capital inflows, and a reluctant state-building process begun partly in response to the influx of capital before national integration was achieved—generated pressures the kingdom proved unable to accommodate (Allan 1982; Hayford 1970). Despite its attempts to prevent the emergence of groups with distinct political or corporate interests, the Libyan military that year ousted the king and assumed power.

The Sanusi Kingdom and the Colonial Legacy

Libya's independence in December 1951 was the culmination of a tumultuous history that in the course of a half-century had witnessed the withdrawal of the Ottoman Empire, Italian colonialism that included a brutal *riconquista* [reconquest] of Tripolitania and Cyrenaica and a transition period following World War II that left Great Britain in charge of the two northern provinces, and French forces entrenched in Fazzan, the country's southern province.[2]

The *riconquista* in particular had proven disastrous to any sense of statehood and unity for the citizens of what eventually became the Kingdom of Libya (Abushawa 1977; Ahmida 1994; Barbar 1980). The Italian fascists destroyed whatever remained of earlier attempts by the Ottoman Empire to create an embryonic state and bureaucratic institutions in its North African territories in the nineteenth and early twentieth centuries. The colonial occupation of Libya had been more a matter of Italian national pride rather than of economic interest and had left no room for Libyans within its bureaucracy or within the administrative organizations they foisted upon the country. In contrast to neighboring Algeria, Tunisia, or Egypt, the colonial economy in Libya did not create clear domestic financial, commercial, capitalist, or agricultural classes that tied their fortunes to colonial interests. Neither a local bourgeoisie nor an indigenous class of patrons, clients, and brokers emerged, which the occupying power needed to maintain or extend a centralized administration. The hinterland, which in neighboring Tunisia and Algeria had been economically incorporated as the colonial state extended its purview,

[2] Fazzan barely figured in the designs of Italy and was considered part of the French sphere of influence at the time. The future Libya was referred to, at the time, as the "two colonies" (Cyrenaica and Tripolitania). Only after World War II, in the discussions leading up to independence, would Fazzan be joined to the two northern provinces, against the wishes of France.

became increasingly isolated in Libya as traditional trading patterns were disrupted. Particularly in Cyrenaica, kinship obligations and patterns of tribal identity were reinforced as the primary expression of local social structures. Client-patron networks that had started to develop during the Ottoman period among the urban elites of Tripolitania and Cyrenaica withered away (Anderson 1986a; Gaber 1983).[3]

The *jihad* [religious war, resistance] against the Italians had been led in part by members of the Sanusiyya, a religious movement centered in Cyrenaica (al-Ashhab 1952; Dajani 1971; Shukri 1948). The Sanusiyya provided a consistent focus for opposition in the eastern province—where most of its *zuwaya* [religious lodges] were located—until 1932, when the Italians finally crushed the resistance led by Umar al-Mukhtar. Opposition proved less hostile among urbanized Tripolitanians, and the differential response to the Italians would continue to mar relations between the two major provinces of the kingdom in the events leading up to independence (Villard 1956, Chap. 2; Pelt 1970, Chap. 2). The issue of Libyan independence was finally settled by the Great Powers in the wake of World War II. Unable to agree on the terms of a United Nations' trusteeship plan for Libya, the country's future was turned over to a Four Power Commission of Investigation and, finally, to the United Nations General Assembly in September 1948 (Villard 1956; Pelt 1970; Khadduri 1963).[4]

The creation of the kingdom introduced into the now-unified provinces of Cyrenaica, Tripolitania, and Fazzan an alien concept in the essentially tribal society, where political affiliation had at best been confined to a provincial arena and, most often, to social and political movements in the early part of the twentieth century that barely reached be-

[3] My own account differs slightly here from that of Lisa Anderson (1986a), whose study relies heavily on the highly partisan *Jihad al-Abtal fi Tarablus al-Gharb* (The holy war of the heroes of Tripoli) written by Tahir az-Zawi, who eventually became *mufti* of Tripoli. Despite local attempts at political representation—particularly the Tripoli Republic in 1918—the impact of the Ottoman period on local structures was perhaps less pronounced than Anderson argues. The Italian-induced "reversal" was therefore more of an actual continuation of a benign laissez-faire that had left substantial power to kinship relations. See Barbar 1980, Gaber 1983, and Martel 1991.

[4] Henry Villard, the first U.S. ambassador to independent Libya, aptly summarized the considerations that had led to the kingdom's creation: "A glance at the map shows the strategic value of Libya . . . without which there might have been little interest in the emergence of an Arab kingdom in North Africa. . . . [I]f Libya had passed under any form of United Nations trusteeship, it would have been impossible for the territory to play a part in the defense arrangements of the free world" (Villard 1956, 23–33).

yond the cities in which they were located (Rizqana 1964; Roumani 1973).[5] Libyans overwhelmingly continued to identify themselves with tribe—or region at best—or as part of an Islamic community of the faithful. Urbanized Tripolitania, site of an earlier experiment in creating the Arab world's first republic in 1918, possessed a highly heterogeneous political structure, where solidarity had traditionally been based on territorial and economic interests. Cyrenaica, a more isolated region with a corporate identity that centered around the Sanusiyya movement, had a cultural and structural uniformity that relied on a traditional segmentary tribal system (Roumani 1973; Ahmida 1994).

Tripolitania and Fazzan grudgingly accepted, for strategic reasons, the Great Powers' selection of Idris al-Sanusi, the heir to the Sanussiyya movement, as king of Libya. Idris's own reluctance to rule over all three provinces, however, only reflected the more general suspicions Libyans had expressed to the United Nations' commissioner about creating a truly unified political structure for the country (Pelt 1970).[6] Their first sustained exposure to the concept of the modern territorial state at the hands of the Italians had been uniformly deleterious, unattractive, and uninspiring—and that collective memory continued to provide fertile soil for the king and his successor, who continually expressed their suspicion of modern statehood and who espoused alternative visions of political community.

But Libya in 1951 hardly possessed the resources to act upon those convictions. The country faced such enormous economic and social difficulties that both the British government, in the discussions leading up to independence, and the International Bank for Reconstruction and Development (after 1951) repeatedly expressed more practical concerns about the country's viability and continued existence (Farley 1971; Four Power Commission 1948). The country's population of approximately one million people (300,000 in Cyrenaica; 750,000 in Tripolitania, and 60,000 in Fazzan) had an estimated annual per capita income of $30.

[5]Perhaps the most ambitious example of those had been the establishment of the Tripoli Republic in 1918. See Anderson 1986; Roumani 1973.

[6]Idris's ambitions were limited to ruling his native Cyrenaica, a desire he repeatedly made clear to the U.S. ambassador. As Khadduri and Villard have noted, "He was not very anxious to rule over Tripolitania and . . . would have been satisfied with the Amirate of Cyrenaica, but accepted the throne of Libya as a patriotic duty in order to supply leadership for a divided country" (Khadduri 1963, 319); and "the unfailing subject of interest to him was the past, present and future of Cyrenaica. . . . [H]e gave the impression that he would be content to reign over that territory alone. As King of a united Libya he seemed to some people rather the reluctant monarch" (Villard 1956, 42).

Libya was one of the poorest countries in the world. Cyrenaica's infrastructure, including much of its agricultural areas, had been destroyed during the war. Whatever trade took place in Tripolitania was overwhelmingly with Tunisia and other countries to the west, while Cyrenaica's trading patterns were oriented toward Egypt. Until the discovery of oil in 1959 and its marketing in 1961, the country's major revenue sources were sales of scrap metal left behind by the belligerents during the war, sales of esparto grass, and rent from military bases leased by the United States and Great Britain. Despite the inflow of people into urban areas during the colonial period, 80 percent of the country's population still lived at subsistence level in the hinterland.

From a state-building viewpoint, the dismal economic picture was exacerbated further by a lack of existing institutions through which the state could extend its reach and by the lack of enthusiasm for creating such institutions. This weak sense of statehood and the lingering hostility and distrust of unity was reflected in the constitutional compromise that was adopted at independence between the supporters of a unitary system in Tripolitania (who also favored continued close ties with the United States and Great Britain) and those advocating provincial autonomy for Cyrenaica and Fazzan. The result was a loose federal system with multiple overlapping jurisdictions that included a National Cabinet and bicameral Parliament, along with provincial Cabinets and Assemblies. The country had three provincial governments and one national government—with their own ministers, representative assemblies, and executive departments—and three capitals and a winter capital (later an administrative capital) in al-Bayda', where the first Sanusi lodge had been built (International Bank for Reconstruction and Development 1960; Rizqana 1964).

The constitution furthermore failed to specify what the precise political relations between provincial and national governments were. No arrangements were made concerning national versus provincial budgets, except to note that the federal government was obliged to make up provincial budget deficits. Not only did the national government have little control over its expenditures, its extractive capabilities were curtailed as well: because taxation policies were determined by provincial agreement, neither a national income tax nor a business tax was established (Khadduri 1963; Hayford 1970). Provincial tax prerogatives extended to trade and the banking sector, and questions of jurisdiction precluded foreign investment. Any national development policy could only be implemented after bargaining between the three provincial governments and the national government. Not surprisingly, during the first decade of its existence, observers worried about separatism and noted that although Libya superficially looked like a unified state, in effect the federal government remained utterly dependent on the provincial governments for the implementation of any legislation (First 1974).

In light of his own suspicions and of the differing political interests of Tripolitania and his native Cyrenaica, the king soon after taking office banned all political parties—a ban that would be maintained for the remainder of the monarchy's existence. Although it always contained a careful representation of all the major tribes, the country's parliament was reduced to little more than a rubber stamp for what the king and his *diwan* [royal household] decided. Until 1960, this *diwan* consisted mostly of Cyrenaican tribal elites that had proven their loyalty to the Sanusis in the preindependence period. They also found their way into the Council of Ministers, the diplomatic corps, and the national bureaucracy. Tribal alliances were thus maintained, and locally powerful families were consistently recruited by the king and his advisers, more often on the basis of expediency than competence. By the end of the 1950s, politics in Libya had become the assertion of "family, factional, tribal, and parochial interests," and government positions were eagerly sought after for the influence in awarding contracts they afforded (First 1974, 80). The king repeatedly bemoaned the corruption that took place in this highly personalized and barely regulated environment while remaining unaware of how the lack of clearly defined regulations and legal procedures, as well as the informal political arrangements, exacerbated it.

That this state of affairs did not lead to opposition, particularly from Tripolitania, was due to many factors. Although increasing amounts of rent from the leasing of military bases had started to accrue directly to the government, the constitutional provision concerning the subsidizing of provincial deficits had a trickle-down, distributive effect that made everyone a beneficiary of those rents. Furthermore, the multitude of provincial and national bureaucracies, the civil and diplomatic service, the new administrative positions, and the foreign military bases created enormous employment opportunities for all Libyans. By the end of the 1950s, the government had become the biggest employer in the country; its payroll was estimated at 12 percent of GNP.[7] It supported an estimated forty thousand employees, most of them indirectly through the provincial administration and bureaucracies. In addition, the military

[7] See also International Bank for Reconstruction and Development, 1960; Anderson 1986a.

bases and the oil prospecting companies directly or indirectly employed another estimated one hundred thousand.

But no group had yet emerged that possessed clearly articulated economic or class interests—which was partly a reflection of the country's obliterated identity during its colonial history. In the absence of a commercialized economy or a centralized administration, Libya until 1960 relied overwhelmingly on kinship for economic distribution. Kinship also provided the basis for the recruitment of the country's new political and economic elite at the national level and formed, haphazardly, the backbone of the state's bureaucracies, which in turn became the distributive outlets for the country's growing revenues. Notables and tribal chiefs of the Cyrenaican hinterland dominated the top state bureaucracy between 1951 and 1960, but by that time it became clear that economic growth had started to undermine the king's reliance on kinship for political power. The parliamentary elections that year introduced new political figures, many of whom no longer had tribal connections to the Sanusis (Hasan 1973). In the aftermath of the elections, and as the country's first oil boom started, kinship increasingly yielded to broader patronage networks that were maintained by rapidly growing revenues.

In a more ominous development for the country's future, Libya had already started to rely extensively on rent by the end of its first decade of independence. Between 1951 and 1960, foreign aid to the country quadrupled (International Bank for Reconstruction and Development 1960). By that time, the combination of British and U.S. aid and the leasing of military bases accounted for 35 percent of Libya's GNP and the overwhelming share of the country's revenues (Luciani 1987). Merchandise exports had become only a tiny fraction of the country's rapidly increasing imports. Exploration fees paid by international oil companies, and then oil revenues, soon added to the country's riches. Political and economic structures characteristic of the distributive state were already becoming visible. The state had started to expand through bureaucracies and administrative offices that had little regulatory purpose and were meant primarily to provide employment and distribute state revenues. Several of the ministries were little more than personal fiefdoms, ruled by notables and tribal elites in a highly personal fashion. The lack of the state's extractive power had been enshrined in the constitution in an attempt to make the country's federal structure more palatable to the provinces. Finally, as a legacy of the colonialism that made the concepts of state and political community unattractive to ruler and ruled alike in what remained essentially a tribal society, and as a result of increases in rent, the majority of Libyans stood passively on the sidelines and showed little interest in the political life of the country (Hassan 10 December 1989).

Libya's First Oil Boom: State-Building and Institutions

By 1960, despite its deeply traditional and prebureaucratic society, Libya had started to show the impact of rapid capital inflows. The parliamentary elections that year provided a telltale indication of the political interests that those inflows could generate, even if the country remained a rural, bare-bones economy. There was, as yet, no danger that the elections could alter the monarchy's careful manipulation of the political system at the national level: the combination of Sanusi-allied elites and the king's own power to appoint representatives to parliament guaranteed his continued dominance of the system. Until 1960, the state had primarily to mobilize enough resources for ensuring the basic requirements of a mostly agrarian economy. The lack of a class with clear economic interests at independence and the monarchy's ability to create provincial bureaucracies during the first decade had facilitated that mobilization in a manner that avoided conflict, within a society that displayed lingering doubts about a national community.

The tasks that lay ahead, however, were of a higher magnitude: the growing evidence of enormous oil reserves meant that the kingdom would be asked to promote sustained development in an economy that seemed destined to be dominated by a rapid but unpredictable economic surplus in the form of oil revenues. The reserves dramatically changed the relationships between the new "state" and the economy and marked the beginning of rapid institutional expansion. Oil revenues extended, in an undreamed-of fashion, the state's capabilities to provide patronage and consequently affected both the monarchy's reluctant state-building efforts and the country's political process. Indeed, the commercialization of oil in the 1960s had an economic impact on Libyan society far beyond the 1970s oil booms—not simply because of the increase in revenues but, more importantly, because the first deliberate attempt at unifying the state in 1963 and rent-generated economic growth coincided, leaving the monarchy to face two distinct but related challenges.

A glance at an economic map of Libya in 1960 hinted at the profound changes that lay ahead. A patchwork quilt of eighty-four petroleum concessions, whose exploration rights were assigned almost exclusively to U.S. and British companies, divided the country's territory into neat geometric patterns. By late 1963, Libya had 437 producing wells, and petroleum made up 98.7 percent of the country's exports (International Bank for Reconstruction and Development 1960; Bank of Libya 1965; *SA* 1963). The high quality of its oil and its proximity to Europe provoked a rush to develop the Libyan fields and led to an economic boom that in the course of a single decade propelled annual per capita income from $50 to $60 in 1960 to $2,000 by 1969. During that entire decade, Libya's economy grew at an annual rate in excess of 20 percent, fueled exclusively by an output of oil that increased from twenty thousand barrels per day in 1960 to almost three million barrels per day when the military coup took place in 1969. By that time, Libya had become the fourth-largest oil producer in the world (Farley 1971, chap. 8; Waddams 1980).

The rapid exploration and marketing of the country's oil was due in large part to the oil legislation the kingdom had adopted and to the structure of Libya's burgeoning oil industry. The monarchy's first petroleum law in 1955 provided incentives for international oil companies to explore and commercialize the country's resources at an accelerated pace: a stipulation in the country's oil legislation required them to hand back within five to eight years parts of the concessions where they had not successfully drilled (*JR* 19 June 1955, 8 February 1956). In addition, the kingdom had deliberately assigned exploration rights to independent producers. These smaller companies—such as Oasis or Bunker Hunt—had neither the integrated structure, the capital flow, or the kind of global diversification of the so-called Majors, the international cartel of companies that dominated the industry worldwide. As a result, it was in the smaller companies' interest to bring Libyan oil to market as rapidly as possible; as the future would show, this move left them highly vulnerable to pressures from the local government.

On the eve of oil, Libya thus found itself in a position to either strengthen or weaken the monarchy as it stood poised to embark on its vertiginous path of development: there was no politically seasoned group or class that could be expected to challenge the king, but, at the same time, the country lacked a state apparatus that could administer the oil industry or regulate or even plan for development. On the contrary: the constitution had deliberately provided for provincial autonomy in economic matters, including taxation, and had never articulated the boundaries of the national or provincial governments' economic authority. The national government granted concessions to the oil fields; but international companies were worried about the lack of clarity concerning precise property rights and the enforcement of rules announced by the national government. Furthermore, an infrastructure was needed to bring oil to the coast, and this endeavor required provincial cooperation because pipelines needed to cross their boundaries. Then, suddenly, there was also a political reason for developing a more functional state apparatus: contrary to earlier expectations, most oil fields were located in Cyrenaica and Fazzan. Although both provinces had been opposed to unification during the first decade of independence, the provincial governments—particularly the Cyrenaican tribal elites, who had once forced the king to withdraw a similar proposal in 1955—realized that only real financial, administrative, and bureaucratic integration promised to let all three provinces enjoy the benefits of oil (Khadduri 1963). This required formal institutions and mechanisms to allow for state control of the economy.

The abolition of the federal formula in April 1963 and the ensuing unification, therefore, was the most critical event of the monarchy. The unitary form of government promised to concentrate planning, administrative, and economic power at the national level and create, for the first time in the country's history, a unified state apparatus. The urge to create this apparatus, however, had not come about as the result of political willingness or of the provinces' administrative capacity. While some nationalist groups, particularly in Tripolitania, applauded and encouraged it, unification was overwhelmingly a response to the country's need to develop oil riches and to achieve economic, bureaucratic, and legal integration. Furthermore, the strengthening of the state apparatus posed acute state-building problems the monarchy had deliberately avoided during its first decade. These problems had been exacerbated by the conditions under which the state had first emerged and by the limited progress Idris made during the first decade in extending its powers; he was content to engage in a policy of benign neglect, if not outright laissez faire.

From both a constitutional and an institutional viewpoint, the 1963 amendments to the constitution and the subsequent reorganization of the country centralized the state's power immeasurably at the expense of the autonomy of the provinces and of the municipalities within them. The new constitution formally assigned authority to the national government for all transactions involving customs, companies, ports, finance, transportation, and economic development; and, most important, it gave the national government control over all tax revenues—usurping, in effect, most of the previous provincial prerogatives. At the same time, the Cyrenaican, Tripolitanian, and Fazzan legislative assemblies were abolished, as were the provinces' individual juridical systems. A new administrative system for the provinces was disclosed, dividing the country into ten *muqatta* [districts] and a number of subdivisions. The king was given the power to make appointments to these local administrative councils, either directly or through the Ministry of the Interior. Automatic subsidies to the provinces were halted. Reflecting the changes that had taken place, the country's name was changed from "The United Kingdom of Libya" to "The Kingdom of Libya" (Hayford 1970, Chaps. 4 and 5). Finally, outstanding border disputes—except for the Aouzou strip on the Chadian-Libyan border, which Idris considered part of Libyan territory—were settled as oil companies needed clear property rights to the areas assigned to them.[8]

The adoption of the unitary system, at least according to the amended constitution, thus gave the king—and his *diwan*—inordinate power. The evisceration of the provincial bureaucracies and the new administrative organization enabled Idris to staff the new governmental organizations that started to proliferate in 1963. Oil revenues now accrued directly to the government, as did whatever company and individual taxes it could collect while promising the state financial autonomy. The reorganization of the country's banking system and the creation of a central bank whose governor reported directly to the *diwan* further enhanced the king's ability to influence the planning and spending process. The state had at its disposal seemingly all the necessary instruments to expand its regulatory and extractive capacities in a dramatic and unprecedented fashion (Shirkazi 13 September 1989; Hasan 10 December 1989).

In reality, despite the constitutional powers and the newly created tools at its disposal, the state in Libya after 1963 systematically avoided extending its capacity to expand. With kinship no longer sufficient as a reliable mechanism for distributing the country's growing resources, and with a need to maintain the political quiescence it had pursued during its first decade in office, the regime turned toward large-scale patronage and distributive measures. In the process, it created groups that developed common economic interests centered around access to the state's distributive institutions. In doing so, however, the state forced upon

[8]In 1954 Libya would invade the Aouzou strip for the first time, in an attempt to claim the area. For a more detailed account of Libya's involvement in Chad, including Qadhafi's similar attempts in the 1970s and 1980s, see Neuberger 1982.

these new elites a power-for-wealth compromise that dovetailed with its efforts at political exclusion. As the economic boom expanded beyond any Libyan planner's comprehension, the second decade of the kingdom witnessed such a dramatic weakening of the state's capacity to regulate the economy that halfway through its life (the plan was projected to run from 1963 to 1968), the country's first development plan was abandoned, and unrestrained spending took hold for the remainder of the kingdom's existence.

The newly created national bureaucracies, which replaced the provincial machinery, provided ample opportunities for the government to provide large-scale patronage. Although Cyrenaican tribal elites received their traditional share of political appointments to the top positions in these bureaucracies, they now also included Tripolitanian businessmen, who were recruited in part to offset growing demands and in part to temper tribal power.[9] Competition for entry into these new national bureaucracies meant competition for rents; appointments were highly lucrative because they provided access to government allocations that could then be used for further patronage. The period from 1963 to 1965 witnessed an explosion of these new or reshaped institutions, which eventually turned into distributive outlets. At the national level, the new measures included expansion of the Libyan Public Development and Stabilization Agency and of the Libyan Petroleum Commission (which became LIPETCO in 1968), the replacement of the Development Council by an enlarged National Planning Council, and the creation of a Ministry of Planning and Development and a number of development funds. By the end of 1965 the country had thirteen ministries, with at least another dozen individuals from research institutes, the Central Bank, and some members of the royal *diwan* possessing ministerial rank and thus the power to dispense revenues (*JR* 1966).

The five most important ministries, which allocated roughly 80 percent of the budget—housing and state property, public works, planning and development, communications, and industry—were headed initially by tribal supporters of the king and by two Tripolitanian technocrats. These ministries, as well as the development funds, became the

[9] The king is normally portrayed as having favored the maintenance and extension of tribal power. In reality, he was quite cautious of overly relying on them, and on several occasions he deliberately played off their loyalties against each other to keep the political system balanced.

most important formal mechanisms for distributing the growing wealth. As financial discipline was lost in the mid-1960s, they also became important instruments of informal distribution. At the same time their regulatory functions—particularly those of the Ministry of Planning and Development, which was in charge of sector development allocations—declined as information gathering declined. The unification of the country's taxation system now put extractive power in the hands of the state, but both direct and indirect taxes on individuals, entrepreneurs, and businesses dramatically declined after 1963. Import duty levels were substantially reduced, and the enforcement mechanisms of both the Department of Taxation and of the Customs Department atrophied (*JR* 1964, 1965). In the midst of the boom, the state's already weak regulatory power declined even further. It failed to enforce investment codes and ignored whatever import regulations still existed.

At the same time, the country's distributive mechanisms and institutions flourished. The proliferating development commissions and agencies, in addition to the ministries, became channels for food program subsidies, for interest-free loans, and for government-sponsored contracts. Particularly after 1965, when public criticism became more vocal, welfare, social security, interest-free loans for housing, and educational allowances were used in primarily urban settings to protect average citizens from high inflation rates. In addition, the king and his *diwan* controlled two more informal but highly lucrative mechanisms to channel wealth. The first consisted primarily of inside information about future contracts that could then informally be used to negotiate commissions with potential foreign contractors. The second consisted of the king's power personally to dispense grants to urban and rural properties that had been evacuated by the Italians and had become state lands. Once an individual had land, he then became eligible for further subsidies through the newly created industrial, farming, and construction funds. This, in addition to the fact that foreign companies needed those with access to high-level civil servants or to the royal family, made belonging to one of the influential Cyrenaican tribes, to the *diwan,* or to the Sanusi family literally a paying proposition because they controlled the economic bureaucracy. Throughout the 1960s, the skyrocketing prices of urban real estate made those who had access to this informal mechanism wealthy overnight (Shirkazi 6 February 1989).

By the mid-1960s, Libya already clearly demonstrated some of the flaws and dislocations typical of most distributive states in the region. The long-term viability of projects was often neglected in the urge to spend. The country's first national development plan was abandoned as massive capital inflows dramatically reduced the relative stringency of the pre-oil years. Large, highly visible programs that had been promoted by well-connected entrepreneurs took precedence over small-scale projects. Corruption became rampant, and the resultant economic differentiation plainly visible. Rural flight increased, despite the fact that the country's oil industry was not projected to employ more than 5 percent of the country's overall labor force. By 1969, two-thirds of the country's population lived along the coastal strip (International Bank for Reconstruction and Development 1960). Increasing numbers of migrant laborers took over from Libyans, and the country's limited number of technocrats massively defected from government positions to more lucrative private sector and foreign company positions.[10]

The distributive measures of the Libyan monarchy, which had originated as an informal process of spending, eventually led the state to lose control over the allocation of resources and to high levels of inequity between the different sectors. State spending also initially reinforced the tribal and narrow social base of the regime: the Cyrenaican tribal elites and Tripolitanian business community controlled the key distributional institutions through close, most often informal, access to bureaucrats and the royal family. In contrast to Iraq and Saudi Arabia—where the infighting between the state and business coalitions led to repeated crises that prompted the state to intervene—in Libya the historically low level of group identification, in addition to the rapid and massive influx of oil revenues, effectively prevented sustained conflict under the monarchy.

Significantly, however, it also allowed the state to take a passive role in regulating economic behavior. Institutionally, the state had not been strengthened. For most Libyans, it lacked intrusiveness but also held few attractions beyond its role as purveyor of increasingly handsome economic rewards. Economically, after a decade of virtual nonregulation at the national level, the rapid inflow of oil revenues had forced the government to intervene, but it used that intervention to strengthen its distributive capabilities—an easy task in light of the continued oil revenue inflows—at the expense of extraction and active regulation. This early preference exacerbated the traditional distrust or apathy many of its citizens had already displayed toward the modern state in the early

[10] This development had already been singled out by officials from international financial institutions in 1960 but accelerated rapidly during the boom period. See International Bank for Reconstruction and Development 1960.

years of its creation. By that time, Libya had become a classic distributive, capitalist state whose economic expansion depended on the price of oil and not on a domestic tax base.

The unwillingness or fear of creating nationwide institutions that could develop corporate interests extended to the kingdom's military establishment. In an important sense, Idris's Libya did not even hold a monopoly on the use of force—the most basic Weberian trait of the state. Since independence, the regular Libyan military under the monarchy had failed to reflect a national identity. What eventually became known as the Royal Libyan Army had found its origin in the Sanusi Army, created among exiled followers of the Sanusiyya during World War II. Just prior to the 1969 coup, the Libyan army had almost seven thousand men under arms who were advised by sixteen hundred British officers. Most of the recruits were lower middle-class, and professional qualifications were generally considered of secondary importance; the army, like other state institutions, was primarily seen as a mechanism to provide employment.[11]

The army's power, however, was carefully held in check by a more informal mechanism: militias drawn largely from tribal forces, with recruitment based on kinship solidarity, that served directly at the discretion of the king. The most important of these militias, Idris's personal Cyrenaican Defense Force (CYDEF), consisted of recruits from tribes loyal to the Sanusis. The militias outnumbered the regular army—they contained an estimated fourteen thousand men by 1969—and were better equipped. Their primary function was to balance and check the power of the regular army. The king clearly—in a pattern his successor would perpetuate through his attempt at creating a "People's Army"—was suspicious of a professional standing army.

Similarly, the king carefully circumscribed the power of the *ulama* [religious scholars]. Based on their traditional role, during the first decade some of its members had found their way into the executive branches of the provincial governments, within the Supreme Court, within some of the country's Islamic institutions, and in the country's cabinet. Thereafter, however, they were systematically replaced through government decrees that included the creation of a Committee for Senior Ulama, headed by the shaykh of the Sanusi Islamic University, which had been established by the king in Cyrenaica. Even his own Sanusi

[11] Libya also had a tiny navy and air force of about five hundred men in 1969.

ikhwan [brethren] did not escape Idris's more general attempt at preventing the development of corporate interests. Keenly aware of the resentment his role as head of a secular government caused among some of his tribal supporters, Idris reestablished the Sanusi lodges that had been closed by the Italians but did not allow them to reemerge as the autonomous institutions they had once been. The local shaykhs were now appointed as government employees and were supervised by a general director who reported directly to the chief of the royal *diwan* (Hasan 1973).[12] Both the lodges and the Sanusi-affiliated education institutions, however, played the same strategic role and had the same distributive purposes as the new national bureaucracies and the administrative institutions: they allowed the king to sideline more traditional opponents and supporters who could no longer be accommodated into the country's modernizing structures.

By 1969, when the monarchy was overthrown, the state had, willy-nilly, become more centralized. The abolition of the federal system in 1963 indicated that economic requirements had been a primary motive for the unification. Since then, the newly created state institutions had been elaborately used for distributive political and economic purposes. The political apathy, the general pattern of rent-seeking, and the contempt with which the young middle-class revolutionaries would hold that state when they came to power indicated that centralization and seeming autonomy had not translated into relevance or strength.

At a time when the country's basic bureaucratic and administrative institutions had not yet been centralized, the state's financial autonomy prevented a true national integration. In effect, it resulted not in its ability to forge institutions that could be used for better regulation but led to its opposite: centralized before they were capable of penetrating society, they helped to "institutionalize traditional social divisions . . . rolling back previous gains in national integration" in a pattern reminiscent of Saudi Arabia (Chaudhry 1989, 119).

Although oil, the state's distributive measures, and its use of state institutions for that purpose had managed successfully to slow down economic differentiation that could have provoked political conflict, the socioeconomic changes engendered by oil created demands that were,

[12] Contrary to the image often portrayed of him, the king was clearly aware of the secularizing trends around him; he never expected the re-establishment of the Sanusi university to be anything but symbolic, and he saw it in part as a political action (Hasan 2 October 1989; Hayford 1970, chap. 9).

almost by default, not based on economics but focused on cultural, ideological and, to a lesser extent, religious issues. Although the king repeatedly decried corruption and nepotism—and was personally seen as a devout Muslim—critics eagerly seized upon the actions of his family members and of the royal *diwan* to attack the regime (Khadduri 1963). The growing nationalist feelings, primarily among the country's younger population and officers in the Libyan army, were inspired by the rhetoric of Egypt's president Nasser. Among the demands they voiced, the insistence on national control over the country's national economic resources and the removal of foreign military forces figured prominently.[13] Even though Idris had anticipated several of the later nationalist, almost symbolic demands that wafted across the region, the rapid economic growth during the 1960s in Libya had provoked a cultural polarization that found its roots within regional Arab nationalism, corroding further the already tenuous links between the monarchy and civil society, and weakening whatever political legitimacy the state possessed.

The persistence of the Libyan monarchy, while royal houses crumbled around it in neighboring Egypt and further afield in the 1950s, did not signify that it was a strong and viable system that had garnered the allegiance of its citizens. Rather, like the Jamahiriyya that succeeded it, the longevity of the Sanusi family is more accurately explained by the extensive corporatism, the distributive power of the state, and the inability or unwillingness to imagine a better alternative. When that idea finally germinated among a group of young military officers, its slogans proved almost as diffuse as those of the monarchy: the three words president Gamal Abdul Nasser of Egypt eventually used to define his revolution—*Huriyya, Ishtirakiyya, Wahda* [Freedom, Socialism, Unity]—replaced the kingdom's *Allah, Malik, Watan* [God, King, and Country]. Of crucial importance for the future of Libya, however, was that these slogans were touted once more by a group that failed to express its ideals or objectives in purely Libyan nationalist aspirations. As the king did, the new leadership would call for a political community that did not match Libya's territorial boundaries. Rather than long for a more limited community,

[13] The Qadhafi regime heavily promoted the image of the king as simply a pawn in the hands of the United States and Great Britain. Unfortunately, this image has found its way, uncritically, in most writings on Libya. For a more subtle view from a local insider who extensively interviewed political figures of the monarchy period, see Hasan 1973.

however, as Idris had done, the military officers would aim at a supranational, pan-Arab entity.

Conclusion

To the majority of its citizens, the Kingdom of Libya could not be imagined as a continuous and political community at independence in 1951. The entity that had been created was only a state in a minimalist, territorial sense: it possessed juridical statehood, but all the state-building tasks lay ahead. During the first decade of independence, the federal system, with its multiple overlapping jurisdictions, reflected the uncertainty, unwillingness, and outright fear of the Sanusis to cultivate that sense of statehood.

Perhaps not surprising under those circumstances, political development during the monarchy retained a strong insistence on ascriptive politics by its leader: a defining of subnational political identity, the Sanusi concept of a Cyrenaican political community. Virtually from independence onward, the Sanusi monarchy operated independently of local elites, tribes, or individual citizens to help generate revenues for the maintenance of the newly created state. This luxury would prove of dubious value to the state-building process. Whereas in countries such as Kuwait and Saudi Arabia, oil revenues afforded local rulers the freedom to (at least temporarily) turn away from historical allies, in Libya the Sanusi monarchy had no historical allies, except for a loose array of Sanusi-allied tribal soldiers it judged necessary for its physical survival.

No single group proved capable of organizing or firmly establishing its economic interests, in part because whatever groups emerged with corporate interests had been created almost ex nihilo when oil was commercialized after 1961. The development of class or corporate identities that takes shape and molds political participation under most state-building experiences was avoided early on and was later prevented by the further atomization of political and economic interests. The state bureaucracies that grew at an exponential rate throughout the decade were turned, in a not-so-subtle fashion, into arenas for rent-seeking and personal advancement, not into venues for the articulation of group or class interests. As a result, none of the country's grand families or tribal elites had developed national interests that allowed them politically to transcend personal, local, and regional preoccupations by the time the 1969 coup occurred. Atomized, lacking cohesion, having developed no historical record of class memory or class tactics during the colonial period and the first decade of independence—and acting more as a group with common interests than as a class—they would, not surprisingly, be easily and rapidly removed by the military officers after 1969.[14]

This lack of cohesion had been exacerbated by the weakness or absence of political mechanisms that could be used to settle conflicting claims as oil revenues increased. The initial advantage kinship provided to the monarchy as a basis of support was easily offset by the refusal of several groups inside Libya—and even by the king himself—to represent the entire country. As the state apparatus expanded, and personal power gave way to the more impersonal mechanism of an expanding bureaucracy after 1961, the Sanusi monarch proved increasingly unable to manage the social, political, and economic challenges the country faced.

The simultaneous process of state-building and rentier-type development during the monarchy thus created, in a highly spectacular fashion, state institutions that could be used for patronage and distributive purposes but did not significantly extend the state's capacity for intervention and regulation. It simultaneously generated a political and economic system marked by political exclusion and by extensive rent-seeking by individuals. Beneath the visibly corrosive effects of rapid capital inflows—the active rent-seeking, the depoliticization, and the extensive distributive mechanisms of the state at the expense of regulatory capabilities—the much larger pattern of state-building under the monarchy stood starkly revealed. The Sanusi monarchy's minimalist state represented a critical choice that, as the following chapters show, would not be reversed. On the contrary, in a process that showed remarkable similarities in its aversion for a modern state, the revolutionary government after 1969 would fully employ the country's resources to extend a "tradition of the rejection of states" (Davis 1987, 258).

When that coup took place, Libyans had known a truly unitary state for only six years. And much of what they knew hardly provided a focus of identity and integrity. The combination of growing dependence on external sources of revenues, the uses to which the monarchy had put the state, and the economic and political outcomes of that process hardly inspired confidence. More important, the aversion of Idris al-Sanusi's successor for a modern state reflected not only the reservations the king himself repeatedly voiced but mirrored the calculations many Libyans, including al-Qadhafi and his fellow conspirators, made about the state.

[14]For the importance of this lack of class memory or tactics, see Crystal 1990.

4

From Kingdom to Republic: The Qadhafi Coup

> [In a] government where no man is a citizen . . . [where] the prince declares himself proprietor of all the lands . . . nothing is repaired or improved. Houses are built only for the necessity of habitation; there is no digging of ditches or planting of trees; everything is drawn from, but nothing is restored to the earth; the ground lies untilled, and the whole country becomes desert.
>
> —Montesquieu, *The Spirit of the Laws*

> How can a soldier remain passive and salute a king who has filled the country with foreign forces? How can you accept being stopped on the street by an American? That happened to me personally. When I wanted to enter Wheelus base, I was turned away. . . . When I told them of my position as an officer in the Libyan army, I was told, "true, but you will not enter!" I replied, "it is Libyan territory." Response, "it is futile to argue, you will not enter, period!"
>
> —Mu'ammar al-Qadhafi, in Barrada et al. 1984

On Army Day in August 1969, *The Libyan Review*—a government publication meant for overseas and local expatriate consumption—featured a front-page picture of army units parading in front of the old Spanish fort in Tripoli before King Idris and a bevy of dignitaries. In its main article, the magazine reminded its audience that the celebration of Army Day marked the "anniversary of the establishment of the Senussi army" twenty-nine years earlier. The absence of any reference to a Libyan national army, and the reminder that it had been primarily Cyrenaican tribal forces that had joined hands with the British under the command of the Sanusis during World War II, were small but telltale illustrations of the monarchy's lingering inability to conceive of a national community after almost eighteen years in power.

The overthrow of the Sanusi kingdom in September 1969 was not totally unexpected—by that time, it was almost universally considered a political anachronism. The immobility of its political system, its conservative positions in inter-Arab politics, and the growing split between the regime's elites—who possessed few nationalist credentials—and the more ideologically inclined younger Libyans had already led to political incidents throughout the 1960s. The king's careful political calibrations, his attempts at projecting a more nationalist image, and his use of distributive largesse muted some of the criticisms and delayed their impact. But, almost by default, in the absence of alternatives, the Libyan regular army had emerged as the only organization where corporate interests could develop despite the king's efforts to maintain the Cyrenaican Defense Force (CYDEF) as a counterweight. The king, furthermore, had miscalculated: when the coup took place, CYDEF stayed in its barracks, providing a clear sign that tribal loyalty alone was no longer sufficient to defend particular regional interests against those determined to use the coercive power of the country's national army.

The military's assumption of power, possessing coercive capability and imbued with an ideological fervor to reverse some of the monarchy's policies, raised interesting questions about the future of state-building in Libya. Would the young military officers use the power at their disposal to counter the benign neglect that had marked the monarchy? Would they perfect the state by extending its ability to regulate and simultaneously incorporating citizens that had been sidelined and excluded during the monarchy? By the time of the 1969 coup, in a fashion typical of most distributive states, elaborate patterns of patronage had emerged that dominated the country's economic life, and the country's emerging elites had traded economic wealth for political power, while average citizens were largely ignored (except for the increasing economic largesse they received after 1965).

The replacement of the monarchy's bureaucracies, the creation of new administrative boundaries across tribal lines, and, above all, the nationalization of the foreign oil companies during the first four years of the military regime further concentrated power at the pinnacle of the country's political system. Until the second oil boom in 1973, however, the country's new leaders provided few clear answers to whether they would use their power to extend the state's capacity beyond pure coercion and distributive largesse. They seemed genuinely concerned about greater equity and other populist issues and paid close attention to ideological matters linked to pan-Arabism. But much like that of Idris al-Sanusi, the discourse of Mu'ammar al-Qadhafi—who became the *primes inter pares* and soon thereafter the leader of the new regime—indicated a lingering hostility to the notion of the modern state. By mid-1973, the new regime had consolidated itself but had made only marginal progress in institutionalizing its political experiments or in better regulating its economy.

Political Consolidation and Mobilization

Despite the insistence by the country's new leader, Mu'ammar al-Qadhafi, that the events of 1 September 1969 had been a *thawra* [revolution] and not simply a *inqilab* [military coup], the takeover had all the characteristics of a classic *putsch.*[1] It had been a bloodless event, indicative as much of the relative incompetence of the old regime in relying on the CYDEF forces as of the organizational skills of the country's new military leaders. Confusion reigned for several days about the identity of the officers who had led the coup and about their program. Not until a week after the event was Mu'ammar al-Qadhafi's name, as the country's new commander-in-chief of the army, made public, and it took another four days before he was identified as the chairman of the fourteen-member Revolutionary Command Council (RCC) that would rule the country. In January 1970, four months after the coup, Libyans finally were told who the RCC members were: Colonel Mu'ammar al-Qadhafi, Major Abd as-Salam Jalud, Major Bashir Hawadi, Captain Mukhtar Abdallah Gerwy, Captain Abd al-Munim Tahir al-Huni, Captain Mustapha al-Kharubi, Captain al-Khuwaylidi al-Hamidi, Captain Muhammad Nejm,

[1] "It is impossible to give the specific date for the beginning of the Libyan revolution. . . . No one can determine the beginning of any revolution. This differs from a coup which is a casual event occurring at the pleasure of senior officers. . . . A revolution is the opposite, even if the practical application of the idea partakes of the same appearance as a military coup" (Qadhafi, cited by First 1975, 101).

Captain Ali Awad Hamza, Captain Abu Bakr Yunus Jabar, and Captain 'Umar Abdallah al-Muhayshi (First 1975).

Libya's coup had been perpetrated by individuals whose socioeconomic and political backgrounds stood in sharp contrast to those who had provided leadership during the monarchy. All Free Officers, as the coup's army supporters became collectively known, were military men who came from less prestigious tribes and families than those who had been affiliated with the Sanusi regime; most Free Officers were from rural backgrounds. They represented both Libya's middle class and its hinterland, and had all attended military academy primarily because they had not qualified for university entrance, which required an education certificate that had been restricted under the monarchy.[2] As such, Libya's new leaders provided a marked contrast to those who had been in charge of the monarchy, and their populist rhetoric was no coincidence: they came largely from social milieus that Idris had bypassed.

Nowhere was the contrast with the monarchy more sharply visible than in the rhetoric of the new regime. To those familiar with Egyptian politics after its 1952 revolution, there was unmistakably an element of déjà vu in the events that unfolded in Libya after 1969. To Qadhafi, as to countless other young Arab nationalists in the 1950s and 1960s who had closely read Gamal Abdul Nasser's *Falsafat ath-Thawra wa al-Mithaq* [Philosophy of the Revolution], the Egyptian president symbolized all that the Arab world had seemingly lost: courage, vision, and a promise for a better future, independent of the West. Nasser's emergence after the 1955 Bandung conference as a nationalist leader and his success in nationalizing the Suez Canal the following year had turned him into a symbol of Arab unity (Nasser 1970). Qadhafi was willing to commit his country's resources to the pursuit of unity with Egypt: "Tell President Nasser we made this revolution for him. He can take everything of ours and add it to the rest of the Arab world's resources to be used for the battle [against Israel, and for Arab unity]" (Heikal 1975, 70).

To Qadhafi, the possibility for grandeur had not yet been exhausted, and oil could serve as part of an Arab *nahdha* [renewal]. When Nasser died in 1970, the young Libyan revolutionary anointed himself as successor. Even today, almost three decades after his initial meeting with Nasser, one of the most prominent pictures throughout Libya remains that of a young, deliriously happy Qadhafi walking arm in arm with the

[2] All except two of the RCC's members had graduated from military academies in 1963.

former Egyptian leader; Qadhafi still considers his meeting with Nasser one of the defining moments of his revolution (Qadhafi 14 July 1989).

There was another important dimension to the coup. The RCC and its allies represented a small, highly politicized group in the midst of a largely apathetic population. The collapse of the kingdom provoked no organized opposition, partly because monarchy itself had been an untried political concept in Libyan society. The king's disappearance and the removal of British and U.S. military bases shortly afterward never translated into much popular support for the new rulers. Most Libyans initially remained politically indifferent to the new revolutionary regime in Tripoli. In many ways, the revolution got off to an inauspicious start: a small core of revolutionaries with vague ideas about what they wanted to achieve but with enormous resources at their disposal, and a population with few clear interests beyond sharing the growing riches of an oil state (Hasan 10 December 1989).

The RCC did not initially present a clear political program. On 16 September 1970, Qadhafi announced for the first time the broad nationalist goals of the revolution: removal of all foreign troops from Libyan territory, neutrality, national unity, Arab unity, and the suppression of all political parties (*SQ* 1969–70). In addition, there were numerous references to socialism and Islam—the latter to allow the new regime to establish its own religious credentials, in contrast to those of the Sanusis. None of the rhetoric, however, indicated what political structures the RCC hoped to create or how it envisioned recreating local society to support its revolution. In fact, RCC members had given little thought to the internal aspects of their revolution, in part because there had not been in Libya—as in neighboring Algeria, for example—the struggle, persecution, and conspiratorial circumstances that forged a clear political agenda in their minds. Qadhafi's focus on broader pan-Arab concerns hid from view this ideological vacuum, which would lead in the early 1970s to internal struggles as different groups within the RCC tried to fill it in their own fashion.

In the year following the coup, the RCC clearly intended to destroy the power of the monarchy's elite groups—Sanusi army officers in the regular army, the CYDEF, upper bureaucrats and businessmen in all three provinces, Cyrenaican tribal and rural elites with direct access to the king and the *diwan,* and some of the country's regular *ulama*—but the restructuring this entailed was clearly beyond the capacity of the new regime in the first few months. The monarchy's distributive policies had created large bureaucracies that could not be reconstituted overnight; the new regime had to continue relying initially on many of those who had been appointed by the monarchy. The RCC therefore proceeded gingerly: they incorporated CYDEF and other security forces into the regular army and then removed all officers above the rank of major through early retirement, assignments abroad or, in relatively few cases, through brief periods of imprisonment. Libya's army doubled in size almost overnight and started to attract a young generation of Libyans for whom it was clear that, in revolutionary Libya, the Military Academy had become an important road to power and social advancement (First 1975; Hinnebusch 1982).

The regime's consolidation continued throughout the first year. Under the country's new constitution (14 December 1969), the RCC became the highest authority and nominated the Council of Ministers. Within a year, most of the civilians were removed from it as the RCC assumed supreme judicial, executive, and legislative power. An anticorruption campaign started in early 1970 to remove more of the old regime's top bureaucratic elite; but again, for lack of adequate replacements, the central bureaucratic and administrative institutions of the government were left untouched. The government's top civilian participants, however, resigned in increasing numbers. Sulayman al-Maghribi, the country's prime minister, left by the beginning of 1970, and by October that year all ministries, except the technocrat-populated Ministry of Oil, were held by RCC members.

The regime then turned toward a systematic policy of mobilization. On 14 January 1971, Colonel Qadhafi announced at Zawiya the country's first attempt at popular rule: the creation of popular congresses that would appoint representatives to a new parliament and directly elect the country's president. The Zawiya speech was followed by an intense campaign of personal appearances by RCC members, including Qadhafi, throughout Libya, meant to make the populist intentions of the RCC clear to the population.[3] Despite the publicity surrounding its creation, the popular congress system was almost immediately abandoned. Qadhafi concluded at the time that an attempt at self-government was premature and politically still too risky (Ibjad 8 October1992; Abu Khzam 6 June 1989).

Indicative of the lack of ideological and programmatic direction, the RCC then turned toward a more centralized system of mobilization. The result was the creation of the Arab Socialist Union (ASU) on 12 June 1971—

[3]The following RCC members participated: Jalud (Khums), Hamza (Gharian), Hawadi (Ajdabiyya), al-Hamidi (Sabha), Qadhafi (Tubruk) (Bleuchot 1983).

symbolically on the first anniversary of the American evacuation of the Wheelus base (*JR* 27 June 1971). The ASU, based on Nasser's single political party in Egypt, was regarded as a vanguard party that would simultaneously mobilize the population and reinforce the RCC's attempts to further dismantle the tribal system and to curtail potential political activity by the old regime's elites. A structure of national, provincial [*muhafadhat*], and local [*mudiriyyat*] assemblies was created to cross old tribal boundaries and to destroy the power of traditional institutions and that of traditional regional identity. In order to reinforce the regime's actions, the old titles and former ascriptive prerequisites for leadership were changed or abandoned, and whatever social, economic, and religious community affairs had traditionally been handled by local dignitaries were now channeled directly toward the national administration (El-Fathaly, Palmer, and Chackerian 1977). Elections for the local and provincial congresses took place in December 1971 and January 1972. Its chosen delegates attended the first national ASU congress, personally presided over by Qadhafi. But whatever enthusiasm the ASU initially engendered among the country's leadership also dissipated quickly, and by the third congress in 1973 the party had lost all favor with Qadhafi, although it would linger on in name until 1977 (Mammeri 1977). Much like the abandoned popular congresses, however, the ASU had not been able to mobilize the population or to neutralize opposition leaders. In many urban areas the elections had not generated new revolutionary leadership but had retained politically neutral, better-educated middle-class citizens. In rural areas personal, tribal, and regional solidarities persisted, reinforced by lingering patronage systems the new regime had not been able to modify. The ASU had functioned as one more barrier between the country's leadership and the people. Qadhafi's solution, soon formulated during the Popular Revolution and then more systematically elaborated in the Green Book, was to draw nearer to the people simply by abandoning political or bureaucratic intermediaries between the revolutionary leadership and the masses.

The Popular Revolution and the Pursuit of Legitimacy

Qadhafi's preoccupation with the Libyan bureaucracy and administrative institutions dated back to the early months after the revolution. The ASU had in part been an attempt to reshape the monarchy's traditional administrative divisions, in a fashion that cut across tribal boundaries. But, particularly at the national planning level, the fast pace of economic development provided Qadhafi with little choice but to rely on substantial remnants of the Sanusi bureaucracy. Because of the educational opportunities provided to them under the monarchy, many of those who had taken over from the purged national bureaucracies after 1969 were second-generation Tripolitanian and Cyrenaican elites, few of whom shared the revolutionary leadership's outlook. Their socialization and background increasingly clashed with the views of the RCC members and with those of the party organizers of the ASU. As a result, many of the bureaucrats appointed as part of Qadhafi's efforts to replace the tribal leadership were better educated than RCC members.[4]

Almost no technocrats could be found within the RCC or among the Free Officers movement at large—although several would consistently argue for more technocratically oriented solutions to the country's economic problems. The inclusion of overwhelmingly nonmilitary technocrats into subsequent new governments threatened to divide the RCC. But Qadhafi, partly to balance the RCC itself and partly for technical reasons, preferred civilian technocrats. In July 1972, the regime's most powerful figure after Qadhafi, Abd as-Salam Jalud, was charged with redesigning the country's Cabinet. Until then the crossover between the RCC and the Cabinet had been marked by a certain fluidity, but the division now hardened. Civilians occupied fifteen of seventeen portfolios, including the crucial Ministry of Planning.

As part of its continued attempts to further break down the residual power of the monarchy's bureaucratic structures, the regime on 16 April 1973—during a speech at Zuwara, on the anniversary of the death of the prophet Muhammad—launched the popular revolution as an alternative to the Arab Socialist Union.[5] In announcing the new measure, Qadhafi termed the ASU experiment a failure, arguing that the party had not functioned as a link between the country's leadership and the masses. Rather than mobilization "from above," the popular revolution represented mobilization "from below"—a clear intensification of Qadhafi's attempts at direct popular rule. Its five-point program represented a tabula rasa on which the true Libyan revolution would be constructed: (1) the removal of all opponents of the revolution, (2) the arming of the general population, (3) an administrative revolution, (4) a cultural revolu-

[4]El-Fathaly, Palmer, and Chackerian (1977) provide a wealth of data on these secondary elites, recruited both before and after the popular revolution.

[5]Ever since then, Zuwara has been referred to in Libya's revolutionary literature as *niqad al-khamis,* the City of Five Points, referring to the official five-point program Qadhafi announced as the underlying basis of the popular revolution.

tion, and (5) the suspension of all laws applicable at the time (*SQ* 1972–73).[6] The popular revolution was meant to "[destroy] the classical bureaucratic system, by giving the public the whole power and authority to change, dismiss, and elect public officials on all levels . . . removing all the legal and administrative obstacles in the way of revolutionary change" (El-Fathaly, Palmer, and Chackerian 1977, 41).

The first stage involved an attack against local and regional bureaucrats Qadhafi considered hostile to the revolution. Several mayors, managers, and governors—including the top bureaucrats of the Libyan Petroleum Institute (LPI), the national radio and television station, and the Libyan Arab Airlines—were removed from office. In August and September of 1973, the governors of Gharian, Darna, and Benghazi were removed, and in Tripoli the entire municipal council and the president of the country's main university were forced to resign. The second stage involved the creation of popular committees by workers within their place of employment. Most public organizations, institutes, and communities were taken over by these elected committees, which were given legislative and executive power. By the end of August, twenty-four hundred committees had been approved by the RCC, and many of the public enterprises had been purged of 'recalcitrant' elements (*JR* 2 September 1973).[7]

The power of the committees, however, appeared almost purely advisory, while the real power remained with the RCC. The 12 October 1973 law, which finally promulgated the popular committee law, furthermore stipulated that the committees would be restricted to nonvital sectors of the Libyan economy, but these sectors were left unspecified (*JR* 22 November 1973). Qadhafi objected to these restrictions and refused to sign the law, as a gesture of clear displeasure with the RCC's limitations on the competence of the popular committees. His refusal reflected the continuing debate within the RCC over which direction the revolution should take. The exclusion of vital sectors from the committees' area of competence, as well as the restructuring of popular committees at the universities in December, indicated that those within the RCC who

[6] By the time of the announcement of the popular revolution, several of its ideas had already been discussed at the Higher Council on National Orientation, created by Qadhafi in September 1972. In November that year, a first general meeting had taken place to discuss aspects of what eventually became unified into the Third Universal Theory.

[7] The actual law on the popular committee structure was not promulgated until 12 October 1973.

shared the views of the country's top technocrats and who were opposed to popular rule still strongly defended their viewpoints, even at the expense of Qadhafi himself.

As the Libyan leader acknowledged in his Zuwara and subsequent speeches, Libya's revolutionaries had made few structural changes in Libyan society since 1969, and the popular revolution was an expression of that frustration. He was convinced nonetheless that Libyans shared the (still undefined) principle of socialism that had led the Free Officers to wage the revolution. The years since 1969, he argued, had not been a true revolution but only an introduction to the real revolution, where "people govern themselves by themselves" (*SQ* 1973–74). People needed more vigorously to remove nonrevolutionaries and bureaucratic elements that obstructed the true revolution. The Zuwara speech thus contained the seeds of the three major components that would form the basis of Qadhafi's increasingly dramatic political pursuits after 1973: (1) the destruction of representative systems, (2) the dismantling of the state, and (3) the assertion of the Third Universal Theory as the ideological reference for Libya.

Since coming to power, the new regime had managed—imperfectly, in light of existing constraints—to force the economic elites who were once the backbone of the Sanusi monarchy to withdraw from the country's political life. It had also tentatively drawn up new institutional, bureaucratic, and political structures for the country. The popular revolution thus seemingly vindicated Qadhafi's desire to create a local leadership that differed substantially in outlook from the educated officials and tribal chiefs that had been part of the monarchy's institutional structure. Recruitment from among the lower-middle and lower class produced a layer of low-ranking officials closer to the masses and, of greater importance, hostile to the bureaucratic politics of their predecessors (El-Fathaly and Palmer 1977). But their inadequate education repeatedly exacerbated their actual functioning and frustrated both the people and the part of the regime that often labeled them as intransigent and lazy.

In addition, the rapid reform of part of the prerevolutionary bureaucratic network created great confusion. The government's inclination was simply to add more government agencies often with overlapping authority rather than to streamline the already existing institutions. The Ministry of Agriculture and the Ministry of Industry, for example, had corresponding departments of agriculture and of industrial research that performed virtually identical functions—and in each case their areas of jurisdiction were separated, and then joined once more, on at least two occasions. Often public corporations and administrative departments pursued the same goals, relying on vague guidelines and directives. To make matters worse, bureaucratic offices, even of the same ministry, were often left uncoordinated and physically shifted location regularly, in a fashion that became almost standard practice after 1973.[8] Clearly, the country's bureaucracies were emerging—or were maintained and expanded—as important political outlets for the regime in creating its own networks of patronage, but in a much more inclusive, populist fashion than had been the case under the monarchy. By the end of 1972, Libya's administrative and bureaucratic structure had nearly doubled, and the resulting confusion about areas of competence and jurisdiction were such that Libyans developed a special deprecatory vocabulary to describe it.[9]

In the quest for legitimacy for his revolution, Qadhafi skillfully interwove historical, symbolic, cultural, and pragmatic factors that resonated within the traditional but modernizing setting that Libya represented when the coup took place. Central to that quest were his confrontation with the West, symbolized in the demand for the removal of U.S. and British military personnel from Libya and in the struggle over greater control with the oil companies. Although the success in each case was linked to decisions made under the monarchy, Qadhafi quickly claimed each as an achievement of his revolution. The developments in the oil sector added to Qadhafi's stature inside the country. The RCC moved with seeming impunity as it insisted on considerable increases in royalties and taxes in 1970 and 1971. The increase in the posted price of Libyan oil and the hike in the new regime's share of profit not only increased the country's earnings but, more importantly for Qadhafi, vindicated his calls for economic sovereignty.

Equally important, they propelled him within the region to a stature that, for the first time, commanded respect for Libya's actions. The sight of Egypt's Nasser visiting Qadhafi in Benghazi and the willingness of the region's two most powerful countries (and eventually others) to consider unity plans with Libya provided a sharp contrast to the virtual ostracism

[8] A precursor of Qadhafi's later attempted to shift ministries away from Tripoli and create a new capital at Jufra to control the country's bureaucracies.

[9] One of the common words used was *tabika,* literally meaning " boiling stew" (see El-Fathaly and Palmer 1980, 107–120). The confusion also led to a profusion of hilarious cartoons by Muhammad Zwawi in local newspapers that poked fun at the Libyans' lethargy in responding to the revolution and at their traditional, conservative lifestyles.

Idris had previously been met with.[10] Qadhafi's wrapping himself in Nasser's pan-Arab cloak and assuming the leadership of the Arab unity movement—no matter how outdated by 1970—upon the Egyptian president's death resonated particularly among younger Libyans. Similarly, Qadhafi and most of his fellow RCC officers represented Libya's hinterland and a socioeconomic background that had largely been excluded from the first decade of the country's oil riches. During the initial years of consolidation and mobilization, this "hinterland culture" and the emergence of educated members of less prestigious tribes provided, at least ideologically, a powerful focus for the regime (El-Fathaly and Palmer 1980). It would lose its importance as urbanization and economic differentiation among the regime's own support coalitions started to take place but would linger as an expression of Qadhafi's vision of statelessness: the creation of a political community that reflected the consultative aspects of an earlier, tribal *shura* [consultation].

Although sensitivity to Islamic concerns led to symbolic actions that contributed further to Qadhafi's legitimacy—the closing of nightclubs and churches, the banning of alcohol, and the readoption, in principle, of Islamic criminal penalties—the Libyan leader's pronouncements at this early stage of the revolution already indicated what he would later spell out more clearly: that religion constituted a direct relationship between an individual and God and should therefore not be used for political purposes. In light of the collaborationist role the traditional *ulama* and the Sanusi-allied *ulama* had played during the colonial period and the monarchy, the clear warning to the country's religious establishment did not raise any popular objection.

Finally, legitimacy was also bought. Laws appeared in the country's official gazette, *al-Jarida ar-Rasmiyya,* ensuring that the regime's distributive largesse was applied to a wide segment of Libyan society. Not only did national expenditures for health care, education, and literacy increase dramatically between 1969 and 1973, but, through government-sponsored mechanisms, individual consumers also profited directly. In the wake of the coup, minimum wages for workers were raised, free housing or interest-free loans were provided (the repayment of which

[10]Libya eventually proposed unity plans on seven different occasions: (1) in 1969 with Egypt and Sudan (the Tripoli Charter); (2) in 1971 with Egypt and Syria (Benghazi Treaty); (3) between Egypt and Libya in 1972; (4) with Algeria in 1973 (Hassi Messaoud Accords); (5) with Tunisia in 1974 (Djerba Treaty); (6) with Chad in 1981 (Tripoli Communiqué); and (7) with Morocco in 1984 (Oujda Treaty).

was waived for Libya's poorest on the first anniversary of the revolution), and workers were allowed to share in company profits. Farmers became eligible for confiscated Sanusi or Italian land and farms and were able to purchase all necessary implements and livestock at an estimated 10 percent of their real value. Land could be purchased interest-free; until the farm became self-sufficient the farmer was eligible for a government salary. Subsidies to build houses, particularly in the countryside, were easily available from a banking system in which the government had taken an across-the-board 51 percent holding in 1970 (*SQ* 1969–70).

Small business also profited handsomely: the RCC quickly moved to implement a "Libya first" policy that required that all government contracts be assigned to Libyan firms. In its wake, business boomed. Virtually anyone could seek government tenders for construction or imports, and government banks provided financing of up to 95 percent for all commercial business ventures. Individual entrepreneurs, providing only 5 percent of the total capital required, could then sublease parts of their projects to foreign firms for substantially higher fees. Industrial projects were eligible for 100 percent government financing. The impact of these measures was such that in Sabrata, for example, within two years of the revolution, the three companies that had monopolized all government contracts under the monarchy were joined by almost thirty others that were now contracting with the government. In Tripolitania alone, an estimated forty thousand new grocery licenses were issued between 1969 and 1976 (El-Fathaly and Palmer 1980).

The object of these initiatives was in part to increase the legitimacy of the regime, but they also further burdened the country's bureaucracies, which were still experiencing the replacement of their personnel in the wake of the coup. They became even more inefficient, making Qadhafi's harangues against them a self-fulfilling prophesy that would lead to their evisceration after the mid-1970s. The government's initiatives also led to the emergence of countless high-profit and high-cost businesses that proved extremely inefficient. In addition, it turned many Libyans into *kafils,* sponsors of expatriate laborers and demonstrated all the social dislocations distributive states exhibit. Over and over again, Qadhafi singled out these social and economic perverse effects but never showed any understanding of how the combination of populism and distributive largesse was at the root of many of the country's problems (Qadhafi 6 June 1989).

The distributive measures of the regime during its first four years in power indicated its populist aspirations and showed how consumers, small entrepreneurs, and workers formed one part of the new patterns of patronage that had started to emerge; the RCC and the Free Officers constituted the remaining part. As Qadhafi stood poised to pursue his populist, stateless utopia in earnest, however, Libya remained dominated by the RCC. The regime adamantly refused to permit the development of any autonomous popular organization or initiative, and Qadhafi's reference to a People's Militia at Zuwara hinted that, in ways reflective of the monarchy, not even the military would be allowed to develop and pursue its own interests. Nor would opposition parties or syndicalist activities be allowed to reappear, Qadhafi said, because "whoever is opposed to the people's revolution is opposed to the people" (*SQ* 1972–73, 505).[11]

From Concession to Participation: Oil and Development

Amidst the initial political confusion, the campaigns to replace the monarchy's elites in the country's bureaucracies, and the expulsion of the remaining Italian settlers, the Qadhafi government paid little systematic attention to the economy during its first few months in power.[12] Overwhelmed by the tasks that faced them, RCC members constantly expressed concerns about the political and economic implications of the role that oil now played in the local economy. Their concern was heightened by the fact that oil production in 1970 reached a new record of almost three million barrels per day, a rate of production that was considered damaging to the long-term health of the oilfields. By then, oil provided Libya with 98.7 percent of its revenues and made up 99.82 percent of its exports. The oil industry, however, directly employed only 1 percent of the active population and had led to a structurally unbalanced economy, characterized by undesirable social and economic ripple effects that the young officers repeatedly decried (*AAN* 1969).

[11] On 30 May 1972, law number 71 made any political activity outside the ASU a crime, punishable by death under certain circumstances. Since in the original text (*JR* 1972, 1338–1341) the Arab word *hizbiya* was used as a criterion of what constituted forbidden political activity, the word could be interpreted to encompass any action that was potentially divisive to politics in Libya.

[12] The Libyan oil industry and the role of the country's leadership during the early 1970s have been examined in many publications. This truncated account relies in part on Allan 1981, Wright 1982, Waddams 1980, and the concise quarterly and annual reports provided by the *Economist Intelligence Unit* and the *Annuaire de l'Afrique du Nord*.

At the same time, the RCC had neither the educational background nor the skills or experience to regulate and plan for what had become one of the world's most sophisticated oil infrastructures. With outright nationalization impossible at the time, the RCC turned its attention to the one aspect of oil production it could influence: its pricing mechanism. In doing so, from late 1969 through the first months of 1972, the new regime relied on advantages it enjoyed over the oil companies that emerged simultaneously and almost accidentally. In less than five years the combination of these fortuitous circumstances and the brinkmanship of the new regime allowed it to dramatically increase prices for Libyan oil. The initial victories over the oil companies then catalyzed the reversal of the multinationals' domination over the country's oil industry and to the successive nationalizations that took place after 1973.

The Sanusi government's oil legislation, described in Chapter 3, had fostered the rapid exploitation of Libya's oil by assigning areas for exploration to small independent producers and to Majors who possessed a long-established market position. This peculiar structure of the Libyan oil industry allowed the new government, through a divide-and-rule policy, to press for higher prices and for greater production control starting in 1970. Also, the position of the independent companies in the international oil market provided Qadhafi with an excellent opportunity to enforce his demands. Independent oil companies did not have the large integrated structure of the Majors, nor their capital flow. Most operated only in one country, or a few at most, thus obtaining a substantial amount of their earnings from a single source. Occidental Petroleum, for example, one of the two prominent independent companies in Libya, obtained 97 percent of its total oil production from that country. In comparison, for Amoseas and Esso Libya, both part of larger multinational corporations, Libyan production amounted only to 3 percent and 5 percent, respectively, of their global output (*AAN* 1973).

Independents were clearly more vulnerable than the Majors to threats of expropriation or cutbacks in production. They also had few, if any, incentives to follow the Majors' long-established practice of cutting back on production when surpluses on the global market reduced oil prices. When such a situation developed in 1970, the Majors found themselves in a dilemma: while they were willing to consider a drop in their own production to restore the market, they acknowledged their inability to persuade the Independents of doing so. Taking advantage of the Independents' precarious position—heightened by an acute short-haul shortage in Europe at the time—the Qadhafi government systematically singled the Independents out in its attempt to raise prices. They were ordered to cut back their production substantially and quickly acquiesced to Qadhafi's higher price demands, which were formalized in the Tripoli Agreements (Cooley 1982). Qadhafi's actions, representing the first significant victory for any local government over the multinational oil companies within the region, steadily raised prices through indexation of oil prices and through the regime's insistence on larger shares of profits.

Flush with its victories over the oil companies, Libya's negotiators then turned their attention to the Libyan National Oil Company (LNOC). Their aim was clearly to strengthen LNOC's role in the actual management of the oil industry. That same year, the company took over twenty-three concessions that oil companies had abandoned both before and after the oil price negotiations. In an effort to prevent further loss of control, the multinational oil companies in January 1971 countered with the secret Libyan Producers' Agreement, an arrangement whereby any individual oil company's losses—caused by the Libyan government's actions—would be made up by the other companies. The agreement soon failed, in part because close cooperation between Algeria's and Libya's oil ministers outmaneuvered the companies.[13] The stage was now set for even more dramatic action: the actual takeover of local production. Throughout the remainder of 1971, 1972, and 1973, Libya announced majority shares in most of the oil-producing companies inside the country. On 1 September 1973, the fourth anniversary of the coup and just prior to the October war, Libya announced an across-the-board 51 percent participation of the Majors' holdings.

Although the price increase of Libyan oil between September 1969 and October 1973 (roughly from $2.50 to $4.61) paled in comparison to the virtual quadrupling of prices that occurred after OPEC's actions in the wake of the 1973 war (from $4.61 in early October to $15.76 on 1 January 1974), the Qadhafi regime's actions galvanized the region and seemingly confirmed the Libyan leader's stature as Nasser's heir to pan-Arabism. Just prior to the 1973 October war, Libya had accumulated $2 billion in reserves, sufficient to maintain imports for an estimated four years in case of an embargo against the country. This seemingly vindicated what had, by then, become one of Qadhafi's most often repeated assertions: that Libya had lived without oil for five thousand years and could do so again (Wright 1982). The confrontation with the multina-

[13] Algeria, for example, refused to sell oil to Esso for delivery to Spain after the oil company failed to reach an agreement with Tripoli.

tional oil companies provided him with legitimacy far beyond anything he imagined possible; but it also put at his disposal increasing financial resources that would soon expand beyond already heightened expectations—in a political system that, like the monarchy, had no mechanisms for ensuring accountability.

The rapid increase in oil revenues and the dislocations they generated however, threatened to further exacerbate the country's dualistic economic nature. Besides oil, Libya had few other known minerals, minimal infrastructure, and a small and underskilled labor force. Between 1962 and 1969, the share of petroleum in the country's GDP had jumped from 27 to 65 percent (*AAN* 1969; First 1975). All other sectors appeared in a dismal state, linked in part to the poverty of the country's natural endowments. The population had remained small, hardly sufficient to sustain major economic development plans. By 1969, it remained at just below two million people. Although per capita income had soared to $2,168 by 1970, the increase was due exclusively to hydrocarbon revenues (*MEED* 31 August 1979). Agriculture and manufacturing only contributed, respectively, 2.4 percent and 2 percent to GDP by the time of the Qadhafi coup. Only 1.5 percent of Libya's total area of 680,000 square miles furthermore lent itself to agriculture. Of this, a meager 260,000 acres were irrigated. Most of the country's modernized farms had belonged to the Italian settlers that were expropriated in the wake of the coup. Ninety percent of the available land was left to unproductive dry farming. By 1969, Libya could not produce enough food to feed its own population "for one third of a single day" (Attiga 1973; *AAN* 1970, 453). Nevertheless, 34 percent of the active population still remained involved in agriculture, a sector that by that time only contributed 4 percent of GDP.

During its first two years in power, the regime announced a number of stopgap measures that represented little more than a reaction against the economic policies of the monarchy, by a regime still utterly dependent on foreign expertise and possessing no firm grasp on its economic direction. The measures were essentially conservative, meant primarily to dislodge the previous regime's allies from whatever positions they had obtained. After expropriating the property of the Sanusi government—estimated at 220,000 acres of the country's most fertile land—Qadhafi in February 1970 started to redistribute the confiscated land, and in July nationalized all land owned by Italian settlers. The exodus of the Italian population left in its wake temporary but debilitating shortages of skills.

The manufacturing sector, consisting overwhelmingly of small businesses involved in food and import processing for the local market, was left untouched. In March 1970, the first guidelines for the creation of an industrial infrastructure were put into effect. The private sector, and its control over wholesale and retail trade, was retained but was not allowed to contradict the economic policies of the government. Large industrial projects—in essence the refineries and liquefaction plants along the Mediterranean—came under state control.

The lack of direction and the haphazard measures until late 1972 indicated above all the difficulties the new regime faced in finding adequate personnel to staff many of the positions that had been vacated by the monarchy's personnel. Not surprising, many were retained and, together with the expatriate technocrats, continued to form the nucleus of the country's economic planners. The 1973–75 plan, announced in April 1973, was the Qadhafi government's first systematic attempt to confront the daunting problems of its economy and the role of Libya's society in the country's development. The plan's allocations reflected the regime's preoccupation with agriculture to slow down rural flight (16.6 percent of the total) and with utilities (13.1 percent), and housing (18.4 percent) to provide basic amenities to the people. Chapter 2 of the *Three Year Economic and Social Development Plan 1973–75* detailed the projected goals: a growth rate in real GDP projected at an astonishing annual rate of 11 percent and a diversification of the economy that would decrease the country's dependence on the oil sector. The non-oil sectors were expected to expand at a much higher rate than the oil sector: 16.5 percent, versus 5 percent annually. According to the Plan, the share of the non-oil sector in the country's national income was expected to rise to almost 50 percent by the end of the projected period (Libyan Arab Republic 1973). The Plan also aimed at channeling substantial long-term investments into agriculture and manufacturing. In similarly optimistic language, it envisioned that the agricultural sector would be able to meet internal food production and would slow down the migration of the hinterland population toward the coastal cities. For that purpose, the government signed several contracts for land reclamation, for the construction of farms, for agricultural and geological research, and for the drilling of water wells. In 1973 alone, contracts for bringing approximately 356,000 acres of land into production were concluded, largely with Arab and East European companies. These formed only the first part of a much larger project that was meant eventually to bring 1.1 million acres into agricultural production in four major development efforts: (1) at Kufra and Sarir, (2) at the Barce-Tukra plain in Cyrenaica, (3) at the Gefara Plain in Tripolitania, and (4) at several *wadis* in Fazzan.

In all of these instances, however, budgeted expenditures did not necessarily mean actual implementation. Because of the almost nonexistent infrastructure, the new regime's first plan was in effect little more than a list of planned public investments financed through oil revenues. In the wake of the dramatic increase in oil revenues that began in October 1973, the plan's allocations increased dramatically. But, like the monarchy's first attempt at planning for development, it lost much of its coherence as spending increased rapidly (*MEED* 31 August 1979). By 1973, new industrial projects had been started: the construction of three new refineries, a petrochemical plant in Marsa al-Burayqa, and two steel plants that would use the considerable reserves of iron ore located in Fazzan. In the light industrial sector, the General Industrialization Organization concluded several turnkey contracts, primarily for construction materials. In line with the populist philosophy of the government, the Libyan Industrial Bank in April 1973 extended credit to approximately twenty private companies in order to produce consumer goods for the local market. A significant part of the 1973 expenditures, in particular, were targeted toward the extension of electrification networks throughout the coastal strip and to the construction or enlargement of the Tripoli and Misrata harbors.

On the eve of the country's second oil boom, the RCC had proven itself "long in enthusiasm for managing a national economy but . . . very short in experience" (Allan 1981, 179). In light of their collective background and of the general policies during the monarchy, the lack of experience was not exceptional. The young officers faced the daunting task of not only developing plans for their country's future but of convincing Libyan citizens to take part in those plans after nearly two decades during which they had been deliberately excluded from participation. By the summer of 1973, the regime had enjoyed extraordinary success in confronting and wresting power from the multinational oil companies and in removing substantial segments of the kingdom's commercial and landed elite. In the process heavy industry, banks, insurance companies, and hospitals had been nationalized or were put under closer scrutiny. But the new regime showed little interest at this time in the wholesale management of the country's economy. The redistribution of Sanusi land and Italian properties; the projected heavy outlays for housing, roads, and utilities; and the efforts to channel money toward ambitious agricultural projects hinted at the new regime's heavily populist orientation. But the redistributive efforts of the RCC's early years provided, as yet, no clue to its ability to match its enthusiasm for managing a national economy with actual strength.

Conclusion

The four years between the 1969 coup and the country's second oil boom in 1973 were an interlude that allowed the new regime to consolidate itself and to attempt a first wave of political mobilization in support of its self-proclaimed revolution. Libya's new rulers quickly and successfully dismantled part of the old elite structure that had been created as a system of royal patronage. This had been a relatively easy task: economic competition and differentiation had only started to emerge after 1960, and the first oil boom had proven too short a period for these elites, who had no shared history of coordination at any rate, to become either well organized or well entrenched. Furthermore, the monarchy had retained few supporters, even among the Sanusi-allied tribes, that were willing to risk their status by openly opposing the Revolutionary Command Council. The highest ranks of the national administration and bureaucracies, as well as the army, were quickly purged of disloyal personnel; Cyrenaican and Tripolitanian business elites and entrepreneurs were expropriated and removed.

Reducing the power of the tribal chiefs had been more arduous and hazardous and had necessitated new administrative units that cut across tribal lines. For that purpose, the regime attempted to create new allies consisting of modernizing young bureaucrats—primarily from less prestigious tribes—that were at the heart of the RCC's initial mobilization efforts. Equally important were the Free Officers and a new group of junior officers who formed the backbone of the restructured Libyan army that quickly emerged as the focus for social advancement under the military regime. Finally, in a manner that foreshadowed his role in the years ahead, Mu'ammar al-Qadhafi had emerged as the charismatic leader of the revolution, based on a combination of traditional and modern elements he skillfully blended to promote his own standing.

There were also the first signs that the revolutionary regime, like its predecessor, showed little interest in extending the state. The demise of the ASU, the pejorative references to bureaucratic structures that could slow down and frustrate the goals of the new regime, and the increasingly populist rhetoric to circumvent both sets of obstacles indicated Qadhafi's frustration at seeing his plans obstructed. The first glimmerings of what eventually became the Third Universal Theory—Qadhafi's alternative to capitalism and communism—appeared in the Libyan leader's discourse: the distrust of political parties and institutions as obstacles to popular participation that needed to be replaced by direct rule. The announcement of popular rule in 1973 had, temporarily, been the culmination and the expression of that ambition, but it still lacked the programmatic unity the Green Book would provide.

By 1973 the military regime had arrived at an important crossroads: the RCC seemed genuinely interested in extending its efforts at mobilization and at pursuing a long-term economic development strategy. In an even more pronounced fashion, however, Libya's new rulers now possessed both the physical and economic resources to forego or limit participation and to use their distributive capabilities in pursuit of a populist agenda. Most of the regime's actions during the first four years had been of a redistributive nature, to correct what it saw as highly inequitable development during the monarchy. As it stood poised to weather the onslaught of yet more oil revenues that had already led to a loss of control over economic regulation during the 1960s, there were already the first signs that it would not be able to avoid completely the attractions of distributive largesse in pursuing those populist policies. If the monarchy had been marked by the use of distribution for managing political exclusion and networks of patronage, between 1969 and 1973 redistribution had been used for the pursuit of a haphazard process that involved political mobilization and inclusion.

Only after 1973—in the wake of the country's second oil boom and following continued frustration to institutionalize its efforts and make regulation work—would the regime turn toward policies that more closely reflected those of its predecessor. In the process, Qadhafi unleashed upon Libya dramatic and contradictory policies that simultaneously put the state in charge of all economic activity and made it irrelevant as a focus for political identity. State-building proceeded, but in a highly uneven fashion that left the capacity of the country's economic institutions and political system to cope with emerging problems highly differentiated.

5

Thawra and *Tharwa*: Libya's Boom-and-Bust Decade

> Two types of regime, expressed by similar-sounding Arabic words, predominate in the Arab world: one relying for its survival mostly on political capital revolving around categories such as nationalism, populism, radicalism and revolution (*thawra*); the other relying for its survival on kin-based relations, but above all else on financial capital, or wealth (*tharwa*).
> —Nazih Ayubi, *Over-Stating the Arab State*

> With random seizure of property it is irrational on the part of the citizens to produce very much to be seized.
> —Gordon Tullock, *The Social Dilemma*

> The budget is the skeleton of the state stripped of all superfluous ideologies.
> —Rudolf Goldscheid, *Finanzwissenschaft und Soziologie*

Starting in 1973, oil revenues made possible a decade of political and economic experimentation in Libya that combined the two categories quoted in Ayubi's epigraph: the pursuit of a populist and increasingly radical *thawra* [revolution] that relied overwhelmingly on the *tharwa* [wealth] produced by the country's oil revenues—an estimated $95 billion during the country's second and third oil booms that allowed the Qadhafi government to move forward with increasingly spectacular economic and political directives meant to implement the Libyan leader's vision of a stateless society.

Economically and politically, the country had been thoroughly transformed by the end of the revolutionary decade (1973–82): the state's institutions had been put directly into the hands of the people through a system of political congresses and committees, and all private economic activity had been outlawed. The sudden capital inflows allowed the regime to unleash a wave of new economic and political plans and directives—upon an economy that had, until now, been largely unregulated and upon a population that remained indifferent to the regime's mobilizational rhetoric. The formal attempts at planning, however, were matched by virtually unrestrained spending: in an effort to maintain those groups that the regime considered its main supporters, it made major outlays through an unbridled program of welfare measures, military purchases, and government contracts.

Starting in 1975, all economic decision making became even more concentrated in the hands of the country's rulers, who then, in the name of popular rule, put the country's citizens in charge —at least in principle—of the country's economy through the people's congresses and committees. The creation of this congress-and-committee system closely dovetailed with the ideological and political inclinations of a regime whose leader now committed himself in earnest to pursue his vision of a stateless society. By that time, the tension between distributive proclivities and regulatory intervention had become an acute political issue for the regime, pitting factions within the Revolutionary Command Council against each other. Their disagreement provoked an attempted coup in August 1975, led by two RCC members. In its wake, the regime's populist, distributive inclinations were strengthened as technocrats were removed from the top echelons of power. The publication of *al-Kitab al-Akhdar* [the Green Book], a compilation of Qadhafi's ideas on economic, social, and political organization in a Jamahiriyya, provided the ideological template for what was now referred to as the Everlasting Revolution [*al-Fatih abadan*].[1]

[1]The literal translation should be "the revolution everlasting." *Al-Fatih* refers directly to the opening day of September on which the actual military takeover took place. It carries heavy overtones, however, because it means "the opener" or "conqueror" and is a Quranic term that connotes social, spiritual, and even military conquest.

The defeat of Libya's technocrats in the wake of an attempted coup in August 1975 doomed the prospects for a viable public sector: in its wake, the choice between increased participation and enhanced control was consistently resolved in favor of the latter. Qadhafi's economic and political solutions, detailed in the Green Book, were simple and utopian and reflected the nostalgia for the prebureaucratic and precapitalistic society he wanted to recreate (Roumani 1983; Deeb and Deeb 1982): by simply handing over all the state's functions to the people—putting them in charge of the institutions that blocked their innate desire to structure and run their own lives—they were invited, through a system of consultation [*shura*] and choice [*ikhtiar*], to devise solutions to their economic and political problems.

The end of the massive capital inflows in 1982 marked the beginning of a transitory period for the regime. The country's oil revenues were reduced from $21 billion to $5.4 billion between the end of 1981 and 1986; as in other regional oil exporters, this forced the regime to consider new economic strategies in pursuit of sustainable macroeconomic policies and to reconsider its traditional distributive largesse. The effect of the general turmoil in the oil world on Libya was further exacerbated by the country's growing political problems with the West. By the end of 1981, the United States had halted all crude oil imports from Libya. Within two more years, a boycott was extended to selected high-technology exports and products related to oil recovery. By that time also, two of the Majors had abandoned their operations in the country.

The regime had options it could pursue in light of the declining revenues: reduce consumption at home and cut back on its development plans, or curtail its foreign adventures and military expenditures. However, because of its suspicion of borrowing on the international market, Libya had little medium or long-term debt and until the end of 1986 postponed adjustment or economic reform. Throughout the period under review in this chapter, Libya became the last great spender of petrodollars in the region and attempted to postpone economic adjustments for roughly five years. It proved only partially capable of doing so: despite the fact that the regime shifted most of the growing economic hardships toward the expatriate labor force in the country, it was also forced to halt imports of a wide assortment of (primarily consumer) goods and could not hide the severe bottlenecks in the distribution of goods and services.

Qadhafi eagerly embraced the confrontation with the West, particularly with the United States, as a way simultaneously to deepen the revolution internally and to deflect attention from the financial and political problems at home. By the end of 1986, however, a number of developments made clear that the postponement of economic reform was no longer possible and that the regime needed to take additional measures to manage the growing dissatisfaction and increasingly open defiance.

Technocrats versus Revolutionaries: Transition toward a Jamahiriyya

The regime's first four years in power had been, from a mobilizational standpoint, disappointing. Political apathy remained widespread, and few citizens had proven willing to trade the growing benefits bestowed upon them for the more active role the RCC repeatedly demanded of them. If the ASU's socialist rhetoric had been "emblematic . . . unformed and implicit" (Davis 1987, 36), the principles announced by Qadhafi during the Zuwara speech, which marked the beginning of the popular revolution, had been programmatically clear and concise. They laid the basis for the more intensive revolutionary measures that were to follow soon and, for the first time, unhesitantly spelled out Qadhafi's intention to dismantle the state—more concretely, the country's hierarchy of institutions that prevented the masses from governing themselves directly, without intermediaries. Within two years after the Zuwara speech, the five principles were reiterated more systematically in what became the guidebook to the Libyan revolution: Mu'ammar al-Qadhafi's Green Book, [2] which contained what the Libyan leader grandiloquently referred to as The Third Universal Theory, the alternative to communism and capitalism.

The two years following the announcement of the popular revolution were marked by chaos and confusion, in part because the division of labor between the ASU and the popular committees had not been clearly articulated, and no clear political program existed for the committees. Popular committees that were created—often at the urging of Qadhafi or other RCC members—were repeatedly dissolved, only to be recreated later, in rivalry to still other committees. The RCC itself repeatedly stepped in to impose orderly elections for the committees, but the conflict over "orderly" versus "activist" procedures persisted within the top leadership. Qadhafi and his supporters clearly used the chaos and the unpredictability provoked by the activists to their political advantage, as

[2] Green is, of course, the color of Islam.

a method of keeping the political system—and those arguing for more orderly procedures—unbalanced. Although the ASU congress was meant to convene in May 1973, Qadhafi postponed it, hoping to further reduce the power of his rivals within the RCC.

When the ASU finally met in November 1974, its proceedings were monopolized by debates over the direction of the revolution and by intense discussions over which tactics should be used to achieve its goals. The RCC had split between those who wanted a more orderly, planned course of action that included a carefully designed economic plan (the technocrats) and those who wanted to pursue a more activist policy that sacrificed some of the country's riches for the sake of Arab unity (the revolutionaries). The struggle between the two sides continued unabated throughout 1974, and it remained unclear which of the two constituted the most powerful group. During the year, the technocrats seemingly gained the upper hand, at the expense of Qadhafi, who was temporarily sidetracked. He refused to deliver the keynote address on the anniversary of the revolution on 1 September 1974 and did not participate in the direct talks the RCC members had with the population in August that year.

In addition, when the RCC reactivated the popular revolution in the wake of the September anniversary celebrations, the campaign was led by Colonel Jalud, who formally excluded from the committees' jurisdiction all areas where technical competence was necessary. In a number of newspaper articles, Jalud accused the old committees of anarchy, violence, and duplicity against the aims of the revolution (*Al-Fajr Al-Jadid* 12 September 1974, 13 September 1974). To avoid such further confusion, Jalud announced that RCC members would be represented at the regional meetings of the committees and that army officers would participate directly in certain committees. These new measures were confirmed at the ASU Congress and clearly contradicted Qadhafi's declaration a few weeks earlier that "neither the ASU, nor the army . . . were authorized . . . to guide the popular revolution" (*SQ* 1973–74, 1208–1212; *Al-Wahda Al-Arabiyya* 1 May 1974, 40–44). The restructuring of the government in the wake of the congress further confirmed the rise of the technocrats: only four RCC members remained, while a number of newly created ministries were assigned to young intellectuals with no broad nationalist credentials. The reform of the popular committees in 1974 was in part an effort by the RCC to contain what it considered Qadhafi's populist drive toward personal power. Some of the technocrats objected to the costs of his pan-Arab and foreign adventures and the expenses of the aborted unity attempt with Egypt. Also opposition increased within the RCC to the political interference of Qadhafi and his supporters with projects that RCC members felt should be evaluated on purely technical merits.

The end of 1974 thus witnessed the most severe internal RCC disagreement since the 1969 coup. The conflict between the two sides was highly ideological and focused almost exclusively on how Libya's oil wealth should be used. Extended debates within the RCC focused on what role the state should play, how extensive its intervention should be in economic affairs, and how much private property should be abolished in favor of centralized planning. As the conflict intensified, both sides attempted to attract allies within the Libyan army to their side, leading to fears of another coup (Ibjad 5 December 1988; Bleuchot 1983). The unrest that existed throughout the country in early 1975 added to the tension. In order to quell student opposition that had sporadically erupted since 1969, the RCC announced compulsory military service. Despite the measure, the unrest continued and spread further, leading to the first large-scale arrests of students in April 1975. Rumors of attempted coups surfaced throughout the summer in the Arab press, and, at one point in July 1975, army units loyal to Qadhafi surrounded Tripoli (*Al-Jumhuriyya,* 29 July 1975; Ibjad 2 May 1988).

At the same time, the country found itself temporarily in financial difficulties, due to a drop in demand for Libyan oil. A request for funds from Saudi Arabia was denied, and the country had to suspend payments temporarily for some of its imports. The catalyst of the August 1975 attempted coup, led by RCC members Bashir Hawadi and 'Umar al-Muhayshi, centered precisely on the haphazard allocation of the country's financial resources. While the government could not pay its bills, it was supporting several costly foreign adventures Muhayshi and his supporters objected to. Muhayshi, who was minister of planning at the time, refused to give up funds that had been earmarked for local development projects and fled with his supporters to Tunis in the aftermath of the attempted coup (Bleuchot 1983).

The events of August 1975 marked a crucial political, economic, and ideological turning point for Libya—and virtually provided Qadhafi, in its aftermath, with *carte blanche* to pursue his notions of a stateless society while channeling enormous amounts of money toward foreign adventures and military purchases. In the wake of the coup attempt, the Qadhafi government introduced increasingly draconian changes in the legal foundations of the state—transforming the country from a republic into a popularly managed Jamahiriyya—that were, more often than not, settled by outright fiat. It also effectively spelled the end of the RCC as a political institution—even though it was kept on in name and was now composed of the five men who, until late 1996, formed the top elite in the Jamahiriyya: Mu'ammar al-Qadhafi, Abu-Bakr Yunus Jabar, al-Khuwaylidi al-Hamidi, Mustafa al-Kharubi, and Abd as-Salam Jalud. With no institutionalized opposition left, Qadhafi quickly moved to consolidate his own position during the remainder of 1975.

From this point onward, Libya's revolution turned ideological, and collegial decision making yielded inexorably to one-man rule. Throughout the remainder of the year, civilian and military professionals and technical personnel were removed from the country's planning institutes and ministries. Most of those who argued for long-term social investment, prudent investment policies, curtailment of spending on military outlays, and greater efficiency were sidelined. Within a few more years, others, including the country's comptroller Muhammad Mugharyif, were replaced by individuals more sympathetic to the regime's political aspirations. The coup also marked the end of professional and technical criteria for military recruitment and was the beginning of a steady but noticeable influx of individual members of Qadhafi's tribe—and later of his family—into sensitive security and army positions.

Before he fled the country, Muhayshi had pointed out that what Libya needed was a systematic planning effort to put the country's resources to productive use. By 1975, a number of economic developments reinforced that message. Halfway through its first development plan, when the October 1973 Arab-Israeli war broke out, Libya in the aftermath of the conflict found itself awash in petrodollars as never before. From $4.605 at the beginning of the month, prices for the country's crude oil climbed rapidly to $9.061 by 16 October, and then to $15.768 on 1 January 1974. Despite this virtual quadrupling of oil prices, the fickleness of the international oil market throughout 1974 and 1975 demonstrated the country's continued vulnerability. The tanker market collapse in the wake of the Arab oil embargo and the production cuts of October 1973 in support of that embargo reduced Libya's daily output to slightly under 1.5 million barrels per day, while the actual price of Libyan crude dropped from $15.768 to slightly above $11 at the end of the year.

Despite this, the Libyan oil embargo to the United States and to the Caribbean refineries supplying the U.S. market was abandoned only in early 1975, almost a year after most producers had done so.[3] In 1974

[3] *Petroleum Economist* 42 (1975).

alone, the country's petroleum production dropped 26.4 percent, and by mid-February 1975 daily exports fell to 912,000 barrels per day, the lowest level in eleven years. These events forced Libya in early 1975 to divert substantial reserves to the national economy, resulting in the financial crisis that summer. The liquidity problems, in addition to the weak world oil market, were also related to the regime's heavy outlays for foreign aid and military purchases. As a result, Libya's balance of trade, services, and transport dropped from a surplus of $1.8 billion to a deficit of $.5 billion in 1975, which necessitated the request to Saudi Arabia for temporary financial aid.

By that time, before the country's economy became subject to popular rule, the country's technocrats had already started to draw up a new development plan for the country. The initial plans and the outcome of the *1976–80 Five-Year Social and Economic Development Plan* presented two benchmarks—before and after the implementation of the Green Book's directives—that could be used to compare the original intentions of its planners with its outcome as the regime's new economic directives took shape after 1975. In its introduction, the planners summarized the deep structural problems the country faced: expatriate labor still provided 40 percent of Libya's unskilled labor at the end of the 1973–75 plan, 27 percent of its semiskilled and skilled personnel, 35 percent of all technicians, and 58 percent of all its managers. Food production had continued to drop since 1969, while food imports consumed 15 percent of the total import budget. By 1975, Tripoli had swollen to over a half-million people, for which the government had been particularly successful in providing housing and education.[4] At the end of the introduction, its authors cryptically noted that the country's main challenge would be to channel the population's energy into productive economic activities and to ensure that the government's investments were conducive to further productivity.[5]

The Five-Year Plan consisted of an ambitious blueprint for the country's economy, not surprisingly stressing a greater centralization of economic decision making and an increased reliance on technocratic expertise in all the country's economic sectors. The plan's main emphasis was on promoting the non-oil sectors that would be paid for by oil revenues. Projected sectoral growth rates were, perhaps unrealistically, ambitious:

[4] By 1975, according to the government's own statistics, 25 percent of all Libyan children were being educated, a rise from 16 percent in 1969.

[5] *Libya. Economic and Social Transformation Plan (1976–1980).* 1976. Tripoli: Secretariat of Planning.

30 percent for manufacturing, 16 percent for agriculture, and 23 percent for electricity and water resources (Social and Economic Development Plan 1975). Of the plan's total $26.3 billion budget, the government would provide almost $23 billion, and the private sector would provide the remainder. In those sectors considered crucial by the regime—agriculture and manufacturing—investments were overwhelmingly public. In the hydrocarbon sector, the government still depended heavily on private (foreign) investment. Although housing was seen as politically sensitive by the regime, investment in the sector was primarily assigned to the private sector. The large allocations to agriculture were meant to ensure food self-sufficiency in eight to ten years. The plan projected that, by 1980, all vegetable and dairy product needs would be met locally, followed shortly by fruit, meat, and grain self-sufficiency. Foreign labor power was scheduled to be reduced to 40 percent of the country's overall needs, with managerial and professional labor still providing 50 to 60 percent of the country's expertise.

When launched in 1976, the Five-Year Plan was expected to raise few financial difficulties: trade and financial surpluses had recovered rapidly in the wake of the 1974–75 financial crisis. Libya's income that year boomed to $8.8 billion, and a consortium of foreign oil companies discovered substantial offshore oil deposits, approximately sixty miles north of Zuwara.[6] By 1977, Libya's development budgets, on a per capita basis, were outspending the rest of the Arab world fourfold.[7] The ratio of development spending to total expenditure was 72.3 percent, the highest in the region. In retrospect, however, none of the problems identified in the Five-Year Plan was addressed systematically as oil revenues diminished further the concerns of the country's technocrats, as the popular revolution unfolded in earnest after 1975, and as economic development became subject to a political logic that relied heavily on distribution of resources to the regime's clients.

On the contrary: the massive capital inflows, the removal of the technocrats from the RCC, and the populist economic directives combined to relegate concerns about efficiency and long-term growth to almost minor importance. The removal of the technocratic faction from the RCC, the

[6] The consortium consisted of Aquitaine, Elf-Erap, OMV, and Wintershall.

[7] In 1977, the total development budget of all Arab countries was $55.1 billion, for an estimated 144.3 million people ($382 per capita). Libya's development budget of $4.35 billion constituted 8 percent of this total, while its population was only 2 percent of the Arab total, thus spending four times as much. Figures from Sarkis, Nicolas. "Les Arabes pauvres et les Arabes riches." *Le Monde Diplomatique,* August; also cited in *AAN* 16 (1977), p. 569.

turn toward personal rule, and the creation of the popular congress system in effect further lowered the country's inclination to regulate systematically the country's economy. Planning, much like the country's other systems, fell victim to the revolution. By the end of the country's revolutionary decade, planning had given way to virtually unrestrained spending, in a fashion reminiscent of the monarchy. This pattern would be perpetuated after 1982.

The Green Book: Popular Rule

The opening page of the Green Book's first volume—*The Solution of the Problem of Democracy: The Authority of the People*—published within a few weeks after the August coup attempt, unambiguously pinpointed the resources Qadhafi hoped to tap in order to overcome the existing political malaise. The Libyan masses, because of bureaucratic interference and the presence of "archaic elements" within the country, he argued, had not been able to become fully involved in the country's revolution (*SQ* 1 September 1975).

The Green Book clearly represented a turning point for the Libyan revolution: it was simultaneously the culmination and codification of Qadhafi's earlier thoughts and the guideline to a new political and economic system for the country. [8] Although much of its contents had been preshadowed in Qadhafi's speeches since 1969—resulting in a number of initial confiscations, regulations, attempts at curbing the power of the Sanusi elite and a short, abortive effort at popular rule in 1971—the Green Book now became the ideological guide that more systematically extended and intensified the previous social, political, and economic directives of the regime and promoted its author to undisputed leadership within the country. It marked at the same time a gesture of continuity and a radical break with previous efforts to mobilize the Libyan population.

The intensity of the new directives that followed the publication of the Green Book's first part testified to that discontinuity. Undoubtedly, the lukewarm reception of the previous political reforms was part of the

[8] A number of editions and translations of the Green Book have appeared, several published in Tripoli by the Public Establishment for Publishing, Advertising, and Distribution (1975, 1977, and 1978) and the Green Book Center. All citations are to the 1980 edition, published by the Green Book Center. Because the volumes are very short, I omit page references to avoid needless repetition.

explanation: neither the ASU nor the popular committee system proposed in 1971 had represented more than brief, uncoordinated attempts at political coherence. The timing of the Green Book's publication was also a consideration. Sections of the first volume started to appear in *Al-Fajr Al-Jadid* in the fall of 1975. Their appearance thus came in the wake of the August attempted coup, when the technocratic opposition within the RCC had been removed and when the country was starting to experience the inflows of new revenues. The regime judged itself free to address squarely the political obstacles it still faced.

For Libya, 1975 was thus a crucial year: economic problems had proven temporary in the face of the massive revenues, but the political events before and after the attempted coup indicated the presence of resentment and opposition, even within the RCC. The ASU had proven incapable of becoming a rallying point for popular action, partly because of the remaining apathy among the population and partly because its scope and activities had been closely circumscribed by the RCC leadership. The institutional and political changes of the 1976–80 period were meant as a corrective for all that ailed Libya. In contrast to the past, incremental adjustments would be dropped in favor of a total restructuring of Libyan society, including an ambitious new five-year economic plan.

The Green Book quickly became the subject of much controversy and debate, leading to a voluminous literature and several well-publicized international conferences sponsored by the Libyan government that analyzed its content in great detail.[9] Inside Libya, it became a never-ending source of inspiration for collections of commentaries—*Shuruh al-Kitab al-Akhdar*—that applied its teachings to virtually all aspects of the country's life.[10] In truly revolutionary style, having a Green Book–related publication became a virtual conditio sine qua non for all individuals who aspired to become part of the regime's elite (Al-Hesnawi 1987; Abu Khzam 1987; Faluki 1987). Qadhafi himself viewed the Green Book above all as a manifesto for action. It was meant to intensify his earlier mobilizational efforts that had been frustrated because the country's political system

[9] Among a plethora of secondary sources on Qadhafi's Green Book, consult the papers of the international conference on the Green Book held in Benghazi, *International Colloquium in Benghazi: The Green Book, vol. 2,* 1–3 October 1979. Tripoli: Foreign Liaison Office, General Secretariat of the General People's Congress, 1981, and *International Colloquium on Mu'ammar Quathafi's Thought: The Green Book, Part 1* 12–15 November 1981. A sympathetic account can be found in Ayoub 1987; a particularly critical source is Allan 1981.

[10] At least two dozen *shuruh* have now been published by the Green Book Center.

could not express the true voice of the Libyan people (Part 1), because Libyans were not directly in charge of the economic resources of the country (Part 2), and because of the country's archaic social structure (Part 3).

Through each of the three volumes ran an important leitmotiv that encapsulated and expressed the Libyan leader's profound confusion and distrust of the hierarchical bureaucratic structures inherent in modern states: the presence of intermediaries who prevented individuals from directly managing their own lives. This common thread informed the regime's ever more spectacular attempts to bring Libya's society, economy, and political life in line with the directives of the Green Book, starting in late 1975. By 1982, when the revolutionary period of the regime had been completed, Libya was, at least according to its ruler's pronouncement, a Jamahiriyya: a political community marked by consultation rather than representation; where ordinary citizens own the country's resources and exercise authority over the country's administration and bureaucracy through popular congresses and committees.

In the Green Book we find Qadhafi's ideas of statelessness and of people managing their own affairs without state institutions. We find as well the emphasis on consultation and equality and an explicit aversion to hierarchy and to state functionaries as holders of authority. We also discover a repeated insistence on "direct democracy" through which citizens will take control of the state.[11] In this fashion, "Libya's historical problem with state authority was resolved in principle by eliminating the state altogether" (Anderson 1986a, 268). The state, of course, could no longer be eliminated or ignored, but its impact could presumably be circumscribed and reduced. Its institutions could be curtailed, handed over to the masses, and managed by popular committees. To those goals the Qadhafi government committed itself—and virtually unlimited resources—after 1975.

In the opening pages of the Green Book's first volume, Qadhafi summarizes what he considers one of the most basic problems faced by all human societies: political systems that involve representation are repressive. Modern states, characterized by party systems that involve representation, are repressive. Representation involves the surrender by some individuals of their natural personal sovereignty and the pursuit of

[11] Qadhafi referred to it as The Third Universal Theory. The development of his ideas can be gleaned from his speeches collected in al-Qadhafi, 1969–1995. See also Barrada, Kravetz, and Whitaker 1984, which contains extensive interviews with the Libyan leader. For interpretations of Qadhafi's ideas, see Ayoub 1987, Badri 1986, Mattes 1982b, Mezoughi 1984, and St. John 1983.

power by others. Until the publication of the Green Book, Qadhafi argues, all forms of government have been an expression of this "struggle for power between [the] instruments of governing," leading to conflict among political parties, social classes, individuals, or religious sects. In this inherently conflictual process one side inevitably wins. But the victory of one side, even in electoral systems, always means "the defeat of the people, the defeat of true democracy." An electoral victory cannot lead to true democracy because even if 51 percent of the vote is obtained by the victorious party, "49 percent of the electorate is ruled by an instrument of governing they did not vote for." "Representation" therefore "represents a deception," and parliamentary democracies represent a "false democracy" because the people's representatives seize power as soon as they acquire parliamentary unity.

Political parties, as the expression of representation, are therefore nothing but the means that allow a minority to usurp the right to speak in the name of the people: votes can be bought and sold at random. Consequently, poor citizens are the victims of this system in which the rich "and only the rich" are truly represented. Of all the dictatorships in history, those most tyrannical "have existed under the shadow of parliaments." Political parties are by implication the instruments of the rich. The struggle between them is at the expense of the common interest, further escalating power struggles and destroying in its wake "all achievements of the people, and of any socially beneficial plans." Social classes and tribes also pursue their own goals and dominate society in the same fashion political parties do, and therefore cannot serve as the basis for a truly democratic society.

What is needed, according to Qadhafi, is a political mechanism that preserves individual sovereignty in a modern society, and that can generate group spirit [*aql jama'i*] among the population (*SQ* 1974–75). Because states inevitably involve some form of representation—politically or bureaucratically—they cannot ensure individual sovereignty. Not even constitutions can guarantee this innate equality, Qadhafi argues, for they represent once more the interests of the most powerful in society. The Libyan leader's solution therefore is *direct democracy:* a system of direct representation without intermediaries. In practical terms, he envisioned the establishment of popular congresses to which every individual can belong and that in turn delegate power to popular committees in order to enact their decisions at the national level:

> The people's authority has only one face, and it can only be realized by one method, namely popular congresses and popular committees. . . .

> First, the people are divided into basic popular congresses. Each congress chooses its working committee. The working committees together form popular congresses for each district. Then the masses of those basic popular congresses choose administrative people's committees to replace government administration. Thus all the public utilities are run by people's committees which will be responsible to the basic popular congresses, and these dictate the policy to be followed by the people's committees and supervise its execution. Thus, both the administration and [its] supervision become popular, and the outdated definition of democracy—democracy is the supervision of the government by the people—comes to an end. It will be replaced by the correct definition: "Democracy is the supervision of the people by the people." [Green Book vol. 1, 12]

The system of popular congresses and committees the Libyan leader suggested thus consists of a legislative and executive branch, both directly in the hands of the people (see Figure 5.1). It did not include a separation of power, and decisions were to be channeled up from the base toward the top. In effect, the highest level of both branches—the General People's Congress and the General People's Committee—could only implement decisions decided on at the lower levels, but they have, at least according to the Green Book, no independent authority. In addition, members of both branches would be agreed upon not through voting but through consultation [*shura*] and choice [*ikhtiar*]. Under the new system, government ministries fell under the authority of peoples' committees; their secretariats, elected annually at the GPC, were put in charge of the daily business of administration. The General Peoples' Committee replaced the cabinet; the secretary of the General Peoples' Committee assumed the duties of the former prime minister (see Figure 5.2).

Each Basic People's Committee consisted of smaller committees elected by the local Basic People's Congresses that were in charge of a wide-ranging area of administration and whose representatives reported to their counterparts at the national level.[12] In principle, therefore, each local district remained autonomous, not subject to central authority, and possessed its own system of committees that could formulate policies on a wide array of issues that were then channeled up to the national level where they formed the basis of policy making within the ministries.

[12]Initially, the areas of competence for these subcommittees included Youth Affairs, Water, Transport, Health, Justice, Finance, Employment, Electricity, Education, Construction, Agriculture, Housing, Municipal Affairs, Planning, and Post and Telecommunications. Their number would later increase beyond the original sixteen.

LEGISLATIVE	EXECUTIVE	REVOLUTIONARY
General People's Congress (GPC)	General People's Committee (GPCO)	"Direction of the Revolution"
	General People's Specialized Committee (GPSCO)	
Municipal People's Congresses (MPC)	Municipal People's Committees (MPCO)	Office of Revolutionary Committees
Municipal Branch People's Congresses (MBPC)	Municipal Branch People's Committees (MBPCO)	
Basic People's Congresses (BPC)	Basic People's Committee (BPCO)	Revolutionary Committees
Syndicates, associations, unions		

Source: Adapted from Moncef Djaziri, "Creating a New State: Libya's Political Institutions," in *Qadhafi's Libya, 1969–1994*, ed. Dirk Vandewalle (New York: St. Martin's Press, 1995), 191. This outline includes intermediary committees and congresses not contained in Qadhafi's original outline.

Figure 5.1. Popular versus revolutionary authority in the Libyan Jamahiriyya

By the end of 1975, the Green Book's populist slogans, such as *lijan fi kulli makan* ["Committees Everywhere!"] started to appear throughout the country. The Basic People's Congresses and the Municipal People's Congresses gradually replaced the ASU's local and municipal committees. Under popular rule, however, the restricted membership of the ASU was abandoned, and all Libyans could now join the new congresses. To reflect the new political system, the ASU was renamed the General People's Congress (GPC) in January 1976. Qadhafi retained his leadership position, and emerged, with Jalud, as the most powerful RCC member at the meeting. Jalud was furthermore appointed as Secretary General of the GPC.

Under the new style of democracy, all RCC members, ministers (now known as secretaries), and upper-level administrators were asked to be present, subject to direct interpolation by all participants.[13] At the same

[13]This measure introduced a good measure of hilarity into the proceedings because BPC members, empowered under the new system, were free to directly question secretaries (ministers) and chose the occasion to vent their anger at several of them. The proceedings also confirmed the extraordinary influence Qadhafi was able to project by this time: there was a general deference to him, and he intervened repeatedly throughout the entire conference. I would like to thank Ibrahim Abu Khzam for making available some of the taped proceedings.

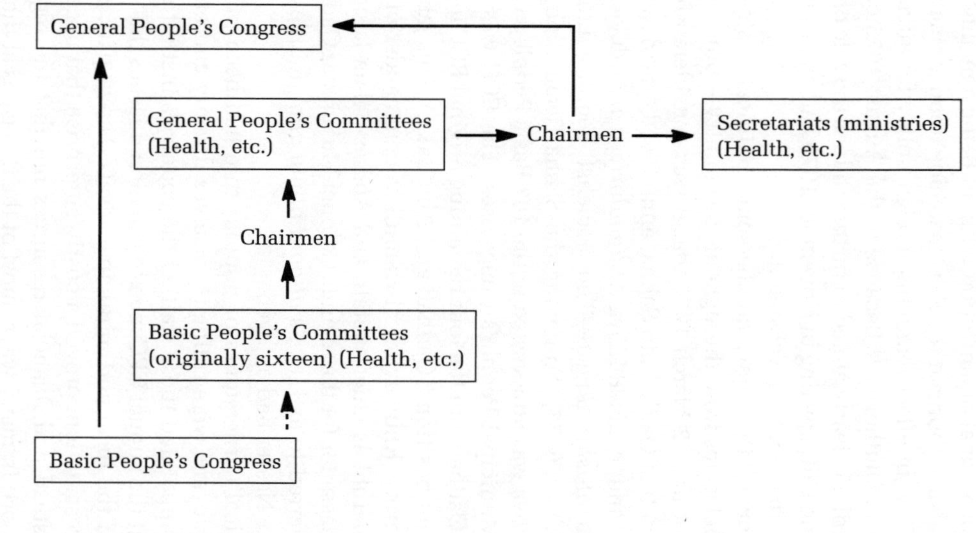

Source: Adapted from John Davis, *Libyan Politics: Tribe and Revolution* (Berkeley: University of California Press, 1987), 21.

Figure 5.2. Popular congresses and committee structure

time, some of the restrictions on the activities and competence of the popular committee system were more clearly articulated—a gesture that hinted at the limited nature of popular rule. Political activities in the future were restricted to the Basic People's Committees; no one could belong to a union or professional organization without being a member of a BPC. The congress also authorized the RCC to decide upon all matters related to foreign policy, in effect removing foreign policy formulation from the BPCs' sphere of authority.[14] Because of the August 1975 coup attempt, however, Qadhafi clearly aimed to further reduce the role of the RCC, and by the second GPC meeting in November 1976 had managed to retain only Jalud within the new government.[15]

The implementation of this new, cumbersome political system—which counted 970 delegates from throughout the country—proceeded slowly, and it was not until 2 March 1977 that it was considered fully functional. It was then that Qadhafi, in Sabha, announced "the dawn of the era of the masses" and renamed Libya *Al-Jamahiriyya al-arabiyya al-Libiyya al-sha'abiyya al-ishtirakiyya*—The Socialist People's Libyan Arab Jamahiriyya (*SQ* 1976–77). Following the Sabha Declaration, all political control in Libya was now vested in the 187 Basic People's Congresses and the 47 Municipal People's Congresses. The RCC was formally abolished, but Qadhafi and the four remaining original RCC members retained important positions: Qadhafi and Abu Bakr Yunus Jabr as heads of the Libyan army; Khuwaylidi al-Hamidi as commander of the police; Mustafa al-Kharubi as chief of staff; and Abd as-Salam Jalud as roving economic ambassador for the regime. Colonel Mu'ammar Qadhafi from now on was referred to as Libya's *al-qaid al-mu'alim,* (guide and master), the same title Nasser had enjoyed.

By 1980, the political cornerstones of popular rule had been put in place: in principle, Libyans were ruling themselves directly and either replaced or directly appointed those staffing the country's institutions. They could discuss at the annual GPC meetings national issues that had been channeled from the local and municipal levels. Direct participation, rather than representation, proved a costly enterprise that necessitated enormous logistical and financial resources but that the regime seemed eager to support. In many ways, most of the delegates at the an-

[14]Text of the January 1976 recommendations can be found in *Ash-Shura* 11 February 1976.

[15]As Bleuchot points out (1983), this gives more credence to Muhayshi's allegations that Qadhafi was trying to abolish the RCC prior to 1975, but that it was too strongly institutionalized for him to do so.

nual GPC meeting were, as the proceedings indicated, inadequately trained to provide answers, or even suggestions, to the increasing technocratic problems the country and its economy faced—a difficulty the regime attempted to solve after 1978 by adding "technocrat advisory groups" that delegates could consult (Ubaydi 6 October 1992; Abu Khzam 6 June 1989).

In several important ways, furthermore, the practice of delegation remained limited. The secretariats (ministries) retained considerable influence and eventually became infiltrated by Qadhafi loyalists. Agendas for BPC committee meetings and for discussions at the GPC level were often determined by them in Tripoli and, after 1977, would be enforced by revolutionary committees. The long-standing war in Chad, for example, was never discussed by the BPCs or the GPC until 1987. In addition, because the GPC met in only three sessions each year, the ministries provided much of the day-to-day functioning of the government, in isolation from the BPCs. Finally, the local institutions of popular rule depended for their survival and functioning on resources, most importantly oil revenues, that were centrally controlled.

The selective areas of competence that were open to debate by the GPC delegates—foreign policy, the army, the police, the country's budget, and the petroleum sector fell outside popular rule—indicated as well the selectivity of *sult ash-sha'ab* [people's power]. And, starting in 1977, the appearance of revolutionary committees in the country's political system, and their growing political power thereafter, clearly showed that popular rule was being supplemented by a rival system of revolutionary rule that was more agile and more responsive to Qadhafi's rhetoric. This split would officially be confirmed and sanctioned by the separation of formal authority and revolution [*fasl as-sulta wa ath-thawra*] at the second session of the GPC in March 1979.

Popular and Revolutionary Means of Governing

Qadhafi concluded the first volume of the Green Book by noting that "theoretically, this [the popular committee system] is genuine democracy. But realistically the stronger part in society is the one that rules." Ironically, in the Jamahiriyya, this split between the formal and real mechanisms of power grew dramatically throughout the revolutionary decade and beyond. The limitations on the popular committee system's sphere of authority and the exclusion of, among others, the army, the police, and the country's intelligence services from the Jamahiri system provided two clear indications that those economic sectors and institutions the regime judged crucial to its survival remained off-limits to popular rule and that the regime firmly retained the ultimate control functions. That the regime also controlled the country's budget without accountability before the GPC added to Qadhafi's ability to manipulate the political system. As repeatedly happened throughout the 1980s and into the regime's postrevolutionary period, economic or political setbacks could now be blamed on the popular institutions in charge of the Jamahiriyya—and not on Libya's ruler, who, in principle, was no longer a part of Libya's formal structures:

> You should understand that since 1977 we no longer have any constitutional prerogative on your economic, political, and administrative matters. Please, let us be clear about this point. You may seek our advice; we are ready to play the role of revolutionary instigators as our presence warrants this. However, we are restricted by people's authority. . . . People's authority has become restrictive even on revolutionaries. . . . [I]t restricts even Mu'ammar al-Qadhdhafi; I cannot act. . . . I have now discovered that since 1990 . . . a town like Tripoli with 1.5 or 2 million inhabitants has been lacking drinking water. I am telling you: I had no such information, I did not know this, because I am not in charge of facilities; nor am I a prime minister, or concerned with this. [*FBIS* 9 September 1993, 19–20]

In this growing split between formal and informal power, the revolutionary committees played a critical role, starting in 1977.[16] They constituted, at least initially, one more wave of revolutionary mobilization but quickly assumed an additional function: to act as a foil to any group, including the army, that could threaten the regime and to hunt down opposition figures inside and outside the Jamahiriyya. Their initial creation in 1977 was aimed at inciting more active popular participation in the people's popular congresses and committees that had been marked by high levels of absenteeism. They were also meant to further reduce whatever residual power certain tribal reactionary forces still possessed and to bring greater coherence and ideological indoctrination to the BPCs (Mattes 1995a, *SQ* 1975–76, Farfar 2 February 1989).

[16]On the revolutionary committees, in addition to Mattes (1995), see El-Fathaly and Palmer 1982, El-Hesnawi 1987, *Al-Lijan ath-thawriya* 1985, and relevant chapters in Mattes 1982b. The committees have also published *al-Zahf al-Akhdar* (since 1979) and *al-Jamahiriyya* (since 1980).

The first revolutionary committee was created in November 1977 at Tripoli's al-Fatih University. The absence of any mention of the revolutionary committees at the GPC Congress that year suggested that Qadhafi was intent on using this new instrument of mobilization independent of the BPC's popular control. By the end of the following year, committees had been established throughout the country, infiltrating basic popular congresses and committees as well as the university faculties. Their role and position remained undefined: they were instructed to defend the revolution and to guide the masses into assuming direct power. This assigned to them the duties normally reserved for a political party, which Qadhafi categorically opposed. In reality, their role quickly became one of ideological surveillance and, after the official announcement of their creation at the 1979 GPC second meeting, of constituting a security mechanism for the revolution (Bleuchot 1983).

A further clue to their real role and to the intensification of the revolution with which it coincided was contained in Qadhafi's 1 September speech that year. For the first time, he started to distinguish between those in power (in theory, the people), and those guiding the revolution. Clearly the revolution and the revolutionaries enjoyed priority: "The revolution divorced from [those in] power shall no longer be in a defensive situation; liberated, it shall in this way clearly assume its role in opposition to the deviations and arbitrariness of [those in] power. . . . The members of the popular committees . . . are not less patriotic or revolutionary than the revolutionary committees, but the latter have announced that they are, as of now, ready to die to defend and consolidate the revolution" (*SQ* 1979–80, 432).

One of the regime's new slogans focused on the role the committees now came to play: *la thawri kharij al-lijan ath-thawriyya* ["No {one can be a} revolutionary outside the Revolutionary Committees"]. This new development clearly increased the power at Qadhafi's discretion, since the revolutionary committees were now empowered to replace "ineffective" leaders of BPCs. This move enabled the Libyan leader to appoint people of his own choice. The revolutionary committees were not permitted to coordinate activities among themselves but were held directly responsible to Qadhafi, who created a special liaison office—the Central Coordinating Committee for the Revolutionary Committees—for that purpose at Bab al-Aziziyya, headed initially by Ali al-Kilani, Qadhafi's personal secretary and a member of the Qadhadhfa tribe. In general, revolutionary committee members were graduates of the *mu'askarat,* a series of special seminars that the Libyan government had started to organize in 1976 in order to indoctrinate candidates with the necessary revolutionary knowledge.

Starting in 1979, the committees met yearly with Qadhafi to draw up a program for the next year. To distinguish further between the formal and revolutionary systems, in December 1978 Qadhafi resigned from the GPC—of which he had remained the secretary general—in order to devote himself to "revolutionary duties" (*SQ* 1978–79, 21). On 2 March 1979, formal and revolutionary authority were officially separated at the GPC second session. The other four remaining RCC members—Jalud, Yunus Jabr, al-Kharubi, and al-Hamidi—and Qadhafi were appointed to head the revolutionary authority structure, while all top positions within the formal authority structure became civilian. As a result of the separation, none of the formal institutions could challenge the revolutionary institutions.

The rapid expansion—and the eventual excesses—of the revolutionary committees' activities toward the end of 1979 were therefore not surprising. By the end of the year, they had infiltrated the institutions of the formal authority structure—the popular committees, the popular congresses, the Municipal People's General Committees (MPGC) that had been created as an additional layer of administration in 1979—as well as the universities and the professional organizations (Mattes 1995a; al-Hesnawi, 11 December 1989). By 1987, just prior to their curtailment, some members of the revolutionary committees' coordinating office (as well as members from Tripoli's Green Book Center, the regime's main propaganda office) became secretaries (ministers) in charge of economy and trade, scientific research and planning, and education (Monastiri 1995; Mattes 1995a). It marked the apex of the influence of revolutionary authority within the country's political system.

Between 1979 and 1987, however, the revolutionary committees—except for the Libyan army—became the single most powerful group within the country.[17] At the January 1980 GPC meeting, from which Qadhafi and other former RCC members were now absent, the country's new civilian

[17]El-Fathaly and Palmer (1982, 259) maintain that the revolutionary committee members "effectively outrank all others [in the army]," and the assertion is accepted by Mattes (1995). Judging from the interaction I witnessed on both formal and informal occasions between army officers and revolutionary committee members during visits to the country between 1988 and 1995, this was certainly not the case. When questioned closely about this, and particularly in light of his later announcement concerning the paramountcy of the committees, former prime minister al-Ubaydi confirmed that the army remained the ultimate power source. (Al-Ubaydi 11 December 1989). Al-Ubaydi's information is corroborated by the fact that although there was an attempt made to establish revolutionary committees within the army, they never managed to gain a foothold.

prime minister, Abd al-Ati al-Ubaydi, announced that "all People's Congresses, no matter what their level, as well as the Secretariat of the General People's Congress, and the secretaries of the Basic People's Congresses are under the permanent control of the revolution and the revolutionary committees" (cited in Mattes 1995a, 97). By mid-1980, the revolutionary committees produced their own weekly magazines, *Al-Zahf al-Akhdar* [The Green March], and *al-Jamahiriyya,* which quickly became the voice of the regime and the pulse by which Libyan political life could be measured and judged.[18] They had also established themselves within the Libyan police by that time, where they started to assume special intelligence and security functions that further strengthened Qadhafi's control. From the ideological vanguard, they had moved on to become the regime's most important tripwire against potential opposition.

Beginning in 1979, the committees dominated not only the activities of the BPCs but were put in charge of overseeing their elections and were granted a veto power over their candidates. They effectively controlled the agenda of the GPC, in total contradiction to the 1977 directives adopted at the creation of the Jamahiriyya. Their power increased even further in 1980, when they were officially put in charge of *tahrid* and *tahrik* [motivation and mobilization of the masses], *tarsikh* [solidifying the role of the masses], *mumarisat al-riqaba ath-thawriyya* [exercising revolutionary control], and *himaya, difa',* and *da'wa* [protecting, defending, and propagating the revolution]. The latter, in particular, represented ominous developments, as they now empowered the committees to hunt down and physically liquidate [*al-tasfiya al-jasadiya*] "enemies of the revolution" abroad and at home and to create revolutionary courts to judge dissenters—both of which the committees proceeded upon with great zeal and with little control over their revolutionary methods, which condoned violence (*SQ* 1980–81; Ibrahim 1983; Burgat 1995).[19] After the publication of the Green Book's second volume concerning economic relations among citizens, the revolutionary committees were furthermore used to implement its directives and to combat growing evidence of corruption and misappropriation of funds. The long-anticipated takeover of the press (including television, radio, and printing plants) by the committees took place in October 1980 and completed their original activist phase.

[18]Both were often used by Qadhafi to publish his own unsigned front-page articles.

[19] Ibrahim's book specifically endorsed violence as a legitimate tactic. He later became minister of education and scientific research.

The power assigned to the revolutionary committees at the 1980 meeting to create revolutionary courts [*mahkama thawriya*], based on the "law of the revolution" [*qanun al-thawra*], indicated the regime's effort to make its legal system dovetail with its political strategies. As in most other countries with revolutionary pretensions, since 1969 Libya has witnessed the use of the legal system to foster, guide, and perpetuate the political directives of the country's leadership. The years immediately following the coup were characterized by an attempt to put forward the *sharia* as the only source of law applicable in Libya—an effort guided in part by the leadership's search for legitimacy and its almost visceral rejection of western influence.

Such a system, however—with its emphasis on codification and clearly prescribed legal remedies—hardly served Qadhafi's conception of a continuous revolution in which constant (and most often unpredictable) upheaval was a sine qua non. The well-established principles of Islamic law that dealt in great detail with contracts and commerce and the *sharia* protections of private property rights were at odds with the intentions of the regime. At the Zuwara speech, Qadhafi had announced the suspension of all laws then in force. Although clearly rhetorical, it marked a transition toward a system of law more attuned to the revolutionary principles of the regime. This trend was later reconfirmed at the creation of the Jamahiriyya in Sabha, by which time the guidelines of the Green Book had become the guiding legal norms of Libyan society, superseding the regime's first constitution of December 1969. In a major debate at the Moulay Muhammad mosque on 3 July 1978 and in speeches thereafter, Qadhafi attempted to prove that Islamic legal rules could not be used as a guideline for economic and political intercourse in modern societies and denied that those who argued for their application had any special right to do so—thus invoking the wrath of the *ulama* (Mayer 1995). He also argued that the prophet Muhammad's actions and sayings—which have traditionally provided important guidelines for property rights and commerce—could no longer be authenticated and were therefore of no value.

The regime's turn toward a more radical revolutionary socialism after 1975 brought about a sustained period of neglect of individual liberties, legality, and the rights of individuals. In this effort, the creation of a parallel system of justice to circumvent the ordinary courts proved to be an important part of the implementation of Qadhafi's revolutionary agenda. The revolutionary courts were staffed by revolutionary committee members, not by regular judges, and were not bound by Libya's penal code. Because normal legal safeguards were routinely disregarded, the revolutionary court system led to many well-documented abuses throughout 1986 (Amnesty International, 1991). The elimination of the private practice of law in May 1981—a measure that also included all other professional occupations—removed the last obstacle to a revolutionary court system (*JR* 29 May 1981). It marked the beginning of a seven-year period in which the regime paid scant attention to formal legal rules—a period dominated by an arbitrary and increasingly repressive revolutionary justice system that enforced the directives of the regime and strongly contributed to the growing tension inside the country.

The manipulation of the Jamahiriyya's legal system and the separation of formal and revolutionary authority in 1979 indicated clearly how the real center of power in Libya after 1975 narrowed considerably and how all major political and economic decisions were increasingly made by Qadhafi and a small group of loyalists. In the aftermath of the 1975 coup, whatever collegial decision making still existed had yielded to Qadhafi's personal rule. The Libyan leader's one-man rule, however, relied on a careful management of those coalitions that supported him, on the creation of new (temporary) allies under the guise of revolutionary indoctrination whenever necessary, and on the ability to keep all groups and individuals unbalanced. The revolutionary committees—whose existence had not been part of Qadhafi's ideological blueprint detailed in the Green Book—were meant to invigorate the revolution. In reality, they represented one more wave of mobilization, and their role shifted from revolutionary vanguard to an instrument meant to ensure the physical survival of the regime. Their rapid rise and eventual curtailment, in the span of a single decade, was symptomatic of the precariousness and unpredictability of politics within the Jamahiriyya.

The regime's ability, in Marx's words, to execute a "*coup d'état en miniature* every day" presented few difficulties during the boom period, since virtually everyone profited directly or indirectly from the massive inflows of oil revenues—despite the considerable expenditures on economically questionable projects inside the country and on the foreign adventures Qadhafi found himself increasingly embroiled in within the region and beyond. The nature of the country's economy (in which all revenues flowed directly into government coffers), the structure of its political system, and the further evisceration of regime opponents and their replacement by new, thoroughly indoctrinated "revolutionary" supporters explain the rapidity and the ease with which the new regime could make even more dramatic distributive policies the cornerstone of its economic and political strategies throughout its revolutionary decade.

But by the end of 1981 there was little to suggest that the popular revolution had been more successful than the ASU in mobilizing the population and in making them active participants in the country's management. Indeed, the revolutionary committee movement had initially been a sign of frustration and of the regime's inability to mobilize the country's population. In a similar vein, the state's takeover of the country's economy after 1977 also reflected that frustration, and its radical nature added to the population's own frustration and further depoliticization and to continued rent-seeking behavior.

The Green Book: Popular Management

In the second volume of the Green Book—*The Solution of the Economic Problem: Socialism*—Qadhafi elaborated his economic vision of the stateless society. Central to his ideas is the concept that everyone should equally share and profit from the country's productive capacity. People must become "partners in production" by abolishing the conventional wage system and profit motive. Salaried employees are nothing but wage workers who are exploited by those owning the enterprises in which they work. Even under Marxist doctrine, where the state owns all enterprises, the "wage-worker [remains] like a slave to the master who hires him." Workers should therefore become direct partners in the production process—as described in one of the volume's slogans that soon dotted the country's urban landscape: *shuraka' la ujara'* ["Partners, not wage earners"]. The injunction against using wage labor applied to employment in both public and private enterprises. No "exploitation of man by man, and the possession of some individuals of more of the general wealth than they need" should be allowed. Workers must "abolish the bureaucracy of the public sector and the dictatorship of the private sector" by directly taking control of those enterprises.

Qadhafi thus aimed at not only restructuring the country's economy so that everyone could become a partner but also sought a more radical redivision of wealth: to eliminate ownership, except of those goods and services individuals and families need, including food, housing, and clothing. To allow one person to possess more than what fulfills these basic needs—to own several houses, for example, "will [prevent] another from obtaining his. . . . Renting . . . is the beginning of a process of controlling another person's needs." Hence the appearance of another slogan throughout Libya: *Al-bayt li sakinihi* ["The house belongs to {him} who lives in it"]. The wealth of the nation should be shared equally, and this equality could be accomplished only if no individual is dependent economically on another. Services—such as hiring taxis or employing maids—could no longer be allowed, because they did not constitute a productive economic activity.

The impact of these directives within Libya after 1977 was enormous and led to a further dismantling of state institutions for regulating the country's economy. The new measures resulted in policies that, paradoxically, made economic nonmanagement or very crude management possible: the state by 1981 was in charge of virtually all economic activity, but it deliberately stepped back from regulating in favor of popular management—partly because of lingering weakness and unwillingness and partly not to upset the distributive, conflict-free arrangements it increasingly relied on after 1975 for its own survival. Libya, in ways both intended and unintended, became a centrally unplanned economy: its leaders retained control over the country's spending mechanisms, barely extending the state's economic reach beyond distribution throughout its revolutionary decade.

Between the end of 1977 and 1982, the regime systematically implemented the economic directives of the Green Book, aided by the revolutionary committees. Extending its nationalization of all nonoccupied dwellings throughout the country in 1976, the government reduced apartment purchase prices by 30 percent in late 1977. In March 1978, a series of proposals were submitted to the BPCs dealing with the "*al-bayt li sakinihi*" policy, and on 6 May the government promulgated a special real estate law that implemented the new measure (*JR* 8 May 1978). The confiscated properties were redistributed by the state—primarily to low-income earners. Numbers of renters suddenly found themselves owning their apartments and houses, paying only a small monthly mortgage to the government.

The "partners, not wage earners" slogan had an even more profound effect. Throughout 1978, Qadhafi repeated the need to put all enterprises and industries, both private and public, under the authority of the people, who would receive all the benefits produced by the enterprise. Following his 1 September speech, and guided once more by the revolutionary committees, a first wave of takeovers of businesses took place that quickly reduced an entire layer of merchants and businessmen to passive onlookers in the country's economic life. Although the Qadhafi regime had initially been tolerant of small-scale private businesses, entrepreneurs, retailers, and farmers—they had in part formed the initial base of its support—the new measures proved that they were no longer seen as crucial to the regime. In 1976, when the GPC debated and adopted the 1976–80 development plan, Qadhafi's attempts to nationalize all internal commercial transactions had been rebuked by the large number of businessmen at the congress. Within two years, they had clearly lost their power to prevent the implementation of the new measures. By the end of 1980, the more important large industries were put in the hands of Basic Production Committees—selected groups of workers within each business or enterprise. Popular Committees replaced their administrators. Only the banking system and oil-related industries were, once more, saved from these takeovers.

Individual traders saw their role greatly reduced and finally abolished. The few who remained until 1980 were subject to close supervision by the secretariat of finance, who, by withholding permits or permission for international financial transactions, in effect eliminated private trading. Only the agricultural sector still fell outside the socialist embrace—at least in theory. In reality, most of the land in the countryside had fallen under the public sector since 1970, depending heavily on government investment or subsidies. In 1977, in order to prevent large-scale individual farming, all land became government property. In line with the Green Book's directives, individuals could lease only enough land to satisfy their own food requirements. By 1978, only the lands in the coastal strip remained private. Owned to a large extent by the remnant of the old land-owning class, Qadhafi did not confront this powerful group with its entrenched landed interests until 1980. By that time, however, the internal marketing of agricultural products had become highly centralized.

That year also marked the end of private commercial and retail transactions within Libya. In his 1 September speech, Qadhafi echoed his previous ideas contained in the Green Book that the country's entrepreneurs (estimated at forty thousand) constituted a parasitic element of society because their economic activities were unproductive. Although in principle the BPCs had not yet confirmed the measure, Qadhafi's insistence had gradually halted the possibility of obtaining provisions for local entrepreneurs. To replace them, the government created state supermarkets; within a few months, 180 had been established throughout the country. Revolutionary committees closed down the few remaining private enterprises. Simultaneously, all imports were restricted to ten import agencies that purchased everything from oil technology to basic foodstuffs.[20]

[20]Information based on mimeo consulted by me at the GPC, Tripoli, 12 December 1989.

The curtailment of the power of the private business sector soon extended to the legal community and other professionals, who were no longer allowed to have private practices. The takeover of private and public enterprises by popular committees continued unabated throughout the year. Indemnification proceeded rapidly, and in the wake of several measures to consolidate production in certain manufacturing enterprises, overall output seemed to have suffered little (perhaps in itself an indication of the previous inefficiency). Finally, in 1981, the GPC's general secretariat announced the state takeover of all export, import, and distribution networks, and *waqf* [religious endowment property], thus undermining whatever economic power the *ulama* still possessed.

By that time, in March 1980, the government, in order to control private wealth, had decided to demonetize the Libyan dinar, force all Libyans to declare their assets, and exchange their accumulated old currency at government banks. Only one week was allowed for the exchange, and the amounts that could be exchanged were limited to one thousand Libyan dinars. It represented the most radical of the regime's populist measures, further undermined the confidence of the population in participating in the country's economic life, and led to enormous spending sprees inside the country.[21] It was also highly effective. In a country where cash transactions and savings were a long-established tradition, the measure directly affected every citizen who had no choice but to declare his wealth or to risk losing whatever part of it was not exchanged into the new currency. The demonetization, however, was only one more measure indicative of the inability of the government to regulate the local economy. It represented "a rather blunt instrument, necessary only because the government and the banking bureaucracies were not capable of monitoring and controlling all the personal and business transactions of a complex national economy. The instrument, if blunt, had the virtue of being much less expensive to deploy than a full blown inland revenue system" (Allan 1981, 241).

By the time of the demonetization measures, the country's banking system had already lost many of the functions of an active financial intermediary and had become little more than "a repository of surplus funds" (*MEED* Special Report, 1980). By 1980, it consisted of five commercial banks, two specialized loan banks, and a single foreign investment and trade bank. The commercial banks, with their emphasis on

[21]On the eve of the deadline for exchanging old currency for new bills, all gold in the Tripoli and Benghazi *suq* had disappeared, bought up by anxious Libyans.

private sector loans, had become largely nonfunctioning. The specialized banks—the Industrial and Real Estate Bank and the Agricultural Bank—were originally created to provide interest-free loans for small-scale manufacturing firms, to subsidize housing loans, and, in part, to serve as conduits for state investment. By the end of the decade, their functions also dramatically declined as the one-house policy came into effect and as manufacturing was nationalized. The Real Estate bank was reformed in 1981, with a more specific purpose of providing interest-free loans to poorer families (*Central Bank of Libya* Annual Reports, 1978–82). The country's Central Bank remained the country's most important financial institution, and it was carefully kept outside the popular committee system.

By the end of 1981, the Qadhafi regime had attempted a set of radical asset and income adjustment policies. Successive nationalizations had put virtually all economic activity into state hands. Small factories, commercial firms, agricultural land, urban real estate, and private residences had been confiscated and were either redistributed or kept by the state. Through legislative actions, simple administrative measures, and controls over its supermarkets, the state controlled all basic necessities and food distribution—a mechanism it would subtly but effectively use to reward or punish the behavior of its citizens.

The takeovers of the different sectors and the interference by the popular and revolutionary committees brought an initial wave of confusion and further inefficiencies. Their effect was exacerbated by the fact that national planning, despite the continued centralization, was often uncoordinated with initiatives within the different sectors of the economy. This piecemeal approach added to the general confusion.[22] In effect, Libya's planners, trying to implement the 1976–81 plan, faced a fourfold challenge: (1) drawing up development plans in the face of a fickle international oil market, (2) extending regulatory control over an economy and population that already exhibited many oil-induced rentier characteristics, (3) controlling the country's administration and bureaucracy, which were now in the hands of the people, and (4) averting sustained political interference, legitimized in the Green Book, from the country's leadership. Starting in 1977, the interference became particularly acute through the interference of the technical committees, most of which were government appointees, assigned to the secretariat of the

[22]See Gazzo, *AAN* 15 (1976).

GPC. Not surprisingly, during Libya's revolutionary decade, the country experienced the largest exodus of well-educated technocrats, which prompted an even greater reliance on foreign expertise.

In retrospect, the achievements of the 1976–80 Five-Year Plan differed significantly from the original intentions of its technocratic planning team and showed the corrosive impact of both the popular management style the country had adopted and the politicized nature of planning that took place as the popular base of the regime narrowed. The Qadhafi government continued to make heavy investments in education, in order to reduce its dependence on skilled expatriates. By 1979, Libya had twenty thousand university students, a sixfold increase since 1969. Almost 40 percent were in technical areas. But the takeover of the universities by the revolutionary committees and the Green Book's implications for education were deeply disturbing, in a country that heavily relied on technological solutions to its economic problems, even in agriculture. Qadhafi's notion that "knowledge . . . should not be made available via organized courses and curricula" (Allan 1981, 303); the publication by one of the country's future ministers of planning of an economic textbook that "reflects the insights of the Third Universal Theory" (Farhat 1983, 4); and the teaching of an economics course at al-Fatih University titled "Econometrics according to the Green Book" were only a few of the worrisome ideological intrusions on economic planning.[23] This unconventional view was even more alarming in light of the rapidly escalating brain drain after the 1975 reforms. By the end of 1979, an estimated one hundred thousand Libyans lived outside the country. Many of these were the best educated, often with advanced degrees from western universities (Monastiri 1995; Vandewalle 1991a, b).

The immediate impact of these developments was the need for continuing high levels of migrant labor. This applied particularly to areas requiring managerial, professional, and technical personnel. In manufacturing, almost 50 percent of the labor force was non-Libyan. By 1980 the need extended to nontechnical areas, primarily agriculture and construction. As expectations for Libyans were constantly raised, a large

[23]These were my observations at al-Fatih University, November 1988. During a more recent visit to the campus in June 1992, one of the university deans in charge of curricular development quickly stated that "they had done away with all that nonsense."

number moved into the tertiary sector: "The large numbers of non-national migrants [whose entry into the labor market is uncontrolled] have allowed Libyans to move out of productive operations into those which they consider desireable, namely service occupations in the government. There are insufficient 'desireable' service posts to absorb all Libyans, however, so as numbers of Libyans shun the undesirable jobs which they relinquish to non-nationals, they are opting out of the modern sector altogether" (Wright 1982, 261).[24]

The labor force of the modernized part of the agricultural sector was almost exclusively expatriate. Most Libyans in the sector remained in the traditional part, characterized by low levels of production and investment. The absorptive capacity of the agricultural sector also proved limited. Under the monarchy's economic plan, allocations of 12 percent of the (much smaller) budget had already proven difficult to invest efficiently (Allan 1981). Under the Qadhafi government's first plan, the allocation was increased to 17 percent of a budget that reflected the much higher inflow of oil revenues. As in Saudi Arabia, the Libyan government opted to invest heavily in agricultural projects that, under normal economic conditions, would have proven financially unfeasible. Massive loans were extended to agricultural research projects to improve the quality of individual farms and cooperatives and to facilitate the commercialization of their products (*JR* 9 October 1976, 22 January 1979).

The agricultural project at Kufra and the Gefara Wheat Project provided two excellent examples. In the Kufra project—started under the monarchy, then dropped and readopted by the revolutionary regime—several thousand acres of soil with low organic content were irrigated by means of advanced technology. Staffing was up to 80 percent expatriate, and few Libyan farmers settled in the area. Efforts to raise cattle at the project were abandoned in 1977, and it reverted to its original purpose of grain production after that year. Although certainly feasible, the project was utterly uneconomical. Transport costs to the coast alone, per ton of grain produced at Kufra, exceeded world prices in 1979. Total cost per ton was estimated to be between ten and twenty times the world price for grain in the late 1970s. The Gefara Wheat Project was started amid great fanfare in 1972, with similar advanced irrigation technology. Production between 1973 and 1979, however, was far below the levels set at the outset of the plan. By 1976, parts of the projects had been abandoned, and yields per acre remained dismal, even when average

[24]See also Birks and Sinclair, *Arab Manpower,* 137.

rainfall was above normal (as in 1975–76). It is ironic but telling that the regime's planners did not account for the uncertainties of long-term crop prediction—something both the Ottoman Empire and the monarchy had done routinely in their agricultural forecasting (Hajjaji 1981; Hajjaji 8 December 1988).

Inflation, rising prices of industrial imports, a fluctuating oil market, and heavy reliance on a few countries for oil exports added to Libya's difficulties. In 1974 alone, an inflation rate of 25 percent forced Libya to spend an additional $1.041 million for imports (*AAN* 1978). Throughout the remainder of the decade, inflation hovered around 20 percent, forcing the government to alter its development budget accordingly. Rising prices of food, and particularly of high-technology and machinery imports, added to the burden. Libya's industrial development suffered from repeated delays, which the government interpreted as tactics by the international purveyors to let the high inflation rates work to their advantage. Libya also developed no strategy to deal with technology purchases, took no advantage of access to international capital markets, nor developed a financial system that could have dampened the wildly fluctuating revenue income. It relied almost exclusively on its own reserves and actual income to ride out the turmoil created by the fluctuations. The country had no outstanding debt in 1980, but its unsophisticated method of financing a burgeoning economy produced occasional cash flow shortages.

Libyan policy makers seemed unconcerned about the fact that the production and marketing of oil proved highly unstable throughout the 1970s. Until 1974, the real price of oil remained consistently above the nominal price. Thereafter, however, the rate of inflation constantly depressed the real price. Furthermore, Libya's dependence on oil revenues now amounted to 99.9 percent of all its income. Four multinationals, however, still produced 80 percent of the country's total production by 1978.[25] By 1977, the United States became the biggest single purchaser of Libyan oil. This situation remained unchanged until after 1980. During this time, European buyers had started conservation measures, and some governments expressed reluctance to rely on what they perceived as an unpredictable government.

Despite new contracts for off-shore production in 1979, by 1980 the spontaneous takeovers of the economic sectors by the regime's militants—although still restricted to the non-oil and nonbanking sectors—

[25]Oasis 33.5 percent; Arabian Gulf 17.4 percent; Occidental 16.4 percent, and Esso 12 percent (*AAN* 1978). The smaller producers still in Libya included Mobil and Amoseas.

had a chilling effect on company-government relations. Although profit levels were estimated at more than double those of oil production in the United States, the growing animosity with Libya forced several U.S. companies to reconsider their investments in the Jamahiriyya. This did not particularly worry the Libyan government in 1979. The threshold had not yet been reached where anti-U.S. rhetoric prompted actual divestment. Furthermore, the uncertainty in the oil market after the Iranian revolution more than doubled the price of Libyan crude, and by extension the profits of the oil companies, between December 1978 and December 1979. Also, a lucrative spot market existed in Amsterdam where excess oil could be dumped at prices that reached as high as $45 per barrel in the fourth quarter of 1979. As a result of the 1978–79 price hikes, Libyan revenues were pushed to unprecedented levels, which allowed the government the luxury to keep production levels untouched. By that time, the real price of oil, even after discounting for indexation and inflation, consistently lagged behind posted prices, indicating that a buyer's market was in the making. With its reliance on only a few European countries and the United States, Libya was particularly vulnerable. If, as would happen in 1981, the United States started to boycott Libyan oil imports, fully one-third of the country's income would be lost without a readily available alternative.

The quadrupling of oil prices in 1973–74 had created even greater imperatives for managing Libya's financial problems if serious inflation were to be avoided and sustained development to be pursued. The country's leadership, partly to sidestep enormous strains on the feeble economic institutions that existed, needed to decide whether oil production should be limited and how to recycle and to invest the revenues. In reality, as the technocrats before the coup attempt had pointed out, this would have demanded the creation of more elaborate and integrated information-gathering institutions for the country and many legal, disclosure, and accounting requirements that clearly would have limited the revolutionary energy of the regime (Shirkazi 18 December 89). The availability of oil income also allowed for rapid accumulation without, however, the need to mobilize domestic savings through taxation or through other policies that could have curbed consumption throughout Libyan society. By 1981, the few taxes that had existed during the monarchy had been eliminated, and Libyan citizens paid only a symbolic *jihad* tax, meant to pursue the struggle against Israel.

Similarly, an effort to control the country's rapidly growing inflation, for example, would have necessitated a deliberate and sustained management of the revenue flows. As expressed in the 1976–81 plan, the country would increasingly need to rely on technical expertise for state decisions, on integrated and centralized policy making at the national level, and on the establishment and implementation of more rational criteria for the country's burgeoning bureaucracy. In effect, the political goals pursued by the country's leader and the imperatives of economic development were incompatible, while the populist measures taken after 1977 immeasurably added to the country's economic difficulties and deepened its distributive characteristics.

Like the king before 1969, the Jamahiriyya's leaders tended to use economics to solve strategic political puzzles. The Libyan government's priority consistently remained focused on distribution—admittedly draconian by now—rather than careful management of the country's economy, which could protect it against the nefarious impact of fluctuating international capital inflows. In the process, the regime's actions had provoked a massive brain drain, left local and international investors with rapidly decreasing confidence in the absence of clearly defined guarantees, and led to prestige projects that the regime would privilege, even during the economic downturn of the 1980s (Wright 1981). In the process, heavy outlays for military purchases had taken place in an effort to placate the country's single most powerful group of regime supporters. The outlays were little noticed because of the unorthodox and opaque nature of the country's budgets.

In an extraordinary fashion, Libya's oil revenues during its revolutionary decade thus allowed its ruler to distribute resources directly—through loans, subsidies, government jobs, contracts, and the provision of services—to groups it judged necessary for its survival while allowing it to use its rule-making authority to create rents for its direct supporters by effectively restricting market forces. The monopolization of imports by certain state agencies and the rationing of foreign exchange were two of the most powerful mechanisms the state used for that purpose. Whatever productive activity existed when the regime came to power—admittedly already low in light of developments during the monarchy—declined in favor of unproductive profit-seeking activities that made economic efficiency decline even further.

Postponing Reform: The Last Great Spender of Petrodollars

Despite the declining oil revenues after 1981 and the growing need for economic reform, the half-decade following the end of the country's third oil boom witnessed an unabated spending of the country's diminishing resources. Shortly after the demonetization in 1980, the Libyan government announced both a long-term plan for the country's economy, *Long-Term Development Prospects, Issues and Policies 1980–2000,* and a new five-year plan.[26] The latter was formally adopted by the GPC in January 1981 and reiterated the basic priorities of the two previous plans: self-sufficiency in basic foodstuffs, provision of adequate housing and social services, growth of the manufacturing sector and the development of heavy industry, and creation of a local workforce able to assume positions in a technologically oriented economy.

The new plan's expenditures were set at $57.46 billion with a reserve of $5.07 billion, making total allocations ($62.53 billion) almost two and a half times those of the previous plan. Some general new trends could be deduced from the official reports. The government wanted to reduce substantially the contribution of hydrocarbons to the economy, consistent with the instructions of the long-term development plan: oil production would be reduced to a level sufficient to meet the country's economic needs, and non-oil contributions to the GDP were to increase from 35.7 to 53 percent in 1985. By 1981, Libyan planners already knew that the investment goals of the 1976–80 plan had been overly ambitious and that most expenditures had remained significantly below allocations in all sectors. Despite this indication of a lack of absorptive capacity, the regime plunged ahead and awarded a staggering amount of contracts during the initial two years of the new plan. Libyan contracts, by themselves and as a percentage of the Middle East total, witnessed a phenomenal growth. In 1981 alone, they amounted to 18.5 percent of total international contracts in the region (COMET 1982).

Heavy industry was singled out for large investments, particularly in steel and petrochemicals. The Misrata steel complex was envisioned as the nucleus of many industrial projects, including an eventual rail link to the Wadi Shatti iron deposits. Further investments were made in an aluminum smelter in Zuwara, the chemical industries at Abu Kammash, and the petrochemical complex at Ras al-Unuf. By 1985, the plan estimated, they would serve as regional centers for future industrial development.

Agriculture remained the most troublesome sector, plagued by highly inadequate water supplies. The Gefara Plain was slowly depleted of its

[26]For an overview consult Allan 1981 and Committee for Middle East Trade 1982.

reserves, and some of its farms had already witnessed the intrusion of sea water. Under the new plan, the total of irrigated land would be reduced to eighty-eight thousand acres. The Kufra, Maknussa, and Sarir projects again received substantial commitments, but preliminary plans were being drawn up to bring massive amounts of fossil water from aquifers near Tazerbu and Sarir to the coast. The 1985 objective for cereals was put at 50 percent of total need, a dramatic downward revision from earlier plans. Almost half of the allocations for the agricultural sector remained committed to land reclamation.

By 1980, total development spending had reached $10 billion per year. In 1981 alone, however, this still left $11 billion at the discretion of the government and allowed major allocations in defense, international adventures, and outright consumption. As financial resources became more scarce afterwards, tradeoffs would have to be made by the Qadhafi government. The renewed involvement in Chad in 1981 indicated, however, that international adventures would not be curtailed. The available evidence also suggests that defense and military spending (in many ways closely related to foreign intervention) grew rapidly, despite the overall reduction of the development and regular (administrative) budgets. Although it is virtually impossible to gather how much of the development budget was diverted for defense, its share of the regular budget climbed from $709 million to $1.149 million (respectively 16.7 and 23.6 percent) between 1982 and 1984 (*MEED* 15 April 1985). The most relevant figure—arms imports as percentage of total imports—indicated that throughout the period of the plan, approximately one-quarter of all Libya's imports consisted of arms.[27] Within two years after announcing the plan, Qadhafi renewed the war with Chad in an attempt to incorporate the Aouzou strip as Libyan territory.

The plan finally also contained outlays for the so-called Great Man-made River Project. Meant to carry five million tons of water per day from aquifers at Tazerbu and Sarir toward Benghazi and Surt, the enterprise had an initial price tag of almost $10 billion but, by 1996, was expected to cost $27 billion. From ecological, economic, and agricultural points of view, most experts considered the undertaking highly problematic. Many feared that much of the water would eventually be used

[27]Although all figures on military expenditures must be used with great caution, consult both the reports published by the United States Arms Control and Disarmament Agency, *World Military Expenditures and Arms Transfers,* and *The Military Balance,* issued yearly by the International Institute for Strategic Studies in London.

for industrial use or human consumption as reserves along the coastal strip were rapidly depleted. Whatever the merits or demerits of the project, it represented a failure for the Qadhafi government. When first studied by the regime in 1974, it had been shelved in favor of developing agricultural enterprises near the water resources. As one geologist commented at the time, "It was a question of either taking the water to the people or taking the people to the water, and the government opted for the latter" (*MEED* 5 June 1981, 25). By 1983, the earlier policy had been abandoned, and the government now decided to bring the water to the people.[28] The war in Chad and the Great Man-made River Project, however, were only the two most spectacular examples of political expediency taking precedence over economic considerations, even in times of difficult economic conditions within the country. The water project in particular seemed contrary to the overall economic policies Qadhafi claimed to pursue. It relied entirely on foreign consulting and technology—almost exclusively from the United States—and on expatriate labor.[29]

As the second five-year plan reached its end, little had changed in the country's professed movement toward a more integrated, post-oil diversified economy. Libya's high dependence on expatriate labor persisted, particularly in sectors using high technology. The agricultural sector remained utterly unproductive; where projects were relatively successful, they were often achieved at a staggering cost that could be sustained only through massive spending. The attempt to create a heavy industry and downstream hydrocarbon sector remained worrisome: the country had no overall strategy to integrate them with the remainder of its economy. In the Jamahiriyya, where many of the technocrats continued to be expatriates with little stake in the development process, the procurement process remained haphazard at best, and the country was further forced to diversify substantially its purchases after the Reagan administration's technology embargo in 1983. Furthermore, by 1986 the country still relied on expatriate labor for 35 percent of all its technicians and 60 percent of all its managers, a major share of which came from the United States and Europe.

[28]The discovery of enormous quantities of water had been made by the Italians during the colonial period. As part of Occidental Petroleum's concession to drill for oil during the monarchy, the company had promised the king—many of whose relatives still lived around Kufra on Sanusi-owned land—to fund several agricultural projects in the region.

[29]Overall initial management of the project was provided by Brown and Root, a Houston-based company. The initial stage of the actual construction was completed by the South Korean firm of Dong Ah.

In the petroleum sector, downstream operations had become uneconomical, if not outright unsound, during the global refining overcapacity of the early 1980s. The most significant ratio to judge the long-term potential of Libya's economy—GDP derived from the oil-related sector as compared to GDP from the non-oil sectors—showed that non-oil activities were slowly increasing as a share of the country's economic output. But this ratio proved inconclusive: the growing share of non-oil activities was perhaps due as much to the contraction of the oil sector in the unstable world market after 1980 as to real growth in the non-oil sector (Shirkazi, 13 September 1989). Finally, a basic underlying problem remained: Libya's small population resource base would forever remain unequal to the demands of its government's ambitious development blueprints.

Libya's strategy for its 1981–86 Five-Year Plan had been predicated on projected oil sales that would match, in both quantity and price, conditions of the late 1970s. By the end of 1981 already, it was abundantly clear that those conditions could not be replicated. From 1.7 million barrels per day (bpd) in the first quarter, Libyan production tumbled to 600,000 bpd by the end of the year (*MEED* 13 July 1981). Total production for the year was 40 percent lower than in 1980. Of the total drop 550,000 had customarily been delivered to the United States. The remainder of the cutback resulted from phaseouts in production or from annulation of contracts by different companies operating in Libya. By the end of the year, Libya was furthermore forced to reduce the price of Libyan crude between $4 to $5 per barrel. Total revenues decreased by 31 percent, while imports increased by exactly the same amount. As a result, Libya's balance of payments for 1981 showed a deficit of $4.8 billion; during the period of the plan, the country's reserves tumbled from $15 billion to $2.4 billion.

The deteriorating relations between the United States and Libya prompted U.S. companies to take stock of their investments. Exxon—represented in Libya by its two affiliates, Esso Standard Libya and Esso Sirte—announced its complete withdrawal from operations in the country on 4 November 1981. Shortly after, on 10 March 1982, the U.S. government prohibited the import of Libyan oil and restricted exports to the Jamahiriyya. In January 1983, Mobil also withdrew from Libya, after several months of unsuccessful negotiations with the government.[30]

[30]Mobil first announced its withdrawal in April 1982, when it was lifting less than ten thousand bpd. It rescinded its policy temporarily in July, when the Libyan government seemed willing to make some concessions. For more details, consult *MEED* 25, no. 41 (26 July 1982) and *MEED* 25 no. 42 (2 August 1982).

Even before Mobil's withdrawal, several other companies in Libya also reduced their production or—as in the case of the French para-statal Elf-Aquitaine—temporarily postponed implementation of contracts concluded with the Libyan government.

Within days of the Exxon withdrawal, Libya started to offer financial incentives to the remaining companies to resume liftings—a strategy it would follow consistently from 1981 through 1984. In the case of its biggest independent producer (Occidental), Libya had already granted a $4 cut in October 1981 to encourage production. The prices set by the government for Libyan crude by 1983 were substantially below the already low 1982 prices. The measure was a sign of desperation. In this most capital-intensive period of the country's development plan, revenues were suddenly cut by one-third as a result of the U.S. oil boycott. From July 1982 until the end of 1984, when a new glut on the world market "allowed" Libya to fall in line once again with OPEC policies, the country consistently produced in excess of its OPEC quota. In the first quarter of 1983, for example, it marketed 1.8 million barrels per day, almost 800,000 barrels above the Vienna OPEC agreement of December 1982.

The continuing internal turmoil also created enormous confusion within the country's institutions. By the end of 1985, several of the country's ministries—including agriculture and industrial development—no longer produced reports that could be relied upon for planning and development, a situation linked in part to the expulsion of an estimated ninety to one hundred thousand foreign workers in the summer and fall of 1985 that provided most of the labor force in both sectors. As a result, in 1986, the board of directors of Libya's Central Bank temporarily discontinued issuing its usual yearly assessment of the country's economy.

Several of the country's research institutions by that time simply began regurgitating data provided to them by expatriate consultants or produced reports that dovetailed with the political rhetoric of the regime but showed little depth or consistency. Reports were often couched in the flowery rhetoric of the revolution. In several publications published at the Industrial Research Center and the Agricultural Research Center in Tripoli, for example, little effort had been made to consistently tabulate and integrate data. When questioned, one of its directors pointed out that in several instances—land reform among them—data had been taken from reports issued by one of the overseas contractors, without any attempt made by Libyans to supervise or check that data. Except for the National Oil Company—which was visibly a privileged institution whose employees could collect data in a relatively easy fashion—this atmosphere prevailed at most institutions in charge of gathering data needed for an efficient planning and management of the country's economy.

Postponing Reform: Confrontation Abroad, Mobilization at Home

Much of the turmoil in the country's economic and planning institutions during the 1982–87 period was sparked by and subsequently reflected in the regime's internal political initiatives and foreign adventures. Although Libya's foreign affairs since 1969 always carried a powerful undertone of ideological fervor, the confrontation with regional and western countries increased in mobilizational importance as the country's economic difficulties deepened after 1981. By the end of 1977 Qadhafi had already alienated most of the governments in North Africa, and a protracted skirmish with Egypt ensued that year. After an acrimonious war of words with Saudi Arabia over oil policies, in October 1980 the kingdom broke off diplomatic relations with the Jamahiriyya (*MEED* 3 November 1980). This regional isolation was further increased by French opposition to Libyan intervention in Chad (Neuberger 1982), by Libya's attempt to destabilize neighboring Tunisia in 1980 (*AAN* 1980), and by U.S. efforts to pressure the Libyan government to stop what it labeled "subversion" throughout the Arab world and Africa (Haley 1984). Although acrimony with both countries dated back several years, the issue in both cases came to a crisis in 1981. In the case of Chad, the French government in January 1981 postponed the implementation of a contract signed between the Elf-Aquitaine conglomerate and the Libyan government and more openly committed itself to oppose Qadhafi's meddling in the affairs of its southern neighbor.

The conflict with the United States, however, was potentially more dangerous. In August 1981, two Libyan jet fighters were shot down by planes belonging to the United States' Sixth Fleet in the Gulf of Surt, which Libya claimed as its territorial waters. The response provoked by the incident was visible in the records of the extraordinary August GPC meeting, convened immediately after the incident. At the meeting, Qadhafi—who for the first time since 1978 was present again at a GPC meeting, in clear violation of his own edict concerning the separation of the popular and revolutionary instruments of governing—advocated the implementation of new mobilizational measures (*ZA* 22 August 1981; *AAN*

1981), which consisted of creating a popular militia of the Jamahiriyya that would gradually take over the functions of the regular army.

Qadhafi had voiced the idea on previous occasions, but the Libyan leader eagerly seized on the opportunities provided by the 1981 events to attempt its implementation. Already in 1977 and 1978, for example, Qadhafi had mentioned the creation of a popular army as a counterweight to the regular army. General conscription, the arming of all Libyan villages, and indoctrination of students with military doctrine had already taken place under the guidance of ex-RCC member al-Hamidi.[31] In reality, the measures had never gone beyond perfunctory meetings of popular militias, or beyond the obligatory wearing of military garb at schools throughout the country.

The Gulf of Surt accident, however, acted as a self-fulfilling prophesy on Qadhafi's behalf: in addition to what were now described as the country's "traditional enemies" in the east (Egypt), the south (France in Chad), and the west (Tunisia, aided by France and the United States), the Sixth Fleet had now crossed Qadhafi's self-proclaimed "line of death" in the gulf (*SQ* 1981–82). When additional political initiatives inside the United States for a boycott of Libyan oil started to gain ground, Qadhafi felt himself further vindicated and ordered an intensification of the previous militarization measures. In his 1 September speech that year, the Libyan leader reiterated the need for further mobilization and called for a new type of vanguard, the so-called Guards of the Revolution (*SQ* 1980–81). Simultaneously, he also announced the creation of People's Bureaus wherever public services were rendered. These included all overseas embassies that witnessed a wave of popular takeovers throughout 1981.

Although the Guards of the Revolution were never constituted as a distinct organization in the turmoil that followed the 1981 anniversary speech, the idea of yet one more mobilizational wave was in part an indication of Qadhafi's dissatisfaction with the revolutionary committees (Hesnawi 30 September 1990; Abu Khzam 6 June 1989). They were clearly in command of the campaigns in the early 1980s against dissi-

[31]An ordinary GPC meeting took place on 3–7 January 1981, where the second five-year plan was discussed, along with the continuation of aid to liberation movements and the need to "militarize" Libya thoroughly. The meeting took place before the Elf-Aquitaine and the Gulf of Surt incidents. Qadhafi used both to implement fully his militarization program on the principle that "a people's war cannot be conquered." See *AAN* 20 (1981) for more details on the January 1981 congress.

dents, both within Libya and abroad, but most of their other prerogatives—to set and enforce agendas at BPC meetings, for example—were curtailed. In 1986, the country's economic and political crises—the latter fostered in part by the U.S. bombardment of Tripoli and Benghazi in April 1986 and by the setbacks suffered in the Libyan-Chadian war—forced the Qadhafi government to rethink the role and the usefulness of the Revolutionary Committees (see Chapter 6). Criticisms of the committees intensified, particularly in the aftermath of the U.S. military action, when the revolutionary committees proved unable to mobilize the population for demonstrations in support of Qadhafi.[32]

The aftermath of the 15–16 April 1986 bombing reconfirmed what many close observers of the country had argued: that the Libyan army remained the single most powerful institution in the country (Burgat 1995; Djaziri 1995). Army units put down the scattered unrest that followed in the wake of the bombing, in which revolutionary committee members had been involved. Immediately following the event, *Al-Zahf Al-Akhdar,* the revolutionary committees' weekly magazine, ceased the publication of articles critical of the army, and they have not resurfaced since (*ZA* 31 March 1983; 20 April 1985). Although the regime could not afford to do away with the revolutionary committee structure as Qadhafi seemingly wanted, their power was even further reduced after 1986. Their loss of power was in part linked to the general resistance they created and in part to the fact that they had not proven an effective counterbalance to the regular army. They never regained the preeminent position they once occupied. Their curtailment would be matched internally after 1986 by the reappearance of a certain measure of predictability and resurgence of the nonrevolutionary institutions in the Jamahiriyya: the military, the police, and the diplomatic corps.

Despite the turmoil created by its foreign policy, the internal effects of the growing economic difficulties and the political confrontations with the West were seemingly more favorable than the country's detractors had hoped. In several ways, they even added temporarily to Qadhafi's domestic support by his skillful manipulation of Libyan traditional distrust of outside interference (Wright 1982). It was also clear, however, that the combination of diplomatic isolation—which made traveling outside Libya virtually impossible—and the growing economic dislocations at

[32]See, for example, "Al-Jaish: hashish wa taish" 1983 and "Libya: Army versus Revolutionary Committees" 1983.

home had substantially diminished Libyans' appetite for the directives of its revolutionary leader. The population met the U.S. bombing of Benghazi and Tripoli in April 1986 with almost total apathy: "One saw more demonstrators in Khartoum and Tunis than in Tripoli where the number of foreign journalists outnumbered Tripolitanians" (*AAN* 1986).[33] Attempts to organize demonstrations in its wake were quickly abandoned for lack of participants, and Qadhafi disappeared for several weeks from the Libyan media.

The Politics of Evocation: Myths, Symbols, and Charisma

The lack of visible popular support in the wake of the U.S. bombing was a clear sign to the Qadhafi regime that its ability to mobilize the population, traditionally provided in part by the more informal mechanisms of politics, had been severely curtailed (Ibjad 5 December 1988; Al-Ubaydi 11 December 1989). Throughout the extraordinary decade of Libya's boom-and-bust cycle, the country's leader incorporated in his discourse powerful assumptions and ideas that, informally but instrumentally, were meant to reinforce the more formal measures of the regime and to overcome resistance to them.

In the Green Book, Qadhafi attempts to portray the Libyan revolution, in an almost scientific fashion, as an inevitable historical process of political development—an alternative to both capitalism and communism. As the country's revolutionary decade unfolded, the growing split between the country's formal rules and processes—embodied in its popular congress and committee system—and the reality of an increasingly exclusionary political system heightened the use of symbols, myths, and attempts to carefully exploit Qadhafi's charismatic qualities in ways that resonated within the culture and the historical experience of Libya. Reading the Green Book and Qadhafi's speeches—painstakingly assembled in yearly volumes of *As-Sijil Al-Qawmi*—reveals not only the Libyan leader's ideas about statelessness, popular rule, and popular management that sustained the Jamahiri experiment throughout the regime's revolutionary decade; they also contain repeated, powerful references to shared traditions, to notions of a common history that has pitted Libyans against the West, and to symbols that powerfully find a

[33]The quotation is from Frachon 1986.

voice within local culture. These indicate the important process of normative socialization that has accompanied the more formal directives of the regime that came to power in 1969 and that reinforced those formal processes. This socialization has been important in reinforcing the regime's attempt at reducing the importance of neutral processes for the articulation of political and economic interests, and, simultaneously, to overcome the lack of institutionalization and mobilization.

There have been, from the beginning of Libya's revolution, continued references made by the Libyan leader to words that hint almost nostalgically at a prebureaucratic, prestate past: *turath* [heritage], *furusiyya* [chivalry], *diafa* [hospitality], *karama* [dignity], *'ird* [honor], and *'ailah* [extended family] are only a few of the words that permeate the vocabulary of the Libyan leader on a regular basis. Dignity, and the indignities at the hand of the West, have continually provided a powerful sense of unity often expressed by Qadhafi: "[Unity] should be our only concern so that we are not humiliated in the future as we have been in the past, so that the horses of the enemy do not stamp on us as they have in the past. . . . The issue of dignity to me is more important than food and drink. You can sit under a tree without a home" (*FBIS* 2 November 1993, 20).

Within the Jamahiriyya, history has provided—and continues to constitute—the most important focal point to contrast those admirable qualities of *asala* [authenticity] to those that are deemed *wafid* or *majlub* [unacceptable or alien]. No single event has played a more important role in making that difference clear than the Italian colonial period. The shared memory of the brutality of the fascists' concentration camps, the capture and hanging of the resistance's most important leader, Umar al-Mukhtar, and the removal of the local population from their own land have provided a never-ending focus for the country's attention. Speaking to the Awlad Abu Sayf tribe in 1993, for example, Qadhafi in a few sentences deftly brought together some of the emotionally provocative symbols of his revolution: "There is no person who has a zeal and pride in Arabism more than the tribe of Awlad Abu Sayf. At the same time, there is no person who rigidly follows Islam and the teachings of the prophet more than that Awlad Abu Sayf. . . . Just imagine if I arm you, and say: This region is a strategic reserve for Gharyan, and Gharyan is a strategic reserve and a second line for Tripoli so that the Western and American enemy, or another, will not advance like the Italians did and entered and occupied this region" (*FBIS* 23 September 1993, 19).

The need for Libyans to be vigilant against the West and to destroy those who would sell out the revolution for their own interests also became a frequent reference, in a fashion that linked those themes to the country's past:

> So I must tell you that the traitors are a bigger threat to our future, freedom, and independence than colonialism. It was the traitors who enabled Italy to go deep inside Libya. The Italians on their own could not have advanced into this desert or these mountains. They would not have managed to catch Umar al-Mukhtar had it not been for a traitor who gave his whereabouts. . . . Now we should seek traitors, those who pave the way for the Americans, and kill them. The Americans today are like the Italians yesterday. The traitors of today are like [those] of yesterday. The traitors of October 1911 are like those of October 1993. [*FBIS* 20 October 1993, 21–23]

The regime also took steps to ensure a more permanent and solid record of the country's history and of its confrontation with the West. In 1979, the Libyan government constructed, in Tripoli, the Libyan Studies Center for the Study of the Italian Invasion, where the country's encounter with the fascists is painstakingly documented, indexed, and published. With generous funding from the government, teams of researchers from the center fan out across the country, trying to create an oral history of the colonial project and resistance. Parts of the documentation appears occasionally on local television, to celebrate the martyrs of "the country's first revolution" (Qadhafi, 14 July 1989). Even today, the country's leader still insists on reparations from the Italian government for its occupation of the country. At the center, pictures taken during the Italian occupation—of concentration camps, of local resistance figures, of Italian biplanes dropping bombs on powerless tribesmen—have been turned into enormous paintings that line the hallways of the building, reminding its visitors of the country's painful past.[34]

Before the creation of the Libyan Studies Center, the government had already ordered the construction of a national museum, to be called the Museum of the Jamahiriyya. The magnificent building, constructed within the Spanish fort on Liberation Square in Tripoli and designed by a Swiss architectural firm, chronologically displays the history of the country on different floors. The Italian colonial period is once more highlighted, complete with Umar al-Mukhtar's glasses and the tradi-

[34]Ironically—although symbolically relevant in its own way—they have been painted by a Korean artist who was brought to Libya for that purpose.

tional *zirt* the country's national martyr wore on the day of his execution. But in what represents an egregious example of manipulating history, the exhibitions jump from World War II to the Qadhafi period, leaving the period of the monarchy completely undocumented.[35]

In Libyan mythology, the 1969 coup was not simply a revolution but, much like Ayatollah Khomeini's later revolution, a reformation and a crusade against the West and against the monarchy it imposed on Libya. The coup represented a sweeping clean of all the cultural accretions of western culture, colonialism, and the new oil-induced imperialism and led to many symbolic actions: burning western books and musical instruments, wearing traditional Libyan dress, and changing the names of the months of the Gregorian calendar (Burgat 1995). Libyan independence in 1951 had been a "false independence" that could now be turned into a true independence, free of western interference (*FBIS* 9 September 1993). In that endeavor, oil revenues were crucial, and Qadhafi's victories over the international oil companies provided a immeasurable sense of accomplishment. To many Libyans, as to himself, Qadhafi was indeed the heir to Nasser's pan-Arabism.

Oil was not only a commodity whose proceeds could be used to implement or take over wholesale the economic, social, and political directives at home. It was also a vehicle the regime used to project Libya's power beyond its borders, in pursuit of its foreign policy goals (Neuberger 1982; Burgat 1995). Oil was also a means to confront the West and to restore to the Arab world the luster and power it had once enjoyed. In a spectacular fashion—which has forever marked Libya's image internationally—the Qadhafi government used the oil revenues at its disposal to confront the United States (Haley 1984). These confrontations would economically and politically prove very costly to Libya after 1980, but during the revolutionary decade they generated popular support eagerly seized upon by a regime whose level of legitimacy had not led to significant institutionalization, despite the gargantuan efforts at indoctrination and mobilization throughout the period examined in this chapter.

There was, in the confrontation with the United States, a self-fulfilling image both the Libyan leader and the U.S. government deliberately or inadvertently fostered. The continual pressure by the United States not

[35]Many books concerning the Sanusi monarchy were simply off-limits at libraries throughout Libya until the 1987 liberalization period. At research libraries, for example, foreign researchers needed permission from the local director to consult them.

only provided Qadhafi with a chance to deflect whatever internal criticism the GPC gingerly voiced, it also created the illusion that the highly unequal antagonism was somehow valid. The very idea, sponsored by the United States, that "the politics and actions of the Government of Libya continue to pose an unusual and extraordinary threat to the national security and foreign policy of the United States" (Bush 1993, 3) seemingly validated the Libyan regime's claims.

In all of this, there is little doubt that Qadhafi tapped into a rich source of general malaise and resentment among Libyans. The oil negotiations and the evacuation of the military bases gave ordinary Libyans a sense of dignity and importance, and he made sure initially to project the Libyan revolution not as the work of a single individual or of a small group of "progressive officers" but as the work of an entire people. He had, he argued on numerous occasions, only been a tool in the hands of the Libyan people. The people had rejected the kingdom and its corrupt pro-western clique—the military officers and Qadhafi had only implemented the wishes of the people.

It was important therefore that the coup be imagined as a popular revolution, no matter how limited the group of plotters had been and no matter how much they lacked a clear program in 1969. It was also important that the Libyan revolution be portrayed as an event of world historical importance, as the Green Book hinted. And it was important for purposes of legitimacy, finally, to portray the revolution as being in tune with the general precepts of Islam. Since 1969, therefore, the regime has consistently described the events of 1969 as not simply an *inqilab* [coup d'état] but as a *thawra* [revolution], despite the obvious difficulties this implied:

> We are proud to say that all the claims that a military coup took place . . . have been proven wrong. . . . [W]hat happened was not a military coup. The record of this historic event confirms that it was a deep-rooted popular revolution. . . . This was not a conspiracy, not a coup. It was a popular revolution and a historic movement. . . . What is taking place in Libya is a historical change that concerns not only Libya. It is the cornerstone of a new civilization and a new era, which humanity has to experience inevitably. It is the era of the masses, the era of all the people and the era of ordinary individuals. . . . People's authority, no democracy without people's congresses—this is a bullet that has been fired, a cry that has been set off in the world. [*FBIS* 9 September 1993, 17]

The passage, taken from Qadhafi's anniversary speech in 1993, combines the attempts to characterize the 1969 events as both a true revolutionary act and an important global event. Each night on Libyan television, before the daily news, a cartoon depicts how the Green Book will eventually spread throughout the world, turning all countries into Jamahiriyyas. In personal conversations, Libyan elites and ordinary individuals alike often compare the 1969 coup to the Chinese Revolution of 1949. The superficial similarities between the two revolutions are obvious: the Red Book and the Green Book; China's Red Guards and Libya's revolutionary committees; the self-management campaigns in both countries; Mao's "countryside versus the cities campaign" and Qadhafi's massive mobilization attempts starting in 1975.

Beyond these, however, the differences are enormous, and comparisons collapse almost completely: in China, the guardians of the revolution were assigned real and virtually unrestricted authority. Libyans, however, never tolerated the abuse the Chinese experienced at the hands of the committees, which in China held the power over life and death. In Libya, remnants of the tribal system, the power of its elders, and the role of Islam tempered both political initiatives and intrusion by the revolutionary committees. The tribal system and its elders continued to command a large measure of loyalty, even if its real functions shifted toward social rather than political objectives. Very few tribal members who became revolutionary committee members, for example, had the power to impose decisions handed down from Tripoli. They were seen as young upstarts, a situation that improved only marginally with the assignment of outsiders. Another lingering impact of the tribal system was the importance of persuasion rather than actual violence in settling disputes. The Chinese campaigns, in which thousands of "undesirables" were executed during and after the Cultural Revolution, had no equivalent in Libya.

Despite flagrant abuses within the revolutionary court system, including executions inside and outside Libya, the control mechanism in Libya has been both more subtle and more pervasive. It functions, in part, through the popular committee system and the revolutionary committees. Infringements can mean, for example, the loss of shopping privileges at national supermarkets. But when the committees' behavior started to raise intense criticism at committee meetings during 1987, some of their prerogatives were scaled back as Qadhafi announced political and economic liberalization measures on 26 March 1987 (Vandewalle 1990). Although the comparison may therefore seem outlandish, that it is even made is of some interest, for it reveals the image some Libyans hold of themselves and of their revolution.

Finally, Qadhafi attempted to portray his revolution as Islamic. In 1969, he had inherited a legal system in which codified Western law prevailed over religious and customary law. Despite the fact that the Green Book elevated religion and custom to the status of the law of society, in practice secular policies displaced them both as sources of law. This break with Islamic law and Libyan custom, however, was never officially acknowledged. The Green Book continues to call for reliance on "a sacred law based on stable rules which are not subject to change" and continues to identify this sacred law with Islam or with the Qur'an. In March 1990, the GPC, at Qadhafi's prompting, passed a resolution that included the statement that Libyans would adhere to the Qur'an as the *sharia* of Libyan society that would destroy imported cultures (*FBIS* 13 March 1990). This statement echoed the themes of many of Qadhafi's own speeches from the early 1970s, when he stressed the need to restore Islamic law as part of a rejection of the cultural legacy of Western colonialism. In April 1990, Qadhafi still insisted that his revolution had reinstated true Islam (*FBIS* 10 April 1990).

Undoubtedly, however, the most powerful informal mechanism of normative socialization has been the reliance on Qadhafi's personal charisma as the revolutionary decade unfolded (Hinnebusch 1984). Charisma is not a random accident: it emerges out of external and cultural crises and often reveals great psychological distress. Rumored to be only twenty-seven years old when the coup took place, Qadhafi, for the first time in the country's short history, provided Libyans with a sense of personal integrity, collective identity, and self-esteem. The effortless removal of the Sanusi monarchy (which had been marked by political apathy, corruption, and cronyism) and of the West with which it was closely allied added to his exceptional qualities. The victory over the international oil companies provided him with a stature far beyond those around him. His initial asceticism and self-effacement, his sense of duty and of honor, his personal honesty—all these were beyond question during the early years of his revolution—are qualities still ascribed to him by close collaborators and citizens alike (Farfar 10 December 1989; Ibjad 5 December 1988). His attempt to portray himself and his audience as following in the footsteps of the country's great historical heroes—he often refers to his listeners as "followers of Umar al-Mukhtar"—creates both a bond of solidarity that Libyans identify with and an implicit common bond of opposition to the West, whose colonial policies led to the death of Mukhtar.

Against the background of the country's history and the wave of Arab nationalism that swept through the region at the time of the coup, Qadhafi possessed character traits that appealed in times of crisis to the hearts and minds of many Libyans: youthfulness, creativity and militancy in opposing the West, and, above all, a will to power that inevitably and powerfully resurfaced each time the regime faced a new (often deliberately self-inflicted) crisis. In this sense, Qadhafi, as other modern charismatic leaders, repeatedly and rationally selected what looked to outsiders like "irrational themes" in order to create "a sense of pseudo-*Gemeinshaft*" (Bensman and Givant 1975, 606). The continual reliance on crises—which reached their apex in the 1980s—represented one more mechanism to prevent the routinization a clearly articulated political system inevitably entails. Charisma is by nature antibureaucratic and demands constant renewal of the charismatic leader's extraordinary gifts and abilities, as well as constant obligations to be imposed upon his followers (Weber 1968; Ashraf 1994).

Throughout the country's revolutionary decade, the Libyan leader therefore put, not surprisingly, a high priority on personalized exchange: continually delivering speeches throughout the country, on all occasions, that reinforced his message and exhorted citizens in a way few recent rulers in the Middle East have effectively managed. At the same time, starting in 1975, charisma yielded to a careful manipulation and perpetuation of its image through the Libyan mass media and allowed him through this manipulation to retain "all the appearance of charisma" (Bendix 1968, 172; also Loewenstein 1966, 86). The efforts to halt bureaucratization and the attempts to prevent the emergence of neutral state institutions slowed down the process by which Qadhafi's charisma became routinized, but its eventual demise was unavoidable. Charisma is inherently an unstable source of authority: not only must the charismatic leader have extraordinary qualities, but his people must share his belief—or at least suspend their disbelief—in his mission. The charismatic leader must constantly prove his worth, and, as the revolutionary decade ended, it became increasingly difficult for Qadhafi to do so. By the end of its revolutionary decade, particularly after the April 1986 bombing of Tripoli and Benghazi, Libya provided a good example that, even in distributive states, "every charisma is on the road from a turbulently emotional life that knows no economic rationality to slow death by suffocation under material interests" (Weber 1968, 1120), despite the advantages enormous financial resources at the disposal of its ruler can provide.

Emerging Problems of Control

If the popular reaction to the August 1986 bombing provided the most tangible evidence of dissipating enthusiasm for the revolution, it was only one of several signs of growing resistance. There were further isolated but increasingly public acts of defiance. Arson cases involving public buildings and revolutionary committee headquarters in several cities took place. Antigovernment graffiti increasingly appeared in public places, despite the vigilance of the country's security agencies.[36] In August 1986, Ahmad al-Warfalli, a prominent revolutionary committee member, was assassinated by opponents of the regime. The murder was widely reported inside Libya to be the work of Islamists, leading to a new wave of repression and confrontation that fall and winter.

The absence of sustained opposition until the country's looming fiscal crisis testifies once more to both the extraordinary power rulers of distributive states possess in shaping and holding in abeyance demands for political "voice" during boom periods, and to the profound process of depoliticization this process induces at the same time. In explaining this remarkable political silence, rulers of distributive states possess great powers to provide their citizens with goods and services, effectively preventing "the scarcity of resources that engenders both social conflict and distinctive social and political identities" (Anderson 1986a, 269) during the boom period. The regime's initial programs, aimed at redistribution, as well as its honoring of the important initial promises it made regarding education, housing, and other necessities, provided considerable support. Many of the actions taken by the government and described in this book as buying off the population do resonate among many Libyan citizens.

Although the tactics and excesses of the regime were increasingly perceived as unacceptable by many Libyans, they fundamentally shared Qadhafi's *weltanschauung:* the wish for a more authentic Arab or Muslim lifestyle, a more egalitarian society, and in particular a visceral dislike of the West that can be understood only within the context of the country's history. The lack of Islamic opposition until the mid-1970s, for example, is due to the fact that Qadhafi's own early policies of radical cultural decolonization—prohibition of alcohol, attempts to contain

[36]As I witnessed in Benghazi in spring 1987. Highly symbolic, the graffiti included fragments of poetry written by Mahmud al-Darwish, a prominent Palestinian poet, against Israeli occupation.

the cultural influence of the West and its presence within the region, the closing of nightclubs, the conversion of churches into mosques, the adoption in principle of Islamic punishment—preempted many of the issues that became the foci of Islamist movements elsewhere.

It is important thus to focus on the tasks the state sets for itself and the responses these provoke—or, as in the Libyan case, do not provoke. As Tilly has argued regarding the European experience, demands for political participation are linked—albeit often inadvertently—to efforts by state-makers to "build their armies, keep the taxes coming in, form effective coalitions against their rivals, hold their nominal subordinates and allies in line, and fend off the threat of rebellion on the part of ordinary people" (1975, 663). In distributive states, virtually all of those can be accomplished by spending the oil revenues that fall into the hands of the state's managers, thus containing, during boom periods, the demand for representation in return for taxation.

It is equally important to remember that Libya's leaders came to power with few credentials and lacked the legitimacy during the initial phase of the revolution to ride roughshod over whatever resistance existed. Until 1973, therefore, the impact of the country's revolution was much less harsh than what the rhetoric of the regime suggested (Davis 1987). During these early years, the Qadhafi government preferred to allow exit, which initially provided an important safety valve for the regime. These alternatives—physical exit or political exclusion—remained an essential but unofficial part of the Libyan leader's concept of an Enduring Revolution in the 1970s and early 1980s. To avoid the revolution's unpredictability, an estimated one hundred thousand Libyans left the country. It was not necessarily that, in trying to prevent exit, the government would have needed to use repression, but, more importantly, the amounts of repression required would have necessitated a strong secret police that could in turn have become a powerful organized group.

After 1973, Qadhafi's directives were meant to prevent from emerging any group that could create an independent political base of support—whether as members of a socioeconomic class, as part of the Libyan military, as popular or revolutionary committee members, as members of a tribe or of the country's security organizations, or as intellectuals or students. The system of popular committees extended this process further and ensured that a systematic articulation of interests became even more difficult, in the process creating a control system that constituted the real power. Even the most powerful members of that control system—the Libyan army—however, were never permitted to form a professional standing army and thus to become truly institutionalized or autonomous. Much like the king created the CYDEF forces as an alternative—based on tribal affiliation—to the Libyan army, Qadhafi repeatedly reshaped the army and eventually prevented the emergence of a hierarchically organized military bureaucracy by insisting on a popular army and popular militias as the popular revolution unfolded.

This depoliticization and atomization, brought about by constant new waves of *zahf* [assault] against groups showing the potential to organize, provides an important clue to explain the absence of sustained opposition until roughly 1986. Because a division of labor among citizens virtually disappears in distributive states during the boom period, they are unlikely to develop the interdependence among individuals necessary in productive economies. Common interests are seldom articulated during economic booms, and few group mechanisms exist that allow for any broad-based organization of particular interests. Rather than being merely a reflection of tradition, as is often argued in the study of Middle East politics, the continued reliance on primordial affiliations in distributive states is as often the result of the lack, novelty, or distrust of the more impersonal institutions that accompany state-building and the destruction of alternative mechanisms of expressing political preferences.

When citizens comprehend the wide gap between these formal and informal mechanisms of governing, they learn to cope with a political system they have no chance of reforming. In Libya, as in other distributive states in the region, the coping mechanism has been to live within norms of the system while attempting to maximize individual rent-seeking. The state, much as Qadhafi continually advocated, became irrelevant in several important dimensions to many Libyans' everyday life. This depoliticization is not necessarily due to repression but to the fact that citizens eventually stop making claims on the state and that the state has, in several important ways, succeeded in getting rid of its "civil connections" (Najmabadi 1987, 213). In Libya, this process has been so pronounced that even opposition groups operating outside the Jamahiriyya gave up trying to develop a coherent common vision of the country's economic and political future until the Qadhafi regime disappeared (Roumani 1983; Anderson 1986c).[37]

[37]A multitude of Libyan opposition groups have formed in the West and throughout the Middle East. Some of these regularly publish their own viewpoint. The best-known opposition group is the National Front for the Salvation of Libya (NFSL), based originally in Khartoum and founded in 1981 by Muhammad Mugharyif, Qadhafi's former state

When the regime is, in addition, skilled at providing symbolic outlets for local frustrations, effective opposition can be held in abeyance even longer. Even though Libyans were expressly forbidden to organize on their own or to express their points of view freely, they have not totally been without a voice. Qadhafi's often repeated remark, that every popular congress to which individuals belong constitutes an opposition, may seem trivial but is nevertheless important. The popular congress system has allowed citizen complaints to be brought forward and exposed specific ailments—ranging from corruption to mismanagement—that do not directly target the regime or the structures through which it maintains itself. Qadhafi himself has often encouraged these criticisms, particularly when they could be used, as allegedly an expression of the popular will, to extend his own directives.

Neither the interests nor the grievances of civil society, however, were ever allowed to be articulated within groups that developed organizational networks or within organizations that could express long-term group solidarity. They could never be mobilized as an effective protest movement when opportunities for collective action presented themselves. An effective opposition movement would have necessitated both these entrenched organizational networks and a crack in the regime. Although the U.S. April 1986 bombing constituted one of the most severe crises of the regime's existence and was clearly meant to destabilize it—and succeeded marginally—whatever opposition emerged nevertheless remained localized and ineffective.

Oil and State-Building during Libya's Revolutionary Decade

In his final volume of the Green Book—*The Social Basis of the Third Universal Theory*—Qadhafi reiterated once more his ambivalence

---

comptroller and ambassador to India. The NFSL also had a military wing, the Salvation Forces, which, with French and U.S. support, conducted military actions against Qadhafi in the 1970s and 1980s. For more information, consult Anderson (1986c), National Front for the Salvation of Libya (1992), and Vandewalle (1995b). By 1990, the different groups had started to organize themselves more effectively, led in part by the leadership of the NFSL, but their cooperation remains precarious and shows the deep divisions that, in turn, reflected the different aspirations of each group. For a flavor of the continuing infighting among the groups, see *FBIS* 3 November 1993 and 17 November 1993.

and suspicions of the state: "To an individual, the family is more important than the state. . . . Mankind . . . is the individual and the family. The state is an artificial economic and political system, sometimes a military system, with which mankind has no relationship and has nothing to do" (Qadhafi 1980, 4).

Massive inflows of capital invariably create a crisis in distributive states such as Libya, where they become the overwhelming source of income. By the end of its revolutionary decade, the Qadhafi regime had attempted to solve this crisis in a manner that dramatically altered not only the country's political system but also, more importantly, its country's administrative and bureaucratic institutions. Reflecting Qadhafi's preoccupation with equality, his aversion to hierarchy and to the social complexities associated with the modern state expressed in the Green Book, the country's economic bureaucracy and its administration had been handed over to the masses (Anderson 1986a).

This dispersal of power had not solely been an expression of the pursuit of the Libyan leader's ideological proclivities. As the revolutionary decade proceeded, the atomizing of individuals within Libyan society became a crucial ingredient in the regime's attempt at preventing any group within Libyan society from acquiring an institutionalized base of support; it had become part and parcel of the regime's survival. It forced Qadhafi to steer a course between the Scylla of popular participation and the Charybdis of exclusion—after 1975 he consistently resolved the dilemma by opting for the latter.

This unpredictability and the contradictory process it involved sparked among Libya's population and even among the country's new elites a matching survival ethic that further contributed to the already high levels of rent-seeking and depoliticization that had marked the country since the monarchy. The regime's claims about the inadequacy and inappropriateness of the state and its institutions within an Arab setting—and its simultaneous efforts to enact a stateless society—extended further the ambiguities, uncertainty, and outright distrust of the notion of statehood and of a political community among Libyans. During the revolutionary decade, Qadhafi's pursuit of a stateless society became a self-fulfilling prophecy: whatever negative notions of the state Libyans possessed had been reconfirmed by the use it had been put to since 1951, particularly during the spectacular political and economic campaigns of the late 1970s.

The measures taken by the government after 1975 in the pursuit of a Jamahiriyya—which could swallow one's wealth overnight or throw one at the mercy of hastily convened revolutionary courts headed by Green Men (also known as committed revolutionaries)—made state institutions even more suspect. They no longer represented beacons of predictability or the rules of the game in local society. Nor were they meant to reduce uncertainty among the country's citizens by providing structure to individuals' everyday life. On the contrary: as the Green Book indicated, popular rule and popular management were meant deliberately to introduce and perpetuate uncertainty among the country's citizens, to keep them off-balance, and to destroy intentionally all social, economic, and political mechanisms so that what had traditionally provided structure in their lives disappeared.

Under such conditions, neither long-term investment nor political initiative are likely: in Qadhafi's Libya, the deterioration of state institutions had been dovetailed with a further disorganization of civil society that had, by itself, become an ingredient in the regime's pursuit of its political survival. The country's leader was seemingly not concerned about either perfecting the state or changing it, but rather wanted to smash it. That he needed to do this and could do this was the product of the refractory inheritance of the state during the colonial period and the enormous latitude of capital inflows that a hydrocarbon state afforded him, as well as the political space these inflows allowed and perpetuated during the boom.

Despite the regime's attempt to portray the measures during its revolutionary decade as an indication of growing strength, after 1975 it became clear that they were overwhelmingly a sign of weakness. The economic and political directives, cloaked in the pseudoscientific language of the Green Book, became easy solutions not only for hiding the state's inability to regulate but for foregoing the conflictual process that regulation and the state's adjudication require. Rather than create specific institutional arrangements through which the new inflows of capital after 1973 could be managed, the Qadhafi regime opted for a takeover of an unregulated national economy. In theory, Qadhafi's populist agenda, with its intense insistence on egalitarianism, equality, and redistribution, could have been achieved by stronger state apparatuses for that purpose, by more selective taxation policies, or by regulatory institutions aimed at the economy's sectors. It did not have to result in the wholesale takeover of all the country's productive assets.

From the beginning, however, the Qadhafi government—in a manner reminiscent of the monarchy—never seriously attempted to craft effective institutions to create and govern a national economy. In the presence of enormous oil revenues, the luxury to circumvent regulation and simply take over wholesale whatever economic activity existed proved irresistible. The state's direct participation in the economy represented above all a political and administrative shortcut. By 1982, the state's intrusiveness had increased exponentially—but, significantly, all the spectacular and intrusive episodes throughout the revolutionary decade had been made by fiat and were never negotiated or arrived at through compromise and consultation. By the end of 1982, this contradiction and the split between the intrusiveness and the relevance of the state for the country's citizens characterized Libyan state-building: the intrusiveness masked the progressive evisceration of regulation that made the state and its institutions irrelevant beyond their distributive largesse.

Conclusion

By 1982, a decade of revolution, distribution, and redistribution had, at least in principle, vindicated Qadhafi's often repeated insistence that "wealth and power belong to the people"—a slogan from the Green Book that, by that time, could be found everywhere: embroidered on hotel blankets, painted on countless official buildings, and printed on the labels of bottled water from Kufra. For the overwhelming majority of Libyans, Qadhafi's radical populism resulted in undreamed-of tangible benefits: in 1969, Libyan per capita income had been $2,200; within a decade it soared to almost $10,000.

Less visible perhaps, but equally dramatic, was the impact of the rapidly increasing revenues on the regime's ability to pursue, in a highly spectacular fashion, its notion of statelessness. In that process, the regime reorganized, reshaped, obstructed, or outright destroyed state institutions in the name of popular rule and created a carefully controlled but widespread patronage network managed by former RCC members, the top military elite, and a cluster of Qadhafi loyalists at Bab al-Aziziyya that—despite the implementation of popular rule and popular management—closely controlled access to the country's ministries, the main spending institutions.

The announcement of popular rule in 1977 marked the apex of a process the regime had gradually pursued since it came to power but that accelerated during the oil boom: a populist experiment that would circumvent and destroy the hierarchical structures of the modern state, where citizens governed themselves without any intermediaries and where they directly controlled the country's economy through a takeover [*zahf*] of the state's institutions. "Libya's historical problem with central authority," Roumani observed, "was resolved by eliminating it altogether, at least in principle." (1983, 166). This continuous uprooting of a bureaucratic apparatus that could provide continual and consistent administration had been legitimized in the volumes of the Green Book.

Beneath the rhetoric of popular rule and popular management, however, Libyans were politically and economically disenfranchised. Despite the regime's claims, the popular congress and committee system and the General People's Congress had no real power but were overwhelmingly consultative mechanisms throughout the revolutionary decade. The country's political institutions became instruments to further depoliticize the population, where the "pulse of the people" could be measured without ever precipitating a serious debate over the direction or the goals of development and growth in the country. Indeed, that debate had been summarily settled in the aftermath of the 1975 attempted coup, paving the way for an intensification of Qadhafi's *diktats* on the economy and the country's social and political organization.

Both the destruction of independent civil institutions around which opposition could occur—the old private sector, the religious establishment—and the creation of new institutions more in line with the political aims of the regime—popular and revolutionary committees—were meant to prevent social conflict and promote social support. In an almost paradoxical fashion, the principle of consultation stressed in Libya's "popular" institutions, with its hints of collectivity, encouraged this disaggregation by actively discouraging the formulation of demands within a collective setting. The creation of the revolutionary committees and the separation of the revolutionary and popular means of governing in 1979 represented thinly disguised attempts to bypass the formal institutions of authority Qadhafi had himself created. The continuing central role of the Libyan leader, despite the lack of a formal link to the country's executive structure, increasingly provided the setting for the personal politics that came to characterize Libyan politics during the 1970s, particularly after 1975.

The management of the country's economy demonstrated a similar growing interference. Libya's oil booms of the 1970s allowed the regime to become the only hand on the country's economic tiller, destroying the private sector and bringing all economic activity under its purview. This wholesale takeover extended further the social and economic symptoms typical of the distributive state already noted during the last decade of the monarchy and the first four years of the Qadhafi government: a further destruction of state institutions in charge of regulatory activities as all enterprises became subject to popular takeovers; a further extension and evisceration of whatever remained of the country's participatory institutions in the name of popular rule; and the even greater concentration of state spending that did not result in any noticeable penetration of local society. The state's ability to solve problems and to manage economic growth—historically already low—diminished further as spending unfolded at a dizzying pace.

Despite Qadhafi's incessant complaints about delays in administrative procedures, the irresponsibility and laziness of public employees, the lack of accountability, the emergence of corruption, and the lack of personal initiative, he—like Idris al-Sanusi before him—remained seemingly unaware of the broader structural constraints that perpetuated these symptomatic ills of a distributive state. The state's monopoly on collecting rent and its active restriction of this monopoly by engaging in activities that prevented competitive entrepreneurial enterprise consigned citizens to pursue unproductive, rent-seeking activities. These deficiencies were clearly exacerbated by the regime's own inclination to keep economic and other information compartmentalized "for political and security reasons" (Ibjad 5 December 1988). As a small but telling example, even the country's top planners, economists, and advisers to the GPC were often kept in the dark about the financial health of the country's state enterprises.

As this chapter demonstrated, the economic and political imperatives provoked by Libya's oil booms were contradictory, if not incompatible. By the end of the country's third oil boom in 1982, however, neither had yet been put to a sustained test. Starting that year, the regime never again had at its disposal the kind of resources that allowed it to pursue simultaneously these various inclinations. Despite this, and despite the fact that by 1986 the regime faced the deepest crisis since it came to power, it continued to resist reforms.

When it finally adopted such reforms in March 1987, it became clear, as the next chapter details, how the country's past would cast a deep shadow over the country's *infitah* [economic liberalization] strategy and its attempt at political *ouverture.* In a distributive state such as Libya, where depoliticization and economic patronage are intricately linked, the need to recast the power-for-wealth social contract has the potential to introduce deep changes. The transition toward a more market-oriented economy depends in part on the willingness of local governments to provide economic information and incentives and to create a legal environment for their efficient use. Since 1969, to enforce its ideological commitment to statelessness and then to ensure the survival of the regime, the Libyan government deliberately pursued opposite policies. It implemented radical socialist economic policies in which all aspects of the economy, from banking to retail, were dominated by the state and where individuals were first discouraged and later forbidden (in the name of popular rule) to engage in the economy outside the state-controlled public sector.

By avoiding the creation of an internal market system, the regime had closely linked its economic strategy to its political goals. The announcement of People's Power in 1973 symbolized the formal acknowledgment of a policy of disarticulation the Qadhafi government had pursued since it came to power: the eradication of all organized civil institutions in the country. The unpredictability of the revolutionary legal system and the evisceration of property rights in the 1970s had reinforced that tendency. In the process, the regime had broken the financial power of any potential group through a series of measures ranging from its "partners, not wage earners" policy to outright destruction of property. The nationalization of oil and land and the monopoly over imports and exports gave the state control over all sectors of the economy but kept economic regulation low. In the absence of any need to adjudicate between groups engaged in economic relations, the Libyan state became a crude monitoring agency without the legal or financial institutions required in a market system.

By the time of the 1987 reform efforts, the political institutions and the use to which they were put in the Jamahiriyya could no longer be disentangled from the broader process of the creation, destruction, or absence of the state's economic institutions and its bureaucracies: all formed an intricate part of the regime's survival. That the regime had managed to pursue this strategy while its local and international political and economic fortunes declined is testimony in part to the extraordinary but highly concentrated power that oil revenues bestow upon the leaders of distributive states: the ability to outspend emerging crises, without accountability, even if such expenditures fundamentally jeopardize the country's economic future. That the economic and political reforms were abandoned almost immediately following their announcement in 1987 provided, as the next chapter details, telltale indications of the larger failure of state-building in a distributive state.

6

Shadow of the Future: Libya's Failed *Infitah*

When profit- or rent-seeking behavior is fully incorporated into familiar situations where external diseconomies exist, serious questions are raised concerning the efficacy of the efficiency-generating policy steps almost universally recommended by economists.

—James Buchanan, "Rent Seeking under External Diseconomies"

[U]ntil less hierarchical ways of avoiding a Hobbesian world are discovered, the state lies at the center of solutions to the problem of order. Without the state, markets, the other master institution of modern society, cannot function.

—Peter Evans, *Embedded Autonomy*

Libya's oil booms in the 1960s and 1970s represented a particular challenge to the state and to the unfolding process of state-building: a crisis of wealth. Between 1982 and 1986, however, the country's annual revenues tumbled from $21 billion to $5.4 billion, and by 1987 the regime was forced to respond to the new challenge it faced: a rapid decline of wealth that could radically alter the implicit social contract the country's leader had imposed upon citizens in return for the wholesale distribution of that wealth.

Economically, Libya's plight mirrored that of other oil exporters in the region. In each country, government expenditures were reduced, and direct or indirect tax burdens increased. Governments were forced to narrow their coalitional base as social contracts became more exclusive. This often meant that compensatory or distributive payments were more closely restricted to what local regimes considered crucial strategic allies or, in countries that subscribed to some form of populism, to those for whom the impact of the adjustment process would be most painful.

Economic and political reforms in distributive states, even more than in productive states, are intrinsically intertwined. A potential withdrawal of economic largesse presents the local government with its most fundamental political challenge: the potential for altering the original exchange of wealth for power. Furthermore, economic reform must be implemented through institutions that in distributive states are used extensively for rent-seeking and for political purposes. Competitive market processes in distributive states virtually disappear, while economic liberalization ultimately depends on the existence or creation of internal markets. *Infitah* strategies thus entail not only greater competitiveness but also demand institutional reform—or the creation of new institutions. Because of its earlier institutional development and the peculiar nature of state-building it is intertwined with, this process in distributive states is often beyond the state's capability. The bust period, in a peculiar fashion that reflects this historical and institutional record, reveals the complex interplay of institutions, distributive mechanisms and political interests of groups that profited from the earlier distributive largesse.

Despite his long-standing objection to *infitah,* so clearly opposed to the economic principles enunciated in the Green Book, Mu'ammar al-Qadhafi in March 1987 announced the Jamahiriyya's own version of economic liberalization, an announcement that was matched by an attempt at opening up the country's political system (*Al-Fajr Al-Jadid* 28 March 1987). Both efforts failed or were abandoned at a very early stage. Much of the rentier state literature has traced this failure of political and economic reform in oil exporters almost exclusively to a lack of political will or to a relative indifference to higher economic efficiency. Observers more often than not have concluded that economic liberalization represents a form of temporary exit—a consumer *infitah*—that leaves the more basic structures of the state's distributive ability, and ultimately its political power, intact (Luciani 1987). This subterfuge has indeed been observed throughout the region, and Libya proved no exception. Of greater interest, however, is what Libya's failed attempt at liberalization tells us: about the distributive state's inability to liberalize after an intense period of *étatisme* during the 1960s and 1970s that seemingly maximized its interventionist capabilities; about the importance of institutional development for economic liberalization; and, ultimately, about the larger link between the failure of reform in distributive states and the process of state-building.

"Revolution within the Revolution"

Qadhafi's calls for a "revolution within the revolution" or an "extension of the revolution" [*tawsi' ath-thawra*] in the weeks following the April 1986 bombing were widely ignored and were seen by some of his close supporters as problematic at best (Farfar 10 December 1989; Ibjad 13 December 1989).[1] In his public speeches between the bombing and the announcement of the country's *infitah* in March 1987, the Libyan leader publicly voiced the complaints citizens in private conversations often conveyed: Libya's regional and international isolation prevented citizens from traveling, the "revolutionary instruments of governing" were nefarious, and the country's economy was dismal.

GPC delegates, at the Sabha congress in February 1987—convened in part to celebrate the tenth anniversary of popular rule—publicly, for the first time, voiced these concerns (*ZA* 15 February 1987; 17 February 1987). They singled out the country's state companies as inefficient and unable to meet local needs and asked for reform of the country's banking system and for tighter control over the country's expenditures. The public nature of the demands, along with their specificity and sophistication, strongly hinted that they had in fact been allowed by the regime—a fact later confirmed by some of the participants and by similar criticisms in articles written throughout 1987 in the revolutionary committees' newspaper, *al-Jamahiriyya* (Farfar 10 December 1989).

In populist fashion, Qadhafi castigated Libyans for their waste and profligacy and dismissed their complaints about the lack of availability of goods they had come to take for granted during the abundance of the 1970s and early 1980s. Ahmad Jalud, meanwhile, in a meeting with the GPC secretariat on 18 July 1987, analyzed the more structural origin of

[1] Although Libya's *infitah* was referred to in the Arab press as a "revolution within the revolution," the expression was never used in Libyan newspapers because it originally referred to Sadat's decision to break with Nasser's socialist policies—a decision Qadhafi had repeatedly denounced as treason.

the crisis: internal mismanagement and dislocations (exacerbated by the U.S. economic boycott), high inflation, and inefficient distribution (*Al-Fajr Al-Jadid* 20 July 1987). The average Libyan, who was by now standing in bread lines, had more immediate worries. The state supermarket system, once seen as a vital key in eliminating private traders and shopkeepers, and as a source of subsidized goods for the population, had started to falter under the weight of corruption and disorganization. Whatever sporadically appeared in these *suq sha'abi* [popular markets] seldom matched Libyans' daily needs and became the source of much anger and innumerable jokes.[2] An illegal but officially tolerated black market provided little relief for most Libyans because prices were generally beyond the average consumer's purchasing power. In addition, the expulsion of tens of thousands of expatriate workers in the summer and fall of 1985 had virtually brought the local service and agricultural sectors to a standstill.

The country's deepening diplomatic isolation prevented Libyans from traveling abroad, and the lingering and inconclusive conflict in Chad proved enormously costly in both human and material resources. The increasing number of military trials for defectors and the scores of funerary tents in the main cities became sources of gossip that could not be stilled by official pronouncements about the progress of the war. In addition, the public appearance of economic privilege amid the austerity of urban life added to popular dissatisfaction. At the outskirts of the country's major cities, rows of fancy villas owned by top army and diplomatic personnel, municipal committee members, and top bureaucrats contrasted sharply with the more modest housing around them. Although Qadhafi had repeatedly imposed draconian measures to ensure egalitarianism, economic inequities had become evident, and the dismal performance of the state supermarket system was widely rumored to be the result of corruption by top ministry officials.

Qadhafi's response to the political aspects of the crisis consisted of a multilayered attempt to remove some of the regional and international constraints and to curtail the more unpredictable elements of his revolutionary policies at home. The campaign to break out of the country's

[2]Visits by the author to people's supermarkets in Surt and Ajdabiyya in December 1987 revealed enormous quantities of Dutch milk powder, Italian suits, and Chinese tea, but little else. Despite this, a local acquaintance remained obviously proud of their existence and clearly reiterated on several occasions that they represented a real achievement for the country.

isolation focused on diplomatic initiatives within the region and vis-à-vis Europe that, by the time of the revolution's twentieth anniversary celebrations in 1989, had started to bear some fruit (see Vandewalle 1991a, 1995b). The apotheosis of the diplomatic campaign was the announcement of an agreement to settle the long-festering conflict with neighboring Chad before the International Court of Justice (ICJ).[3]

Relations with the United States, however, remained strained. The U.S. government accused Libya of manufacturing chemical weapons in September 1988, and, in a dogfight over the disputed Gulf of Surt, the U.S. navy shot down two Libyan planes in January 1989. The United States also continued to extend systematically its own economic boycott of the country after 1987, a policy that received a boost after the December 1989 Pan Am 103 bombing over Lockerbie, Scotland, which U.S. officials blamed on the Qadhafi regime.[4] When Libya refused to hand over two suspects in the case, the United States intensified its attempts at isolating the country further. It sponsored a United Nations Security Council resolution that imposed an international ban on airflights into the Jamahiriyya and that froze all Libyan funds and resources abroad.[5] In a measure that added to its economic difficulties, Libya was forced to sell or restructure most of its overseas investments. Finally, in July 1996, the U.S. Congress, in a more ominous effort to constrain international trade with Libya, adopted the Iran and Libya Sanctions Act, which included potential sanctions against foreign companies trading with Libya (*New York Times* 24 July 1996).

The internal campaign to restore predictability and legitimacy was aimed primarily at reducing the influence of the "revolutionary instruments of governing." Throughout 1987 and 1988, Qadhafi targeted the security services and particularly the revolutionary committees, singling them out as overzealous, power-hungry, and antithetical to true

[3] Although the referral to the International Court of Justice seems a tactical move on Libya's part—and was advocated as a delaying tactic by some of the country's own foreign policy experts (Ubaydi 3 September 1990)—Qadhafi's willingness to temporarily abide by international norms met with a sigh of relief in much of Africa and Europe.

[4] For the legal issues surrounding the Lockerbie incident, consult Joyner and Rothbaum 1993.

[5] A comprehensive overview of all U.S. actions regarding trade with Libya since 1978 can be found in the biannual messages by the president to the U.S. Congress, published by the Department of State in its bulletin and by the U.S. Government Printing Office.

popular rule. In a national television speech Qadhafi harangued them for having "deviated, harmed, tortured" and promised reforms to curtail their actions.[6] Charges of corruption against some revolutionary committees prompted the minister of justice, at Qadhafi's insistence, to appoint a special committee to audit the assets of those members entrusted with responsibilities in the revolutionary committee movement (*JR* 28 December 1988). Within a few months they lost many of their previous functions, particularly in the police, security, and intelligence operations, where some had started to operate. To further offset their power, Qadhafi in 1988 created the Ministry for Mass Mobilization and Revolutionary Leadership, under the guidance of a long-time regime confidant, Ali al-Sha'iri, whose task it was to further narrow revolutionary activities down to what they had originally been: indoctrination of the masses, "not through violence but through persuasion" (Sha'iri 6 December 1988; *FBIS* 1 September 1988).[7]

The curtailment of the revolutionary committees' activities was matched by a more general attempt at political liberalization. In 1987 and 1988 hundreds of political prisoners were released, with Qadhafi personally taking part in the destruction of Tripoli's central prison on 3 March 1988—an event broadcast for months afterward on local television.[8] He personally also supervised the shredding of thousands of police files collected by Libya's four security organizations, which were kept in part to deny passports to Libyan citizens.[9] In March 1988, Qadhafi traveled to the Libyan-Tunisian borderpost at Ras al-Jadir and took part in its destruction—announcing that all Libyans were now free to travel. Armed with relatively generous hard currency allowances—approximately $1,000 for every family member—almost one million Libyans visited Tunisia in 1988 alone. Although these safety valves may appear as superficial palliatives, in effect they provided breathing room

[6]On Libyan television (3 May 1988) Qadhafi clearly admitted the excesses of the committees, inadvertently revealing the real power structure in the country: "They deviated, harmed, tortured. . . . [N]o one has immunity . . . at all if he has deviated. The revolutionary does not practice repression. On the contrary, I want to prove that the committees . . . are lovers of the masses, that they are for freedom and that they support my resolutions."

[7]For a more complete description of the rise and fall of the revolutionary committee movement, see Mattes 1995a.

[8]Qadhafi's speech from the prison tower can be found in SWB/ME/0092/A/3–5 (5 March 1988). An estimated 400 local and 130 foreign prisoners were released as a result.

[9]The four branches of security were the secret service, the revolutionary committees, the military police, and the military secret service.

for ordinary Libyans, who were now free to travel for the first time in almost a decade and to bring back goods that had been lacking on the Libyan market for years. Those who found themselves financially strapped could exchange their dinars for foreign currencies through an informal but intricate and efficient black market that the government tolerated.

Qadhafi furthermore extended offers to Libyan exiles to return home, promising employment and assurances that they would not be persecuted—in sharp contrast to the policies of the late 1970s. Passports were reissued to all Libyans who had theirs previously confiscated, and the power to deny them to citizens now became the responsibility of the Popular Congresses and no longer belonged to the police or security services. Finally, on at least two occasions—once in Algeria, once in Tripoli—Qadhafi met with several opposition leaders in an attempt at conciliation.

In a remarkable turnaround, Qadhafi then extended his political liberalization campaign and portrayed himself as an advocate of legality, freedom, and human rights. Acknowledging the lack of the rule of law in the Jamahiriyya and the reality of past abuses, he proposed the codification of legal principles through the GPC in order to curtail further transgressions (*FBIS* 29 March 1988). The security and police services were singled out for their excesses, and Qadhafi suggested making them directly responsible to the GPC. In a speech in May 1988, he went even further in suggesting that all punishable crimes be clearly enumerated and codified to halt arbitrary arrests for unspecified crimes (*FBIS* 3 May 1988). Except for cases involving treason, the revolutionary courts were abolished and replaced by regular people's courts. Promising legal redress for wrongs committed by Libyan authorities in the past, Qadhafi then created a new Ministry of Justice in March 1989 (*FBIS* 5 May 1988).

These measures were followed by the proclamation of a remarkable document—*Al-Wathiqa al-Khadra al-Kubra lil-huquq al-insan fi 'asr al-Jamahir* [The Great Green Charter of Human Rights]—in June 1988.[10] When contrasted against the deliberate arbitrariness and unpredictability of the revolution's political and economic rules since the early 1970s, the Green Charter was an exceptional document that indicated, for the

[10] All references to the Great Green Charter are from *Al-Wathiqa al-Khadra al-Kubra lil-huquq al-insan fi 'asr al-Jamahir* [The Great Green Charter of Human Rights in the Era of the Masses]. Tripoli: Al-Markaz al-Alami lil Dirasat wa al-Abhath al-Kitab al-Akhdar [World Center for Studies and Research on the Green Book], n.d.. A detailed analysis of the Great Green Charter and its meaning can be found in Mayer 1995.

first time since 1969, a willingness by the regime to codify those rules in ways that could be challenged by Libyan citizens, and that would simultaneously provide clear guidelines. The Green Charter, however, gave Libyans neither the political or civil rights traditionally assumed under international law nor "the privileges of citizenship" (Djaziri 1995, 197) but reflected once again Qadhafi's ambiguity about hierarchical structures, clearly defined procedures, and a legal system that relied on impersonal categories and decision making procedures.[11]

Adopted by the GPC in June 1988, the Green Charter codified some of the principles Qadhafi had earlier insisted on but lacked many provisions that would have extended human rights to all Libyans. It contained a compilation of Qadhafi's earlier thoughts, some of them foreshadowed in the volumes of the Green Book. Some stipulations, however, were clearly a step back from his earlier pronouncements. Article 11 of the Green Charter, for example, calls private property "sacred [*muqaddasa*] and protected" but concludes that it could be overridden by "the public interest"—without specifying what those interests are (*Al-Wathiqa al-Khadra,* 11). Furthermore, Article 25 specified that every member of the Jamahiriyya had to defend the country "until death," and Article 26 stated that all "acts contrary to the principles and rights" [of the Green Charter] are not allowed." Both articles, particularly in light of the persistence of a much earlier law on political activities—*man tahazzaba khanan* [He who organizes (politically) is a traitor]—created areas that could be labeled as treasonous behavior by the government if it so desired (*Al-Wathiqa al-Khadra,* 16). Finally, although Article 9 guaranteed all Libyans the right to legal counsel and to an independent judiciary, it offered no real guarantees—as the persecution of Islamists in the country was soon to demonstrate. In the spring and summer of 1989, the Qadhafi government attempted to put some of the Green Charter's provisions into practice. In March 1989, the GPC adopted a law calling for the judiciary's independence and extended this call later to include a strengthening of the people's courts at the expense of the revolutionary ones throughout the country.

The efforts to restore predictability and to reduce the previous arbitrariness, however, indicated clearly the larger rules of the game within the Jamahiriyya. The adopted measures proved highly selective: under no circumstances was opposition allowed. Qadhafi continued to argue that, because Libya was a Jamahiriyya where people exercised power directly, there was no need for some of the liberties adopted in other countries;

[11] The legal system of the Jamahiriyya is discussed in Dawi 1984.

there was no room for a free press because the people were free to express themselves at the people's congresses; no right to strike because Libyans were the owners of the factories at which they worked; and, finally, no specified rights for opposition groups because opposition could only take place within the congress and committee system. Indeed, the persecution of Islamists in the 1990s would eviscerate all the protections the Green Charter had seemingly guaranteed under Article 10, which argued that religion "is a personal and direct relation with the Creator, without intermediary." Qadhafi would call for the elimination of these protections in much the same fashion as he had earlier insisted on the destruction of dissident exiles overseas, accusing them of *zandaqa* [heresy], for which the only punishment was death.[12]

The reshuffle of the country's cabinet following the Sabha GPC meeting cast further doubt on Qadhafi's willingness or ability to pursue a more open policy. Umar al-Muntasir, a respected technocrat with close links to European business circles, was named prime minister. His appointment, however, was offset by that of two "Green Men"—dedicated revolutionaries—to important positions. Muhammad Lutfi Farhat, an economist who had written extensively on the "jamahiri system of economic development," became planning minister (Farhat 1983), and Mustafa Zaidi was appointed as new health minister. While playing delicate balancing acts between technocrats and revolutionaries within the GPC's advisory committees, Qadhafi took no chances: a ruling at the Sixteenth GPC Congress in March 1990 reconfirmed the separation of formal authority and revolution [*fasl as-sulta wa ath-thawra*] and allocated to him, for the first time, the right to formally intervene in political matters. It also confirmed, by implication, the right of the revolutionary committees to exist, despite the fact that they had not been a part of Qadhafi's original outline of government found in the Green Book.[13]

[12] Since 1973 there have been periodic arrests (and executions) of Islamist figures. Some of these—such as shaykh al-Bishti (heir to a prominent Tripolitanian family) and the Tripoli mufti, shaykh Zawi—were independent leaders who objected in particular to Qadhafi's pronouncements on Islam and the value of *hadith* and *sunna*. Others, however, particularly those arrested since 1987, belonged to more politically active, "fundamentalist" groups that Qadhafi clearly considers more dangerous to his regime. They include the *Hizb al-Tahrir al-Islami, Takfir wa Hijrah, Tabligh,* the *Jihad al-Islami,* and the *Munazzamat al-Jihad al-Islami,* as well as other groups that have randomly cropped up and claimed responsibility for diverse acts of sabotage inside the country.

[13] The official declaration of the separation of formal authority and revolution had been issued by the General People's Congress in its second special session on 2 March 1979.

Libya's *Infitah*

It is instructive to recall briefly the features and structure of the Jamahiriyya's economy at the eve of its attempted *infitah* in March 1987. State intervention in the local economy was pervasive: the state dominated all manufacturing, agriculture, and foreign and domestic retail trade and owned all banking, insurance, and other major services. State trading companies were in charge of all industrial, manufacturing, and agricultural imports, including basic consumer goods and foodstuffs. The government, furthermore, intervened indirectly through interest-free credit, state spending, subsidies, and price manipulation of goods. By 1987, an estimated 70 to 75 percent of the Libyan population were direct government employees, working either in the country's bureaucracies or in its state enterprises. The government controlled foreign trade and, as a result of the creation of state supermarkets in the 1970s, retail trade as well.[14] The problems the country faced were essentially those found in many centrally planned economic systems, albeit of an even higher magnitude: low productivity, inefficiencies, misallocation of resources, deteriorating living standards, and extremely high labor costs.

Libya's *infitah* measures consisted of two waves: a first effort between 1987 and 1990 that was meant primarily to relieve the economic hardship within the country, and a second wave after 1990 that would substantially reduce state involvement in the economy. Its overall goals were threefold: (1) to extend cuts in state spending, (2) to gradually withdraw subsidies that contributed to such spending, and (3) to promote private sector initiatives in the industrial, trade, and agricultural sectors. All were meant to improve the management capacity of the state enterprise sector, to promote greater efficiency in the use of resources and in planning, and to reduce waste. Under this new strategy, the state would retain heavy industry, while medium and light enterprises would be given over to popular self-management committees.

The first set of reform measures, adopted in 1987 and 1988, introduced the concept of *tashrukiyya* [self-management or collective ownership], which allowed for the creation of cooperatives. Although the 1978 law on "wage earners, not employees" was maintained, under this arrangement some limited private sector involvement was allowed. By

[14]It must be pointed out that government control over the private sector was not total. For example, individual farmers continued to sell primary food items at the *suq al-falahin* that dotted the countryside and appeared sometimes at the edge of Libyan towns and cities.

August 1988, approximately 140 medium- and small-scale companies were turned over to self-management committees and, at least in theory, no longer received the automatic subsidies they once enjoyed. At the same time injunctions against the retail trade were lifted, and the country's *suqs* inside the cities reopened.

At the 1988 anniversary celebrations, Qadhafi announced the remaining measures. They included the removal of the state import and export monopoly, which would now allow Libyans "to import and export in complete freedom" and the removal of subsidies on wheat, tea, flour, and salt. He also stated that farmers would be allowed freely to market their goods, an official acknowledgment of a practice that had been tolerated even at the height of the revolutionary period, when the *suq al-falahin* [farmers' market] had been a common feature at the edges of most Libyan cities. Professionals were allowed for the first time to open private practices, but fees remained determined by the appropriate ministry (*FBIS* 1 September 1988).[15] In an effort to generate more revenues, the Libyan government also announced the creation of Oilinvest, a holding company meant to increase the country's oil refining capability and to market its products on the European market.

The second wave of reforms took place in the early 1990s. In several ways this "deepening" was meant to surpass the first wave of measures, including a more vigorous withdrawal by the state from the economy. Promoting this deepening of the country's *infitah,* Qadhafi argued for a clear division of labor between the state and the private sector in shouldering the burdens of development in order to "take the burden off the public institutions" (*FBIS* 2 September 1992, 19). Unprofitable state enterprises should be closed and, for the first time, he suggested imposing higher fees on government services (such as water, electricity, and postal services) and reducing the number of government employees. In a move that simultaneously reflected his populist inclinations and his efforts to shift the administrative burdens and expenses away from the major cities along the coast, and to further disperse the population, he renewed his call for a decentralization of the country into fifteen hundred separate *mahalla* [administrative communities] that would be responsible for their own budgets.[16]

[15] The official stipulation at the time had been that farmers could market their own produce if they, or family members, were directly in charge of sales.

[16] This measure was seen by some as an attempt to temper the growing influence of the GPC.

Other measures included laws that, if implemented, would create the framework to make the *infitah* measures operable. They included the adoption of *sharika musahima* [joint-stock company legislation], which would enable private companies to open foreign currency accounts and to import equipment (*MEED* 18 September 1992) and the adoption by the GPC in September 1992 of a law that allowed for more private companies, specifying their access to credit from state and commercial banks. The latter were officially established in March 1993 and were entitled to establish foreign currency accounts for individuals and local private companies (*FBIS* 24 March 1993; *JR* 27 March 1993).[17] Wholesale trade was liberalized in July 1993, including the right to establish partnerships for that purpose.[18] In the hope of channeling capital from the black market into private legal companies, stipulations followed that created special opportunities for reinvested capital.

The culmination of the second set of reforms were measures suggested by Qadhafi in the spring and summer of 1993: guarantees for foreign capital investment, promotion of tourism with the aid of foreign companies, and convertibility of the Libyan dinar (*FBIS* 10 May 1993; 13 July 1993). The first was adopted by the GPC in January 1994, in the hope of attracting foreign investment to high-technology enterprises (*FBIS* 2 February 1994). The GPC considered convertibility at its first meeting in 1994 and outlined conditions that needed to be met before it could be formally adopted. Significantly, both the Central Bank and the petroleum sector, as during the populist phase of the 1970s, which had put all enterprises under popular rule, were excluded from all the new regulations.

If fully implemented, Libya's *infitah* would have represented one of the most far-reaching economic reforms efforts in the region. The laws adopted by the GPC equaled or surpassed the stabilization and structural adjustment measures routinely advocated by western financial institutions to the Third World. In reality, as subsequent years showed, very little was accomplished. Many of the new laws were stillborn or never implemented, for reasons discussed in the following pages. The country's bureaucracies were left untouched. The *tashrukiyya* enterprises were never subject to administrative scrutiny, and the legal texts never made clear who should supervise them.

Although public enterprises under Libyan liberalization became in theory more financially autonomous, there was no evidence that the

[17] Law 1, March 1993.
[18] Decree 491, 1993

automatic subsidies of previous years were halted. They were at best lowered minimally across the board and as part of reduced development budgets. Proposals for increased fees on education, electricity, highway, and health care fees were introduced but immediately dropped from consideration. Most of the hardships of cutbacks were passed on to the expatriate labor community inside the country—a tactic occasionally used by the Qadhafi regime that hinted at the government's inability or unwillingness to hurt local consumers. Pricing policies for basic food products, for example, continued, and the government made no efforts to contain parallel markets for goods brought in from Algeria and Tunisia.

At the retail level, where liberalization would have the greatest immediate impact, reform also remained minimal. Private traders were allowed to bring in goods from neighboring countries (no customs offices existed at any rate), but few traders proved willing to invest in new businesses, and individuals restricted their activities to service enterprises—furniture, car and appliance repairs, hairdressing salons—that were essentially risk-free and required relatively little capital. From 1987 through 1989, for the first time since the pre-1973 oil boom, Libya ran consistent trade balance deficits. A 1989 government decree finally redivided the import monopoly among fifteen state companies (Secretariat of Planning 1989). Despite a growing increase in imports from 1987 to 1990, rising oil prices in 1989 and the end of the war in Chad brought Libya's international reserves by 1990 back to the 1987 level—approximately $5.8 billion—and its current account into the black once more.

There were, furthermore, no visible changes in the lending policies of the country's commercial banks, and the government firmly retained its controls on interest rates and continued to regulate exchange rates. As in the past, banks continued to support public enterprises at the behest of their respective ministries and, by extension, of the Qadhafi government. The Libyan government continued to closely control access to capital, imports, and intermediary supplies. Finally, and most importantly perhaps, the Qadhafi government showed virtually no concern for issues of equity that are normally instrumental in pursuing liberalization or restructuring programs. Indeed, the regime could hardly have been expected to express a desire for greater equity, as Qadhafi's rhetoric consistently argued that the Third Universal Theory already provided for a highly egalitarian system for all Libyans.

The variable income tax system, proposed by some Ministry of Finance officials in 1991, remained limited to increased taxes on the wages of foreigners. The new private sector's role remained limited mostly to providing and distributing what the state through its inefficient state supermarkets could not deliver; the state's overwhelming role remained focused on its distributive and welfare functions. By 1993, Libya's cities once again were filled with many of the consumer items Libyans had taken for granted during the boom period of the 1970s—complete this time with satellite dishes, cellular phones, and other electronics goods. As the most visible sign of new times, however, the required currency for the purchase of such items was the U.S. dollar and not the Libyan dinar, whose value on the black market slipped steadily.

Markets, Institutions, and Economic Reform

The failure of Libya's *infitah* dramatically illustrates the challenges distributive states face when implementing broad economic reforms—or more narrow liberalization and privatization strategies—that are meant to reduce the unique and highly peculiar position the state occupies. Even if rulers prove willing to implement reforms when facing severe fiscal crises, they face more profound obstacles that are related to the nature of economic institutions in distributive states and that are linked to the intertwined economic and political objectives those institutions pursue during boom periods. Ultimately these obstacles, as I have argued throughout this book, are the outcome of structural and institutional weaknesses that emerge from the state-building process within distributive states. They are particularly revealed when the state attempts an *infitah* during a fiscal crisis, when a greater reliance on market mechanisms rather than on state regulation is pursued.

From an institutional perspective, the reason for this is intimately related to the type and scope of activities distributive states undertake during boom periods: they overwhelmingly concern themselves with distribution, a relatively easy task that avoids systematic regulation. The purpose of an *infitah,* however, implies the introduction of market mechanisms. It is important, therefore, to recall one of the basic arguments institutional economists have made: to create markets and to make them function properly requires administrative, regulatory, and legal institutions that must be created and maintained by the state (North 1981). Ultimately, the move toward a market-oriented economy and the functioning of those markets depends on the willingness of governments to provide economic information and incentives and to create the necessary legal environment for the incentives to be efficiently used.

Where state activity has been limited to primarily distributive activities, the pursuit of an *infitah* is thus a much more difficult enterprise than simply allowing a private sector to emerge: the state must prove willing to improve its capacities to regulate, to dispense law, to define and enforce property rights, to tax, and to collect information—without antagonizing the social coalitions that form its base of support. The state must simultaneously reduce its distributive role, create new institutions where they do not exist, and pursue institutional improvements that go substantially beyond abolishing the earlier *dirigisme.*

As I have argued earlier, this proved particularly difficult in Libya, where *étatisme,* adopted by the king and extended by Qadhafi, was ultimately linked to efforts to overcome both low levels of political legitimacy and to the inability to regulate from the time of independence onward. *Étatisme* had been, far from an indication of strength, an effort to avoid the drawn-out struggles of regulating private sector activities: rather than pursue the far more difficult task of regulating the economy, in both cases the state simply assumed power over *all* economic activity. Ever since independence, the king and the Qadhafi government deliberately pursued policies that limited and reduced an active, interventionist role for institutions and bureaucracies in the country's economy. The emphasis on distribution and a benign laissez-faire had marked the monarchy. Qadhafi's more radical populist economic policies had brought all aspects of the economy—from banking to retail trade—under the direct purview of the state.

The Libyan leader not only failed to create the administrative, regulatory, and legal institutions that were needed to establish markets internally, but he tried to abolish them outright after the 1977 Sabha declaration with its "revolutionary" initiatives. In effect, a true economic liberalization would have meant creating or strengthening precisely those institutions both regimes had tried to curtail or avoid since they came to power. And it would have entailed not only the creation of internal markets and their attending institutions but also, inevitably, a complete reversal of the political experiments that had made ordinary Libyans superfluous in the daily management of the country's economy. This is qualitatively a much more difficult enterprise, fraught with difficulties and setbacks even in more diversified and integrated economies.

Indeed, both the monarchy and the Qadhafi regime spent considerable effort in using their rule-making authority to create rents for various supporters, and, as a result, restricted the market forces' ability to operate. Their ability to institute tariffs or quantitative restrictions, to ration foreign exchange, and to selectively prevent entry through licensing procedures constituted important ways of creating those rents. It is obvious, however, that even the creation of new rules and institutions as a deus ex machina is not sufficient to make an *infitah* successful. From 1988 on, both the Jamahiriyya's official gazette and the GPC in its proceedings announced a flurry of directives and decrees that, at least in theory, would have provided Libya with a bevy of regulations and reformed institutions to make the transition toward a more market-oriented economy possible. In reality, as the previous section indicated, few of those regulations were implemented, and the state's institutions essentially continued to function (or not function) as before. One important reason for the inability to translate intentions into concrete action is the link between institutions and politics in distributive states. Despite (or perhaps because of) the general depoliticization that takes place, the policies of distributive institutions and, ultimately, the institutions themselves become highly politicized for ruler and citizens alike: they promise access to goods for the citizens and control for the ruler.

The distributive policies of the monarchy and the Jamahiriyya have also included a specific political goal. Suspicious of any corporate group or any organized entity whose motives could be broadly construed as political, the government used its distributive strategy to buy off various groups in the country's civil society and to prevent infighting among them. By avoiding an internal market system that would create groups with differing economic prowess and interests, the Qadhafi regime closely linked its economic strategy to one of its political goals: egalitarianism. The nationalization of oil and land and the monopoly over imports and exports gave the state control over all sectors of the economy but kept economic regulation—both by design and by weak institutional structures—at a very low level. Like the country's political institutions, Libya's economic institutions were meant more for the pursuit of the regime's survival than for regulation (Vandewalle 1995a; Djaziri 1995).

Libya's reaction to the two phases of *infitah* closely reflected the interests of a broad range of groups within the country. The initial phase of the *infitah* met with little resistance and had been carefully dovetailed with the political liberalization effort. The liberalization of trade and the end of the import regulations benefited both consumers, whose scarcities ended, and *bazaaris* [small shopkeepers] who were now free to import food and consumer goods from abroad. More importantly it did not fundamentally alter the privileges of those who had profited most handsomely from the state's restrictive practices in the past: managers of state enterprises, the military, the country's top technocrats, and entrepreneurs with close links to the military. On the contrary, the *infitah*'s first phase had strengthened their position: with their links to the military and top leadership around Qadhafi, they were much better positioned to gain access to credit and were now free to engage openly in imports and exports while continuing to enjoy privileged access to foreign currency for that purpose.

As an unintended result, the first liberalization wave led to an even greater stratification and division of labor that rankled both Qadhafi and the average Libyan citizen: the *bazaaris* and the retail merchants were limited, primarily for lack of capital, to operations that focused mainly on food and on small, often shoddy consumer goods brought in from neighboring countries, while the imports of major capital goods provided lucrative incomes for those with the appropriate connections.

The second wave of reforms would have led to actual state withdrawal from the country's economy and could have hurt virtually every single group. In the end, it was universally condemned and quickly abandoned. Its clearest potential losers included a small but articulate group whose losses would be immediate and deeply felt: the military, managers of highly protected state companies, the country's technocrats in charge of the oil industry, and political elites, including some of the revolutionary committee members. In a country where virtually everything was imported and characterized by an intricate and personal client system, the import control system—which was abandoned during *infitah*'s first phase—had served as a highly effective instrument to reward loyal clients. Continued access to import licenses among the military and top political elite allowed for large personal financial rewards that could be shared by friends, supporters, and tribal members. Real import liberalization, free access to a liberalized banking system, would have meant the end of profits from obtaining scarce licenses and directly affected those most visibly supportive of the regime.

Those who stood to gain marginally were the least powerful but, in light of economic policy since the 1969 coup and the outcome of the *infitah*'s first phase, the most suspicious: urban consumers, small businesses, and farmers. Whatever gains the *infitah*'s second phase promised would also be offset by the loss of wage policies and broad-based subsidies that kept living standards at a level few could have imagined even a few years earlier. In addition, after living for years under inflationary, controlled economic conditions, consumers of these groups expressed little personal enthusiasm for the new measures that could "be swept away once more if Qadhafi decides to do so tomorrow" and which, in essence, asked them to trade an insecure future with few clear guarantees for austerity in the short term.[19]

In light of what they had experienced since 1969, neither the lack of trust nor the urge to prefer rent-seeking over actual entrepreneurial activity was surprising. The country's capital markets, its banking industry, insurance industry, and legal and commercial codes had fallen prey to the revolution and were hardly inspiring confidence either among whatever local entrepreneurs still existed or among foreign investors. In none of those categories were true market forces still at work. Subsidies took over from any attempt at regulation and touched consumers, "commission entrepreneurs," and importers alike. In this extreme form of corporatism made possible by the distributive policies of an oil state, everyone had become a client in an essentially risk-free economic environment that did not foster entrepreneurial skill.

The country's traditional distrust of central authority had been immensely exacerbated by the utter unpredictability of the country's "revolutionary" legal system, the further destruction of regulatory institutions, and the tenuous nature of the country's bureaucracy after 1973. The reliance of the government on oil revenues to pursue its egalitarian policies, furthermore, was matched by an increasing reliance of the population on the handouts these revenues allowed. Large numbers of citizens had become part of the country's bureaucracies, through which largesse was channeled. The result was a vicious circle in which neither political institutions, popular or government political will, or economic incentives existed to move the country away from the consumer mentality it continues to exhibit today.

Under these conditions of rent-seeking and of general suspicion by consumers—or outright opposition by the regime's major clients—economic liberalization faltered, not surprisingly. In the end, no group had an interest or expressed trust in seeing the economic liberalization proceed. Those not profiting from direct access to the country's riches did so indirectly through the more limited but general distributive largesse of the regime. To the regime's closest supporters, the government's professed intention to introduce a more liberal economic system that would

[19] The comment was made to me by a small shopkeeper in Tripoli in July 1992. Having lost his furniture business in the late 1970s, he migrated to Chad, where he lived with relatives, and returned to Libya in 1991. In his tiny shop he sold mostly small household items and candy he himself brought back from Tunisia on a regular basis.

rely on incentives channeled through a price system and on a more accessible import licensing system meant the potential loss of privilege. It is therefore highly unlikely that in light of the regime's reliance on these clients the disruptive reforms could have been implemented without endangering the regime: the social groups that opposed it were among the key supporters of the regime.

Furthermore, a serious attempt at imposing economic regulations after a period in which most administrative and bureaucratic institutions had deliberately been ignored would have proven extremely disruptive at a time when the regime felt beleaguered. It clearly realized that liberalization could entail a loosening of the tools, particularly its centralized distributive ability, by which it had managed local society. In a country where individuals were deliberately left atomized, the possible creation of groups that develop similar economic interests and prove willing to defend them hinted at the possible creation of an opposition Qadhafi had never been willing to contemplate. Qadhafi himself noted on several occasions how dangerous markets could be, how they provided mobility and opportunity for individuals at the expense of the community; how their inherent mechanisms could also threaten the egalitarian policies the regime had pursued so assiduously; how this greater economic differentiation and inequalities could lead to strife; and how a "culture of the market" would negatively affect the daily lives of Libyan citizens. Qadhafi therefore saw *infitah* not only as an economic challenge but also as a cultural issue: it potentially provided an opening to Islamists and others who could point to the regime's own rhetoric of egalitarianism.[20]

Qadhafi also seemingly confused liberalization with handing over private property to citizens at the expense of central control. In a highly publicized appearance shortly after the announcement of the initial *infitah* measures, he threw out thousands of land records and deeds to private houses in Tripoli, announcing that these now belonged to the people who lived in them. He seemed unaware of the deleterious impact this had on confidence among both potential investors and consumers as

[20]"You will see that those who have failed to resolve their economic problems in their countries and who couldn't mobilize popular forces for the development and for the exploitation of the country's resources turn . . . toward *infitah,* as in Egypt. They open the gates to foreign exploitative capital, to sumptuous palaces, to American corporations, to multinationals. In this way they compensate for the accumulated defeats by throwing themselves into the arms of economic colonialism" (Mu'ammar al-Qadhafi, quoted in Barrada, Kravetz, and Whitaker 1984).

the country stood poised to embark on a liberalization effort. The act again demonstrated Qadhafi's distaste for any institution that would consistently gather information and provide continuity—precisely what a sustained *infitah* would attempt to achieve. In the same vein, he deliberately used the intended liberalization strategy for his own populist purposes: destroying borderposts, throwing out land records, proposing to hand over half of the country's oil revenues directly to the population (*FBIS* 10 March 1993), encouraging the black market as "people's markets . . . a spontaneous decision of the people made independently of the government" (*FBIS* 1 September 1988, 18), proposing home education for children to further reduce state expenditures (Monastiri 1995), or, finally, to suggest that "the oil revenue be distributed to Libyans directly; it should be deposited in their bank accounts and used for purchasing whatever they need" (*FBIS* 9 September 1993, 21).

In the end, the country's announced *infitah* faltered and was never implemented. The country had neither the administrative or institutional capability nor the political will to move forward with measures that could have reversed long-standing policies. Despite the state's seeming autonomy and the emergence of a group of technocrats within the GPC that actively supported the liberalization, it was quickly abandoned at the behest of the regime's major client groups. The defeat of the *infitah* in the 1990s repeated what had happened in 1975, when the revolutionaries had defeated the technocrats who argued for less ideological interference with the economy. Even under dramatically more difficult circumstances, the regime prevailed—this time supported, however, by a broad coalition of *infitah* opponents. Once more, oil revenues provided a vital clue: increased prices and demand by 1990 turned Libya's current account deficits around and kept international reserves at $5.8 billion. That the regime was able to avoid sustained economic reform, even in the face of a severe fiscal crisis, testified once more to the resilience distributive states have. That it continued to spend roughly one-third of its oil revenues on the Great Man-made River Project, the Misrata Steel Project, and the Ras al-Unuf petrochemical complex while attempting economic reform further testified to the lack of accountability that still prevails in the Jamahiriyya.

Growth and Development

Long-term development, particularly in open economies such as oil exporters, requires the state's steady and sustained hand on the economic tiller—a strategy unlikely to materialize and be maintained unless the state itself develops in response to the myriad international and local obstacles and opportunities development entails. As Libya has spectacularly demonstrated, the impact of massive inflows of capital and the financial autonomy the state enjoys allows it to limit itself to nurturing specialized state institutions that do not necessarily extend its ability to regulate either growth, development, or economic and social relations among its citizens. The distributive state has the luxury not to perfect itself, and its management of all economic activities masks more often than not an inability to discriminate clearly among economic and social goals.

In oil exporters, underutilization of productive capacity is not due to a scarcity of financial capital but primarily to the rigidity of the country's institutional framework and to the technological structure of local economies. In the international division of labor, they occupy a highly restrictive and vulnerable niche—a unique place in production for global markets that has powerful implications for the country's development and for the welfare of its citizens (Chase-Dunn 1989). Oil revenues allow for rapid accumulation of capital, high profits, and extended benefits to the population. But local development is highly dependent not only on those fluctuating revenues and access to markets but also on the ability to buy many goods and services on the international market. Development under those conditions requires extraordinary stewardship to exploit that particular niche and to create a "multidimensional conspiracy" that promotes the unleashing of both entrepreneurial energy and developmental coalitions that sustain development. As elaborated in the previous section, both rely on social and institutional elements that can only develop over time (Brenner 1976; Duvall and Freeman 1983).

In "transitory economies" such as Libya, where oil revenues last only a few decades, the state's task to create, nurture, and sustain both entrepreneurial energy and developmental coalitions is thus particularly crucial. Effective statecraft assumes a critical dimension in this process, in order to turn an important but very narrow and temporary comparative advantage into assets that can sustain growth and help create a domestic income base for the post-oil period. Local governments can do so in two distinct ways: either by creating a more diversified economy or, alternatively, by pursuing a Kuwaiti scenario, in which resources are invested in such a way that they yield sufficient income for future generations once oil runs out.[21] For reasons described throughout this book, Libya

[21]In the wake of the Gulf war, Kuwait spent a substantial amount of those accumulated reserves in order to rebuild the country. See Crystal 1995.

now faces enormous difficulties in pursuing either strategy. Some of these problems are common to all small, open economies that rely on a single commodity for development and growth, while others are due to the unique behavior of the country's rulers.

Because of their ability to contain balance of payments difficulties, oil exporters are able, at least in theory, to promote higher rates of investment and self-sustained growth and to alleviate existing imbalances between the structure of domestic supply and demand as they arise during the growth process. In principle, they can absorb the surplus labor of the agricultural sector into other sectors of the economy and foster a manufacturing sector by relieving supply bottlenecks.[22] Of particular importance for long-term development and growth is the oil exporters' potential to create this manufacturing sector, which will allow for "the extension of capital and machinery, the application of science and technology and the introduction of new methods of work [that lead to] important dynamic economies of scale or economies of specialization . . . [and create] simultaneous growth of employment and productivity of labor" (Karshenas 1990, 11–13).

This statement makes assumptions few distributive states manage to live up to: the existence of the state as an agent with a highly developed autonomy and with a clearly defined set of economic priorities imposed upon a "formless or perfectly malleable economy" (Karshenas 1990, 24). In reality, as Libya's *infitah* vividly demonstrates, such states have relatively little autonomy or strength and are often captive to the coalitions that develop during boom periods. The structure of their economies reflects the peculiar nature of oil-led development and must contend with realities that both historically condition the capacity of the state to intervene and determine the direction such an intervention will take.

Clearly, in Libya oil revenues have not generated the dynamic processes Karshenas describes, nor the structural flexibility that is indispensable for self-sustained growth, nor the developmentalist bureaucracies considered crucial to that process. The creation of developmental coalitions and of entrepreneurs in a political system where rent-seeking, the atomization of individuals, and the deliberate neglect of state institutions has been pursued over a long time makes these prerequisites

[22]Economic bottlenecks are defined here as "social or technical conditions of production [either in particular sectors of the economy or within the economic institutions of a country as a whole] which limit and condition both effective economic intervention by the government and the operation of the market mechanism" (Karshenas 1990, 7).

highly unlikely. Rather, Libya has opted to ignore systematically those processes, and such action has led to the economic and commercial policies typically found in settings where extensive rent-seeking takes place: where the purchasing of equipment and the signing of contracts are not subject to considerations of economic viability; where oversight and accountability is limited, and where, as a result, public resources are constantly diverted for private ends (Moore 1991). Under those circumstances, concerns about absorptive capacity are routinely ignored and investments are often biased toward large and prestigious projects that are seldom subject to economic limits or to cost-benefit calculations.

Distributive states, however, can pursue an alternative: to "sequester as much abroad as possible" and to use the proceeds from overseas investment for future generations (Little et al. 1993, 9). Libya's confrontation with the West never allowed the country to pursue that option. Its overseas investments in primarily European companies raised questions locally. Partly as a result of these local concerns and partly because of a growing threat of economic boycott against Libyan holdings in the early 1990s, the Qadhafi government was forced to repatriate its investments to safer but often less lucrative regional channels. Investments in European industry and deposits in western banks were steadily drawn down after 1986 in order to avoid recriminations and possible seizure as the United States pressed for a total economic boycott of the country.

The activist international policies of the regime and the resulting U.S.-led boycott only further unraveled the country's development. As a result, Libya's ability to shift from a petroleum-exporting country to an integrated industrial economy or to invest abroad may be irrevocably lost—at least as long as the Qadhafi regime remains in power. The country's economic pattern, particularly under the Qadhafi government, has been one of expansion rather than growth, industrialization at the cost of astounding inefficiency, and undiminished dependency. Libya since independence has faced two distinct but intimately linked obstacles all countries face in the process of development: one of capability and one of inclination (Gilpin 1987).[23] The peculiar combination Libya's rulers chose to pursue must ultimately be traced to oil revenues and to the idiosyncratic process of state-building they afforded its rulers—and much of that combination may prove irreversible under the conditions the country is likely to face in the future.

[23]This distinction and its implications are discussed in Gilpin 1987.

Conclusion

The failure of Libya's *infitah* provided an important indication of the burdens distributive states face in confronting fiscal crises and in implementing long-lasting reform. Such states are characterized by intricate patterns of patronage during boom periods that turn subsequent attempts at altering those welfare and patronage arrangements into highly politicized issues. Particularly in states such as Libya, where distributive largesse becomes part and parcel of populist politics and where the regime's elite support base is narrow, the withdrawal of patronage is seen as politically impossible.

Libya's pattern of development, with its continued reliance on external resources and an intensive *étatisme* since the early years of the monarchy, allowed for a state-building experiment that permitted both active state intervention and the evisceration of institutions necessary for long-term management. In several crucial ways, the economic organization of Libyan society—the result of both the country's history and the impact of oil revenues—simultaneously created and restricted the reach of its government and the construction of national economic institutions. The bust period, in particular, clearly highlights the institutional, social, legal, political, and indeed psychological difficulties in moving toward post-boom structures. The absence of ancillary institutions instrumental in clearly establishing property rights and providing information has been matched by the presence of institutions whose institutional frailties resulted from their primarily distributive purposes. The luxury of postponing or ignoring the need for economic reforms and adjustment had led to the withering—or absence—of those institutions necessary for a true *infitah*.

The result is an economic and political subterfuge that hints at the power and resilience provided to rulers of distributive states, even when they face a severe crisis: a consumer *infitah* matched by a closely circumscribed political liberalization that leaves the basic power structures of the regime intact. Libya's "revolution within the revolution" and its *infitah* were thus foremost a means to ensure the regime's survival and to safeguard its political system. The diplomatic campaigns abroad, the human rights campaign at home, the curtailment of the revolutionary committees and the consumer *infitah* were intended to bring a renewed luster to a tarnished political experiment and to provide some vital exit at a time of great difficulty. The reforms fleetingly tempered the arbitrariness and confusion of Qadhafi's earlier policies, but they have not delivered real institutionalization, accountability or competition: Libya remains a political system where no opposition is tolerated, where arbitrariness remains the rule of politics, and where its citizens continue every day to experience deliberate, state-sponsored unpredictability. Under such conditions, broad-based and lasting economic reform is unlikely to succeed.

III

CONCLUSION

7

Oil and State-Building in Distributive States: The Libyan Contribution

We may imagine a situation in which the [distributive] state continues unchanged until the last drop of oil is exported. At that point, the state may simply fold and the country be deserted, most citizens having accumulated enough of a fortune to allow them to live elsewhere. Today's oil capitals may be turned into ghost towns. . . . Such states would not face a security threat because they would interest nobody.

—Giacomo Luciani, "Allocation versus Production States"

Sovereign states have become increasingly formidable institutions. They influence the self-image of those individuals within their territory through the concept of citizenship as well as by exercising control, to one degree or another, over powerful instruments of socialization. . . . States are the most densely linked institutions in the contemporary world. Change the nature of states, and virtually everything else in human society would also have to be changed.

—Stephen Krasner, "Sovereignty: An Institutional Perspective"

Because of the confluence of historical and material conditions at the outset of its state-building process, Libya came to represent an extreme example of a distributive state. The legacy of the brutal colonial period that made the notion of centralized authority highly suspect to future Libyans, the initial attempts at state-building after independence that coincided with the rapid inflows of rent and oil revenues, and the presence of leaders who were either indifferent to state-building, outright hostile to it, or willing to use oil revenues in the pursuit of a highly idiosyncratic vision of that state: all these contributed to attempts at statelessness that stand in sharp contrast to the realities that force most rulers of other states to perfect the state.

In their attempts, both Libyan rulers skillfully constructed a fractured sense of nationalism that was ostensibly meant to pursue the creation of a national community and a national identity but served the narrow interests of each regime. Both governments represented different historical periods and different images of the world. The king had been the taciturn heir to a religious movement whose conception of a political community was limited to his native Cyrenaica, and he lacked the will to become a strong ruler. His tenure in office was that of a leader of a westernizing and rapidly modernizing client state who ruled with the help of a politically immature and unconsolidated merchant class. Qadhafi has been the brash revolutionary whose vision of political community focused on the Arab nation. Each projected a political identity below or above the Libyan state, and both created new myths out of a reconstructed history to exert control in the absence of political institutionalization and legitimacy.

This use of symbols, however, should not obscure the more fundamental impacts of oil revenues on state-building in Libya that this book has analyzed and detailed: (1) the peculiar nature of state institutions that channeled development into particular patterns, (2) the differentiated strengths and weaknesses of the state as a result of that development, and (3) the trading of power for wealth by Libyan citizens on a scale far beyond that found in other oil exporters of the region, which led to their depoliticization and to the informalization of the country's political life.

State-Building, Institutions and Rent-Seeking in Distributive States

From the very beginning of its creation, those in charge of the Libyan state possessed considerable autonomy, promoted by the fact that external revenues—first the rent for military bases and then oil proceeds—accrued directly to the state. This arrangement gave both its rulers the luxury not to perfect the state, in contrast to an earlier European context that was prompted by the iron triangle of taxation, legitimacy, and participation. The impact of that relative autonomy in Libya left a profound legacy on how the state expanded. In contrast to the traditional European patterns of tax-based spending described in Chapter 2, spending in distributive states creates large bureaucratic structures that excel at distribution and, to a lesser extent, production, but their regulatory and extractive capacities remain minimal. Particularly after oil revenues entered the local economy, these capacities were of little importance to Libya's rulers. Indeed, much of the king's and Qadhafi's aspirations for the local state could be accomplished with much less destabilizing potential by *not* developing or empowering the impersonal, vertical, bureaucratic institutions of the modern state.

The rapid growth of oil revenues as part of the country's overall income in the 1960s and their explosion during the booms of the 1970s further reduced incentives to create or strengthen them. *Étatisme,* direct state intervention in creating jobs, setting domestic prices, and active participation in production, proved to be nothing more than shortcuts that expressed an unwillingness and, eventually, an inability to regulate the local economy and create politically viable structures. To that extent, the insistence by the king and by Qadhafi that the modern state was not to be trusted or relied upon became, almost by default, a self-fulfilling prophecy.

In distributive states such as Libya, where rulers make few compromises with their citizens to obtain revenues, the nature and structure of political and economic institutions reflect that relative autonomy of the state—but, as this book has demonstrated, in a highly peculiar fashion. Because of the unique way revenues accrue, rulers do not have to create elaborate tax gates, rules, or mechanisms to help decide whom to tax, or when, or at what level (Ayubi 1995; Snider 1988). Because the tax base is so inelastic, they are not compelled to create the bureaucracies that simultaneously extract, redistribute, gather information, and—if those in power so decide—discriminate in the pursuit of social objectives, in sharp contrast to the European experience (Bates 1991). Creation of wealth in such states does not rely on the traditional categories and mechanisms of nature, markets, or—as is increasingly important at the end of the twentieth century—effective economic statecraft. It does not require the state to elicit more than perfunctory loyalty or enforce good behavior. Conflicts over distribution and welfare can be avoided as long as distributive largesse can be maintained; the state only adjudicates in a rudimentary fashion.

In countries such as Libya, where state-building and rapid capital inflows go hand in hand, the presence and impact of institutions with purely distributive capabilities is even more pronounced. The absence of effective bureaucratic institutions *prior* to capital inflows makes their creation ex nihilo extremely difficult when rapid capital inflows start, and it introduces inconsistencies that are difficult to overcome once they are created (Chaudhry 1993; Evans 1995). As this book demonstrated, once the first steps toward nurturing distributive institutions have been set, the choice constrains future possibilities in important ways that only become clear during economic downturns. The country's initial institutional choices limited future options and eventually reduced Qadhafi's ability to correct the country's course for myriad, interrelated political and economic reasons. Even more than in productive states, in late developers that are utterly dependent on external capital, "historical developments are path dependent . . . the range of options . . . at any point in time is a function of institutional capabilities that were put into place at some earlier period" (Krasner 1989, 70).

A focus on the peculiar historical structures and institutions that are present when state-building starts, therefore, is crucial in gauging their nature and strength. The historical context, the legacy left by the incorporation of the local economy into the international, is important in estimating the state's potential capacity, particularly in countries such as Libya, where the state did not result from competition among local social forces but rather emerged in response to international developments. To that extent, oil exporters such as Libya represent perhaps the most extreme example of a state response to rapid influxes of capital by not developing, by further reducing, or by undercutting local institutions that can regulate local economies—and by placing the state in control over local economies while simultaneously limiting its task. In a dramatic fashion detailed in this book, state capacity diminishes across state institutions and tasks.

As in other oil exporters, Libya's oil booms were instrumental in creating large bureaucratic structures that simultaneously were responsible for and subject to the distributive policies of the state leaders and that, in turn, lowered those structures' capacities for self-regulation. In the Jamahiriyya this new bureaucratic layer assumed a peculiar dimension because of the popular committee and congress system, in which virtually everyone belonged to one of the country's bureaucracies.

The outcome of this process was an almost classic case in which rent-seeking became the predominant characteristic of the country's economic and political system and, as part of the depoliticization process noted throughout this book, was tolerated or implicitly encouraged by Libya's rulers.[1] Institutional constraints, established under the aegis of the state, determine whether individuals turn toward either rent-seeking or more productive profit-seeking activities. Contrary to the king's pious exhortations and Qadhafi's repeated harangues that all Libyans have become inherently wasteful and profligate consumers, individuals do not "become different moral beings" but react only rationally to an institutional structure that allows them to maximize value individually (Buchanan 1980b, 4). To diminish rent-seeking and the sociocultural patterns woven into it requires the state to intervene actively and abolish differentially advantageous positions that result from distribution and allocation.

This is a daunting task even in normal circumstances, as "rent-seeking is a nonsymmetrical game in which there are winners as well as losers, and the consensus to reach institutional change in order to eliminate such games is difficult to achieve . . . [where] reform in the rent-seeking society depends critically on the history of its evolution, as well upon the ability of political and intellectual leaders to think in terms of, and be persuasive about, general constitutional changes in the whole structure of social and economic institutions" (Buchanan 1980a, 361–367). In Libya, this would have meant the withdrawal of the monopolies the state acquired: permits and authorizations, franchise assignments, approvals, governmental licenses, and quotas—in other words, all the mechanisms through which the state maintained its political presence and power.

Where competitive markets are not allowed to work, crises of suddenly diminished wealth threaten to upset traditional patterns of rent-seeking, potentially inducing episodes of institutional transformation that can ultimately represent efforts to redefine the "basic rules of the game . . . rather than allocation within a given set of rules" (Krasner 1984, 234). In ways that are analogous to what Lustick argues concerning the territorial shape of a state, the nature of institutions created in distributive states "determine what interests are legitimate . . . what questions are open for debate . . . what cleavages could become significant,

[1]For some of the classic statements about rent-seeking in productive economies, see Tullock 1980; North 1990; and Buchanan 1980a, b, and c.

and what political allies might be available" (Lustick 1993, 41). *Infitah* strategies, therefore, are both politically and economically sensitive: they create new institutions for new purposes and priorities, they alter existing ones, and in the process they affect the fate of all those who depend on their erstwhile largesse. The introduction of markets for economic allocation of resources suddenly reduces the need or utility of political allocation. Ultimately, the state's ability to support markets depends in part on bureaucracies being corporately coherent entities in which individuals see pursuing corporate goals as the best way of maximizing their individual self-interest (Evans 1995). Libya's experiment with statelessness since independence has been precisely antithetical to that notion and that pursuit.

The Power of the Distributive State

At first glance, distributive states look enormously powerful: all revenues accrue centrally, giving those in charge of the state the "power of the purse" to create, buy off, or manipulate social coalitions in support of the state's rulers. This largesse has a political equivalent: the seeming ability to persuade those coalitions—more or less inclusive, depending on the individual state—to give up power for wealth and to rule according to the "no taxation, no representation" principle. Oil revenues provide rulers of hydrocarbon economies with the power to seek easy solutions to the problems and challenges their counterparts in productive economies must continually face: issues of accountability, fiscal constraints, and neutral bureaucratic institutions that act as tax gates. Whatever collective goods the state delivers—justice, property rights, protection and enforcement mechanisms—are not provided as the result of bargaining with groups in civil society but are one more sign of the state's distributive largesse.

During economic booms, this impression of strength remains undisturbed. A closer look, however, reveals the state's varying capacity for regulation, its combination of strength and weakness, and the double-edged sword that the state's seeming autonomy represents. In some areas of economic activity, the state behaves as a night watchman. In other arenas, it is a leviathan who systematically uses the resources at its disposal to keep itself in power; who, with great skill, manipulates a complex system of symbols and national myths; who selectively incorporates citizens into its patterns of spending; and who manipulates coalitions of its citizens or, when all else fails, uses outright coercion to achieve its goals.

Libya is far removed from the stateless society or even the minimal or diffuse state Qadhafi has claimed so ardently to pursue. On the contrary, although some of the country's regulatory institutions are extremely weak, myriad bureaucracies and coercive institutions have emerged. Far from the state being at arm's length, it has attempted to dominate all but the most intimate of relations among individuals, devised elaborate control mechanisms, created several security and police organizations, and produced a court system that enforces the regime's ideological proclivities. The hydrocarbon economy, however, contains within itself a dual and contradictory nature. It can quickly and effortlessly create enormous wealth but does not need to expand its income base or diversify its economy for the purposes of extraction. Its allocative ability is determined not by its extractive capacity but by its ability to generate more revenues through increased oil production. As Libya's experiments with the one-house policy in the 1970s and the arbitrary demonetization of the Libyan dinar in 1980 demonstrated, property rights can remain minimal or change at random.

State economic policies are not ordinarily subject to scrutiny and, because of the absence of regular procedures for political discussion, do not rely upon regular procedures through which interest groups—if they emerge—can influence the articulation and adoption of those policies. Distributive states thus have great power to accumulate revenues but in the process create incentives to squander it; they create large bureaucracies and make bureaucratic centralization all but impossible, while simultaneously diminishing the burdens and tasks those bureaucracies must perform; they inevitably promote national integration for purposes of economic development but also create powerful opportunities for eschewing citizenship or statehood. They buy time, and seemingly social peace, for their regimes.

This does not mean that oil exporters are automatically condemned to be wasteful political communities where politics is reduced to ritualized consent and where the state often flexes its muscles for anything but the use of violence. It does mean, however, that there is little incentive and no political or economic logic to do anything but pursue those limited functions during the boom period. Local rulers and elites must deliberately seek sustainable institutional solutions to offset the peculiar weaknesses distributive states experience: (1) their vulnerability to transnational flows of labor and capital, which limits the effective governance of national institutions over the local economy, and (2) their ability to use revenues as a strategic commodity in outspending economic problems and buying off political opposition. Where rulers such as the Sanusi monarch and Mu'ammar al-Qadhafi avoid such solutions over long periods of time, the results can be devastating. Economic policy remains disarticulated and demonstrates little concern for post-oil development; the state's strength is crudely effective but narrow and limited; political instruments and institutions atrophy; and politics becomes symbolic or informal.

The inability to reform economically is linked only in part to the absence of institutions and bureaucracies that could implement the measures, although, as this book demonstrates, the fostering of institutions that rely on technical qualification and complexity is notably absent in distributive states. The inability to reform relates also to the political constituencies and coalitions distributive states create through their largesse. Ultimately, the problem is not only one of increasing economic efficiency but of eliminating the phenomenon that hinders the pursuit of efficiency: using bureaucracies and institutions for rent-seeking. The combination of institutional and political factors ultimately makes sustained reform extremely difficult.

What is most remarkable, then, about the power of the Libyan distributive state is the great disparity of power during the boom period and during times when a sustained crisis demands institutional and political changes. Libya may be a "fierce state," but it proves incapable of "collecting taxes, winning wars or forging a real 'hegemonic' power block or an ideology that can carry the state beyond the coercive and 'corporative' level" (Ayubi 1995, xi). Although the Libyan case is unique—both in the magnitude of the state's unwillingness to adjudicate as it emerged historically and in the spectacular measures the Qadhafi government took to perpetuate statelessness—it also shows remarkable similarities to other distributive states in the region and beyond.

The pursuit and implementation of popular rule and the popular committee and popular congress system, in which virtually everyone belonged to the country's bureaucracy, made the country's bureaucratic structures unique. In the process of their creation, two new sets of ties emerged, in contradiction with each other. The first consisted of the growing importance of close allies of the country's leader, who were increasingly from his own tribe, in assuring his security by being assigned to sensitive police or intelligence positions. The second was a close link between the Libyan population and its ruler—a link hardly mediated by the political institutions of the country but anchored in the social welfare programs the distributive bureaucracies created for that purpose.

By disassembling the notion of the so-called rentier state in order to examine its utility as a theoretical construct, I have argued that the focus of analysis must be on the impact of the huge influx of market–regulated capital on state institutions. In Libya, as in other oil exporting countries, these inflows of capital diminished the extractive and regulatory capacity of those institutions. In contrast to the economic liberalization policies in productive states, where governments often attempt to replace encrusted bureaucracies with management more conducive to market relations—"reimposing the market" (Ikenberry 1986)—in distributive states the challenge is to promote arrangements that make the creation of markets possible, which is an attempt to move away from an economy marked by state institutions that specialize in self-regulation.

The Libyan case, furthermore, indicates that markets do not exist in an administrative, social, and institutional vacuum. To create competitive internal markets, it is not enough simply to do away with those parts of the bureaucracy that own, control, and regulate the flow of goods and services, as is often conveyed by the use of *liberalization* in the literature. The state must actively deploy or redeploy, create or re-create, the instruments at its disposal to perform the difficult task of administration and indirect regulation to define property rights, enforce contracts, cut transaction costs, and, ultimately, promote real competition. The rapid inflow of massive amounts of capital diminishes or postpones this difficult task, particularly in countries such as Libya, where national consolidation occurs at the same time. The result is often what Libya experienced during the oil booms of the 1970s: the distributive policies of the state create broad social coalitions, primarily among consumers, that can undercut state attempts at economic reform in times of crisis. The notion therefore that ample capital inflows eliminate conflict and provide the state with the ability and strength to operate virtually autonomously is simply too static. It is contradicted by the evidence found in Libya and other oil exporting countries, and it is helpful only in explaining developments during the boom period.

Power or Wealth: Politics in Distributive States

At first glance, politics in Libya closely resembles the conventional image of rentier states, where the political dynamics of state-society interaction are rudimentary, one-sided, and often lacking in real content; and where politics is suspended, and rent-seeking dominates the behavior of local citizens. Although some of those observations are too static, arguably nowhere in the region was the wish to return to the diffuse political controls of precolonial times as strong as in Libya, and certainly nowhere did local governments commit the resources and energy to give this vision of statelessness a new lease on life once independence had been achieved.

Because of the absence of clearly articulated social groups when the state was created, and because that creation roughly coincided with the inflow of oil revenues and other rents, the country's rulers were capable of disengaging from those groups in a manner rarely observed, even in other oil exporters. Those factors that allowed merchants in both Saudi Arabia and Kuwait, for example, to retain a strong sense of cohesion long after they traded wealth for power did not exist in Libya. Elites in Libya had not been able to articulate their interests before the distributive process started. Their degree of political mobilization had been low before independence and quickly dissipated further thereafter. In sum, the social contract drawn up implicitly or explicitly by the king and by Qadhafi never involved groups with a clear collective identity. Partly as a result of this peculiar process, neither Libya's emerging class of merchants nor others (except perhaps the military) were capable of constituting or reconstituting themselves as a distinct group with shared political or economic goals. Lacking an organizational structure, defined collective interests, or shared history, Libya's emerging elite after independence was too weak to withstand the onslaught of oil-induced state power and was easily removed by the Qadhafi regime when it came to power.

One of the key elements in explaining local regimes' resilience and persistence in oil exporters throughout the region has been the withdrawal from formal political life of historically influential elites—a compromise both Crystal and Chaudhry have noted in the Gulf countries—in a trade of wealth for power, an exchange of political voice for the active pursuit of rent-seeking. In Libya this price of wealth (Chaudhry 1989) was enormous, reflecting in part the lack of group or class interests as the simultaneous processes of state-building and oil revenues proceeded. In a fashion unmatched in the region, this price of wealth in Libya resulted first in a massive formal withdrawal of whatever weak elite groups existed under the monarchy and was then extended under Qadhafi to a more broad-based coalition that included virtually all of the country's citizens for whom the popular committee system was little more than their leader's chimera but who were pampered and kept depoliticized by the egalitarian policies of the distributive state.

As in Kuwait, Qatar, and Saudi Arabia—but in a broader sense that reflected the Libyan regime's populist aspirations—oil and the power it bestowed on the country's rulers forced virtually *everyone* to choose between wealth and formal power. Oil revenues and the transformations (or lack thereof) they engendered are instrumental in explaining both the longevity of the regime and the absence of concerted and sustained voices of internal opposition. This "striking political silence" (Crystal 1990), commented on by observers of oil exporters throughout the region, reflects not only the authoritarian nature of the local regime but the price paid—sometimes wholeheartedly, sometimes willy-nilly—for wealth, for the regime's economic largesse, and, ultimately for a process of profound depoliticization that continues until today.

The notion that the lack of taxation somehow precludes demands for representation in distributive states is by now almost accepted wisdom (Luciani 1987; Anderson 1986a). Indeed, much of the rentier state literature has argued that this trade-off is so complete that the process cannot be reversed. Although distributive states are clearly able to profoundly depoliticize their societies, to slow down demands for representation, or to suspend such demands over relatively long periods of time, to argue that they totally and irreversibly preclude such demands may be too static and may be "more a snapshot of the first effects of the rentier state phenomenon than a model of the dynamics over time of rentier state development" (Gause 1994, 81).

Such a notion may well be true during boom periods but not during the ensuing bust period. Citizens do not give up making demands for representation or for better government simply because they are not taxed. The state's distributive largesse during the boom period creates a set of expectations that provide as powerful a sense of entitlement as extraction does. Calls for greater political openness and participation in distributive states are likely to emerge under three sets of conditions: (1) when unequal distribution contrasts sharply with the egalitarianism principles espoused by the local regime; (2) when the country experiences a fiscal crisis that threatens the maintenance of distribution; or (3) when the coercive power of the state is perceived as waning, as during political crises (Gause 1995, chap. 3; Crystal 1990; Mattes 1995a; Vandewalle 1995a).

The pattern of depoliticization and the subsequent re-emergence of political demands was subtle but nevertheless visible during Libya's thirty-year boom and bust cycle. For a quarter of a century after the marketing of the country's oil, its leaders' political experiments generated little domestic resistance, for reasons I describe throughout this book: a combination of rent-seeking (which made individual rather than group action a preferred option for increasing one's benefits) (Luciani 1987), the distributive measures of the country's rulers, the skillful use of symbols and rhetoric, and (limited) outright violence. By the end of the 1970s few Libyans, except perhaps members of the Revolutionary Committees and Qadhafi confidants at Bab al-Aziziyya, were not aware that the political mobilization efforts of their government contributed to the process of disenfranchisement (Ibjad 8 October 1992).

The absence of opposition and resistance, however, did not indicate the success of either the revolution or the regime's power. Rather, it was the opposite: it highlighted the fact that, like the Gulf oil exporters, they had "not yet faced the challenges that produce resistance" (Crystal 1990, 179). In fact, as the general resistance to the *infitah* strategy illustrated, Libya's ruler had not created coalitions he could turn to and rely on in a time of crisis. Libya's economic liberalization after 1987 was in essence a consumer *infitah* that in scope matched and perhaps surpassed the consumption frenzy the country had witnessed in the 1970s. That such consumption and such spending on questionable industrial projects could still take place is testimony above all to the selective power oil revenues create. But they also lay bare a structural inability for self-reform. After roughly forty-five years of pursuing statelessness, Libya has become, more than ever, a political community with very little capacity for self-reform; a community where "political change may turn out to be the factor with the highest shadow price" (Mahdavy 1970, 466).

Where the purposely pursued absence of clear formal rules is a dominant feature, however, moral suasion and symbolic and informal politics become highly visible. We find therefore in Libya that the regime paid consistent attention to high levels of rhetoric, references to a common brutal history and to a shared religious heritage, deliberate political confrontations with internal and external enemies, and an indigenous ideological blueprint that is held up as a universal model. All are skillfully used to promote legitimacy and to expend political energy and resources—a political version of rent-seeking—not for political institutionalization but for keeping the ruler and his supporters in power in the absence of clear rules. This process illuminates the more profound confusion found in a political system where the revolution is still what the ruler proclaims it to be, where "the people are the ruler's subjects, not yet the state's citizens" (Anderson 1986a, 271).

State-Building in the Jamahiriyya: Observations on the Future

By the end of 1996, Libya had existed as an independent state for forty-five years. At present production levels, its oil reserves are estimated to last an equal number of years. Barring new major discoveries, and discounting the country's rapid population increase, Libya is halfway through its life cycle as a distributive state. What happens to that state when, sooner or later, the oil that forms its economic foundation is depleted? It is impossible, of course, to provide a definitive answer. But it is possible—in light of local state-building dynamics, the peculiar form of its political community, and the local institutions that emerged in Libya—to discern the likely contours of the country's political features and its social dynamics in a post-oil world; to figure out the parameters of what the combination of "the shadow of the past" and "the shadow of the future" will likely mean for Libya as a state and as a political community.

It is worth repeating that Libya represents an extreme example of a distributive state. Although states that rely extensively on capital inflows and distribution have existed in varying degrees throughout history, none has tied its fate so single-handedly to a single, nonrenewable resource—to the almost deliberate exclusion of virtually all other economic activity—and few leaders of such countries have purposely pursued such elaborate policies that made the state in its multilayered dimensions, except for its economic largesse, seem so unattractive.

Both phenomena, as I have argued throughout this book, are intricately related, and both bode ill for the future. Economic exposure to the vagaries of the international oil market was tolerated in Libya precisely because it allowed both the king and Qadhafi to keep their distance, to weaken or prevent the re-emergence of local groups and coalitions during the distributive part of the state's life. Under those conditions, the pursuit of statelessness and the ability to not perfect the state—or to perfect it only in a minimal, narrowly defined fashion—provoked few objections. One of the unintended results, demonstrated vividly when the distributive state faces a fiscal crisis, is that the local state possesses neither the institutions nor the political power to implement needed economic changes. Even the narrow stratum of new elites that continue to support Qadhafi have not supplied the state with either social support or political participation. In its economic and political dimensions, those developments are harbingers of a much larger looming crisis that will inevitably emerge: Libya's future in a post-oil environment will depend on the institutional arrangements, the collective integration of the local political community, and the financial resources of the regime that will find itself in power after that transition. On all accounts the country will undoubtedly be found severely wanting.

To those who assume the inevitability and durability of the modern territorial state (Krasner 1989; Evans 1995) and who argue that it will remain the sole constitutive element of the international system, Libya's pursuit of statelessness and its unwillingness to rely on the complexity and impersonality of modern bureaucratic structures must seem anachronistic, at best. But if Libya is indeed a bad example of a modern state, its attempted rejection of the appurtenances of state nevertheless represents an achievement of human constitutional and political creativity (Davis 1987). Moreover, in an age in which the possibility of the transformation of states into new forms of political and economic organization—linked to economic interdependence, globalization of financial markets, ecological transborder developments, and other factors—is being argued by other social scientists, distributive states such as Libya may well occupy a unique place, as Luciani (quoted at the outset of this chapter) asserts, and their survival should not be taken for granted.[2]

Libya's development since independence has been highly uneven. Since the early 1980s, Qadhafi's survival has become so closely intertwined with the perpetuation of distribution and patronage that he cannot be expected to reform the country's economy. Whether or not Qadhafi remains the country's leader, Libya's ability to move away from a volatile, oil-dominated economy has perhaps become impossible. Even a "Kuwait scenario," where assets are held in escrow overseas for future generations, has become infeasible in light of the West's economic boycott and threats of expropriation. And no international power will have an interest, as they did at the country's creation, in upholding Libya's principle of territorial integrity if the moment of disintegration arrives.

From a state-building perspective and a more general political perspective, the pursuit of statelessness has been equally destructive. How much loyalty would a post-oil, post-distributive state retain? The

[2] Among a plethora of works that trace the importance of some of those elements on the fate of states, see Herz 1976; Spruyt 1994; Rosecrance 1986; Hall 1986; Caporaso 1989; Czempiel and Rosenau 1989; and Bryant 1987.

Jamahiriyya offers few attractions for its most talented citizens to stay. There are not even the less tangible public goods that nevertheless make citizens often reluctant to leave: social justice, the prestige of the country or its leaders, a good record of human rights, statesmanship in international affairs, tolerance of opposition and democratic liberties (or the "understood complexity" of one's own society that provides a sense of belonging [Hirschman 1981, 265]), and pride in what to outsiders seems to be an idiosyncratic political system. In Libya, the erratic nature of the ruler's experiments and the lack of institutionalized procedures in favor of unpredictable revolutionary assaults [*zahf*], have subjected its own citizens to a complexity it cannot fully grasp—thus providing little to make the state psychologically attractive (Branthwaite 1993).

Both the kingdom and the revolutionary regime have advanced the level of national political awareness in Libya only minimally. I do not mean to suggest that individual Libyans do not possess a sense of patriotism for the Jamahiriyya: some of its citizens feel uniquely and proudly Libyan. They share a juridical nationality that constitutes the basis of a nationalism predicated on a common history. In Libya, this expression of nationalism has been virulent and was based overwhelmingly on the shared memories of Italian colonialism and of western domination of the country's interests after independence. But despite this ideological fervor, Libyans have had to sacrifice little for their patriotism or nationalism. When even a low threshold was reached—the war in Chad, for example, or economic liberalization—the ruler's reaction has been to rescind unpopular measures in a way that reveals how narrow the sense of a national political community, with its own national interests, remains.

The country's two leaders since independence have systematically fostered this lack of national identity. Being Libyan was always portrayed as secondary to the goal of being a citizen of a smaller tribal or regional community under the monarchy or of a greater Arab or Islamic community after 1969—a first step toward a less or a more inclusive political entity. Both have been indications of a lingering uncertainty and an indifference to the notion of a Libyan sovereign state. Neither ruler brought greater political maturity to either social classes or groups, and no group *qua* group—not even the country's tribes—was truly involved in national politics. As a result, the Jamahiriyya's citizens now consist of two groups: "those who are conscious participants in the revolution and those who are not" (Roumani 1983, 151) or, perhaps more accurate, those who continue to make claims upon the state and those who gave up making those claims.

The distributive measures of that state ultimately had a deeply corrosive impact: those few citizens that are included engender "a type of complicity which undermines the legitimacy of the system itself in the eyes of those who are left out" (Karl 1982a, 25). It is therefore almost inevitable that if serious, concerted opposition ever coalesces, it will likely manifest itself in a rejection of the state in its totality and will do more than ask for incremental reforms. In addition, because of the process of depoliticization and lack of institution-building that could have expanded and perfected the state, future Libyan leaders will find themselves and their country ill equipped and ill prepared to handle domestic conflict by any means other than violence.

The estimated one hundred thousand Libyans now living in exile are in part a testimony to the persistent disintegrative effects of the lack of consensus. Their existence hints at the magnitude of the problem for reconstituting—or perhaps, more accurately, truly creating, for the first time—a political community in the Jamahiriyya that coincides with the territorial state. Lacking the ability to regulate or to extract resources, no longer capable of engaging in distributive largesse or to provide even basic services, the post-oil state in Libya will inevitably face an unprecedented crisis of legitimacy. The creation of a new political community will therefore be unavoidably highly chaotic—particularly when considering the unlikelihood that Qadhafi's popular committee system will outlive its creator. In a political system with no agreed-upon rules, few if any economic resources, and a low level of legitimacy accorded to central institutions, the odds of convincing the citizenry at that future point in time "that it has to pay for the state" (if that still proves possible) will not be very high (Beblawi and Luciani 1987, 2). In many ways the attractiveness of creating a new political community out of a post-Qadhafi Libya may be dim, and few Libyans are likely to have accumulated enough of a fortune to pursue an exit option. Ironically, the possibility of statelessness may then be achieved by default—and not as a deliberate policy fostered so arduously by the country's rulers since independence.

Finally, although oil has made several of the more radical politics of the Qadhafi government possible—and virtually released it from the constraints and demands of accountability of popular opinion and foreign patrons alike—oil was not the cause of that radicalism. Whatever political regime emerges in Libya will undoubtedly want to jettison Qadhafi's internal political experiments. But its foreign policy will likely contain elements of the current regime—for the lessons of the past have been engraved upon the collective memory of Libyans and will undoubtedly be part of the politics of legitimacy in whatever new political configuration emerges.

Oil, State-Building, and Politics

State-building in distributive states differs markedly from similar processes in countries that rely on domestic extraction for their revenues. States such as Libya represent a unique form of political organization that resembles neither the Weberian nor the Marxian definition of the state. The power of the state to create or eviscerate domestic social classes and coalitions through the strategic use of oil revenues stands in contrast to the social scientific notions of class formation both approaches insist upon. In contrast to experiences outside the region where the iron triangle of state formation, extraction, and representation emerges over time, the lack of revenue extraction in distributive states allows rulers to keep each part of the process isolated. Where, as in Libya, state-building and the inflows of revenues proceed hand in hand, the power of the state is temporarily and selectively augmented further, and the disarticulation is even greater.

The result of this disarticulation is that, in distributive states, administrative and bureaucratic structures develop in response to the peculiar and limited tasks the state is asked to play. Bureaucracies in distributive states therefore are unique: they are limited to rudimentary regulatory activity that often expresses itself purely in distributive measures. Observers of oil exporters throughout the region have noted not only the growth of these bureaucracies and of their complexity but also the way in which they assume their own identity and interests, that is, how they become politicized.

Libya represents an important exception to this more general rule: even as the state's bureaucracies grew, they remained overwhelmingly neutral. Through an intricate mixture of ideology, the constant reshuffling of personnel, the dissolving of ministries, the threat of further decentralizing the country's bureaucratic system, and the creation of new bureaucratic structures when the old developed a potential to become politicized, the Qadhafi regime promoted and maintained a depoliticization process that encompassed the country's bureaucracies and ensured that bureaucrats never were able to express corporate interests or to create their own centers of power. In contrast to developments in other regional oil exporters—and reflecting in part the fact that no groups with clearly identified corporate interests existed at independence that could infiltrate them—bureaucracies never became independent arenas for politics.

Many observers of Libya have argued that the alternative to a centralized polity will be the return, by default, to a reliance on tribal politics (Anderson 1995; El-Kikhia 1997). They interpret the growing number of appointments by Qadhafi of several individuals of his own tribe to sensitive positions within the Jamahiriyya as a sign that this process is already unfolding. It is important, however, to carefully contrast the Libyan leader's efforts at self-preservation—in part by adopting certain elements of a neopatrimonial style of ruling—to the more structural political, economic, and social process of depoliticization this book has outlined. While a careful look at Qadhafi's inner circle and those who report to it reveals that, in addition to the military, a distribution of elites from old bourgeois families and from major tribes persists, tribal affiliation in Libya has never—not even during the colonial period—provided a focus of sustained political attention or power. In Cyrenaica, where tribes irregularly provided troops to fight against the Italians, their potential for systematic organization was quickly eviscerated by the king after independence and by the extensive patterns of individual rent-seeking the country's rapid development brought in its wake.

With no concrete history of political or economic enfranchisement, tribes in Libya overwhelmingly retained a social identity that was invoked repeatedly by the rulers for symbolic purposes. But in sharp contrast to other oil exporters, where political and fiscal crises led to the reemergence of distinct traditional social identities, in the Jamahiriyya this development did not take place. Oil revenues, as events in Libya so clearly demonstrate, can effectively halt both institution and coalition building. When combined with a lack of articulated interests when the state-building process starts, revenues can also effectively prevent the maintenance or re-emergence of the more primordial loyalties of family and tribe. In contrast to other regional oil exporters, the most severe crisis Libya faced after 1986 did not lead therefore to a sustained and clear rejuvenation of organized interests.

This outcome in Libya was not coincidental. The corporate identities that had emerged historically in both Kuwait and Qatar before the arrival of oil did not exist in Libya when rent started to dominate the country's economy. In Kuwait, Saudi Arabia, and Qatar, the original pact consisted of an exchange of wealth for historically accumulated power among the merchants. In Libya such a pact was never concluded: there was neither an entrenched nor an organized elite, nor was there a tribal structure organized enough to pursue shared interests that eventually led in other regional oil exporters to the "creation or empowerment of groups that could later reshape the state" (Crystal 1995, 200). In Libya whatever meager political transformations have taken place have overwhelmingly been imposed by the state, and no group within civil society has managed to use even marginally the country's state institutions and bureaucracies to assert power: whatever feeble opposition to the regime took place has been outside both the state's bureaucracies and its tribal structure. This phenomenon confirms the distributive state's ability to maintain both the informal and the personalized nature of politics noted throughout this book: as I argued earlier, in Libya the distance between the ruler and the ruled remains until today unmediated. Power retains an uninstitutionalized quality matched in few other countries; sovereignty in virtually all its dimensions remains unchecked.

The contrast between the capacity for coercion and distribution versus regulation, arbitration, and institutionalization furthermore reveals the inadequacy of simply adopting the conventional labels of strong or weak when analyzing distributive states (Migdal 1988; Salamé 1987b). Libya's rulers have been exceedingly capable of preventing opposition, of creating distributive bureaucracies devoid of corporate identities, and of galvanizing the country's population for their regimes' own purposes without invoking tribal identities for anything but social purposes. Anyone who observes Libya at close hand recognizes the enormous skill and intimate understanding of social relations this requires of the ruler in ways that go beyond the purely fierce attributes Ayubi discerns in Arab states (Ayubi 1995). Yet, under both rulers, the state simultaneously lacked some of the most essential prerequisites to turn those skills into the kind of long-term strength that would provide Libya with predictable and institutionalized mechanisms to coopt systematically its population into pursuing broad-based national goals that promote sustained political and economic development.

Libya therefore, as yet, represents an important exception to the more general findings of scholars who argue that social organizations within local societies retain a resilience that can resurface even after long periods of inactivity, and it confirms the findings of scholars who argue that state power should be more carefully disarticulated (Norton 1995; al-Arawi 1988). This implicit reference to the weakness or strength of distributive states brings us back to the broader debate within comparative politics about the precise role of the state in social transformation. The study of the Middle East has yielded two diametrically opposed hypotheses: either the state is captured by social forces, or it is capable of restructuring its society. At first glance, distributive states such as Libya are highly autonomous, particularly where state-building and capital inflows coincided and where social groups have not yet developed corporate interests. Because of the peculiar way in which revenues accrue directly to the state, one should expect to find the state's power highly developed and the state's ability to weaken civil society very high.

Rulers of distributive states often prefer, as I pointed out previously, to maintain their vulnerability vis-à-vis the international economy in order to retain their power at home. This subterfuge provides a first and unmistakable clue that power in distributive states is limited. A further clue is provided by the failed or curtailed *infitah* efforts in oil exporters of the region.[3] The seeming imperviousness to opposition and change, even the relatively low levels of actual coercion and violence, are more indicative of weakness than of success. Libya under the monarchy and Qadhafi has been marked by a relative stability that is more characteristic of what the state avoided than of what it accomplished: it has sidestepped the cooptation that marks state-building in productive economies; it has postponed a severe fiscal crisis that would necessitate political accommodation and force it to allow economic institutions to act more independently; and it has not yet been forced to face sustained and concerted opposition.

This book also alerts us to the fact that, in contrast to what much of the rentier state literature has argued, the dynamics of loyalty and opposition in distributive states are not necessarily linked to the notion of "no taxation, no representation." Profound depoliticization normally occurs in all distributive states as part of economic booms—not always because the ruler's citizens deliberately pursue this option or are forced to do so but simply because representation seems less urgent. As the delivery of affluence assumes an indelible part of citizens' lives, the welfare function of the state becomes a norm and is viewed as a right and an entitlement. Interests aggregate not around the issue of representation—unless that representation is instrumental in gaining more predictable access to the state's distributive largesse—but, more likely, around guaranteeing continued largesse. The notion that depoliticization and immobility is

[3] One notable exception is Iraq, where the government proved capable of summarily and brutally curtailing the interests of entire levels of bureaucracies developed during the boom period. See Chaudhry 1992.

induced and can be maintained purely by distributive largesse is too static, as this book has indicated, but it must be seen as the end result of historical, institutional, social, and economic developments that are suddenly articulated and questioned—if often ineffectively—during periods of crisis.

Developments during the bust period—until now largely ignored by rentier state theorists—clearly show the more dynamic and varied context in which politics in distributive states takes place.[4] Most rulers attempt to avoid, at all costs, cutting back on the social services delivered to their citizens. In Saudi Arabia, Kuwait, Qatar, Iraq, and Libya they did so by shifting the economic burden via taxation to the expatriate population, by exceeding OPEC quotas if needed, or by drawing down their own international reserves. All responded to the crisis by creating or reforming institutions that would allow them to better weather the crisis or to circumvent those that threatened to develop corporate interests. Libya's ruler, in typical fashion, announced yet another wave of popular mobilization that once more masked the inability to respond to a crisis and the unwillingness to consider any institutionalized solution. And in all countries, rulers introduced sometimes draconian efforts to recreate or adapt national myths, to extend ideologies, and to retell local history in order to manipulate changing loyalties and to confront the re-establishment of tradition.

In this book I have shown how the Libyan state's capacity to respond to that fiscal crisis was limited both by the pattern of state-building that had taken place and by the lack of political and economic institutions that process had engendered. In doing so, I have surpassed much of the current rentier state literature, which has focused almost exclusively on the direct impact of capital inflows within states as the single factor in explaining the forms and problems of state-building they face. An abundance of capital inflows alone cannot fully explain local state-building patterns. Any analysis must also be sensitive to the historical nature of the distributive state's integration into the capitalist world economy and to the specific features of its indigenous society. My attempt to pay attention to these points fills a gap noted by several observers, such as Skocpol, who have called for analyses that pay respect to the "inescapable intertwinings of national level developments with changing world historical contexts" (Skocpol 1985, 28). Distributive states lend themselves extraordinarily well to that task. Indeed, it is the interaction

[4] The exceptions are Crystal 1995; Chaudhry 1989; Gause 1994; and Karl 1982.

between the state in the context of underdevelopment and the crisis sparked by international capital inflows that provides critical clues to the state-building and institutional development experience of late developers.

Libya, by factors elaborated in this book, became an extreme example of a distributive state. Commodity booms, however, will provoke similar patterns of state-building and institutional development in all countries where they constitute a large part of local revenues. Revenue collection and extraction—or lack thereof—are causal factors that shape the contours of the local state and that of the institutions through which it succeeds—or fails—in penetrating local society. The focus of this book has been the Libyan Jamahiriyya. But the broader issues it investigates—state-building in late developers, institutional and political development under conditions of temporary economic wealth, and the relative power of state and society, modernity and tradition, formal and informal politics—are of concern both to other Third World countries and to comparative political economists studying them.

Bibliographical Note

This study of state-building in Libya is based on the insights provided by a number of social science literatures. Some of those sources, particularly regarding more recent work on the state in the Middle East and specifically on the rentier or distributive state, may be unfamiliar to an English-speaking audience. Also, because both Parts 1 and 2 of this book rely in part on Arabic sources that are not readily available in the West, I have included them in this bibliographical note. The literature on state formation and state-building, institutions, taxation, and rent-seeking is enormous and unwieldy, and this note necessarily contains a highly distilled list of those works I found, directly or by comparison, of interest in analyzing the distinctive problems a distributive state such as Libya faces as rapid and enormous inflows of capital enter the country. Complete references to the materials can be found in the bibliography. Readers interested in archival sources and libraries in Libya are urged to read my "Research Facilities and Document Collections in the Socialist People's Libyan Arab Jamahiriyah."

Social and Political Theory: State-Building and Distributive States

As Chapter 2 makes clear, most of the literature on state formation and state-building in late developers draws originally on the insights of social theorists focusing primarily on the European experience. Tilly's *The Formation of Nation-States in Western Europe* and *Coercion,*

Capital, and European States, along with Strayer's *On the Medieval Origin of the Modern State* and Poggi's *The Development of the Modern State* are perhaps the classic statements of those early links, as is Anderson's *Lineages of the Absolutist State.* Important comparative viewpoints are provided by Callaghy, *The State-Society Struggle: Zaire in Comparative Perspective* and by Skowronek, *Building a New American State.* Spruyt insightfully questions early assumptions about the mechanisms of state formation—particularly the relevance of war—in his *The Sovereign State and Its Competitors.* Similar attempts to correct conventional assumptions about the benign character of state formation can be found in the highly useful book by Giddens, *The Nation-State and Violence* and Cohen, Brown, and Organski, "The Paradoxical Nature of State Making: The Violent Creation of Order."

Although few theorists have attempted to examine directly the notions of the state itself, Nettl's "The State as a Conceptual Variable" stands out, as does Krasner's "Approaches to the State." In the last decade, Arab political scientists and sociologists have paid increasing attention to the notion of the state in ways that continue to reflect their lingering ambiguity about the concept but that provide historically informed accounts of the encounter of local societies with the West. Among the most important of those are the following (in Arabic): Al-Arawi, *The Concept of the State;* Al-Hirmasi, *State and Society in the Maghreb;* the edited volume by Ibrahim, *State and Society in the Arab World;* Al-Naqib, *State and Society in the Gulf and the Arabian Peninsula from a Different Perspective;* Salamé, *State and Society in the Arab East.* A particularly important source (in English), informed by a Gramscian-Marxist perspective, is Ayubi's recent *Over-Stating the Arab State.*

Although this book has paid relatively little attention to the more symbolic and less tangible parts of state-building, Colson's *Tradition and Contract* and Mair's *Primitive Government* provide insightful early accounts of the importance of these aspects, in ways that can help explain notions of statelessness as expressed by Libya's leader. Some of Mair's early findings are elaborated on powerfully in Branthwaite's "The Psychological Basis of Independent Statehood" and in Lustick's concept of thresholds in *Unsettled States, Disputed Lands.* The question of whether the state is an agent or a reflection of social change is addressed in, among others, the classic work by Evans, Rueschemeyer and Skocpol, *Bringing the State Back In* and in Migdal, *Strong Societies and Weak States,* and his more recent "The State in Society."

The notion of the rentier or distributive state is a relatively new concept in the literature, although it has now been examined in many Middle Eastern countries and in other settings where commodity booms take place. The original statement is Mahdavy, "The Patterns and Problems of Economic Development in Rentier States." Delacroix's "The Distributive State in the World System" is an early investigation of the implications of capital inflows for state institutions. Anderson, in *The State and Social Transformation in Tunisia and Libya,* contrasts the two countries' historical development and traces the different outcomes of state-building for each country's incorporation into the world economy in the nineteenth century. Following Anderson's account, a number of works on the rentier state emerged in the late 1970s and early 1990s that more closely investigated the impact of capital flows in regional countries. Among the most important of those are the edited volume by Beblawi and Luciani, *The Rentier State;* Katouzian, "The Political Economy of Oil Exporting Countries"; Crystal, *Oil and Politics in the Gulf;* Chaudhry, "The Price of Wealth"; Karshenas, *Oil, State and Industrialization in Iran;* and Rubin, *The Fragmentation of Afghanistan* and his "Political Elites in Afghanistan." Two notable applications outside the region, focusing in part on class analysis rather than institutional development, are Becker, "Bonanza Development and the New Bourgeoisie," and Karl, "The Political Economy of Petrodollars."

Social and Political Theory: Taxation, Institutions, and Rent-Seeking

Somewhat surprising, the problems of taxation and the impact of the absence of an extractive process on state-building remain relatively uninvestigated, particularly in the literature dealing with the Middle East. Those works available are, much like the state-building literature, based overwhelmingly on the European (and western) experience. More abstract investigations can be found in Levi, *Of Rule and Revenue,* and in the powerful essay by Goldscheid, "Finanzwissenschaft und Soziologie." Important historical accounts and analyses are found in Furgeson, *The Power of the Purse;* Brewer, *The Sinews of Power;* Webber and Wildavsky, *A History of Taxation and Expenditure in the Western World;* and Hoffman and Norberg eds., *Fiscal Crises, Liberty, and Representative Government.* A more recent and extremely useful comparative study is Steinmo's *Taxation and Democracy.*

The two classic works describing the origins and implications of the transition toward modern states and the underlying dilemmas of states versus markets remain Gerschenkron, *Economic Backwardness in Historical*

Perspective and Polanyi, *The Great Transformation.* What some of those implications entail, particularly as late developers attempt to make transitions toward market-oriented structures (described in Chapter 6) can be found in two works by Chaudhry: "The Myths of the Market and the Common History of Late Developers," and her "Economic Liberalization and the Lineages of the Rentier State."

Finally, from among the voluminous literature on institutions and rent-seeking, these works have proven particularly insightful to me: different contributions in Buchanan, Tollison and Tullock's *Toward a Theory of a Rent-Seeking Society* and Krueger's original article, "The Political Economy of the Rent-Seeking Society." An interesting application of some of this literature can be found in Repetto, *Paying the Price.* North's *Institutions, Institutional Change and Economic Performance* and his *Structure and Change in Economic History,* along with North and Weingast's "Constitutions and Commitment," proved immensely helpful in conceptualizing the impact of institutions and the importance of their historical development in the process of state-building in a late developer such as Libya. Although this book contains numerous references to other sources, works cited form the bedrock on which many of its arguments are based.

Libya: The Sanusi Monarchy and the Jamahiriyya

Except for specialized journals, relatively few publications in the quarter-century since the 1969 Libyan military coup have paid systematic attention to unfolding events inside the Jamahiriyya. The country's increasingly open confrontation with the West, which dates back to the early 1970s but escalated dramatically in the 1980s, led to both popular and scholarly works that by now have easily surpassed several hundred in number. Although part of those accounts was unavoidably impressionistic—access to the country remained extremely limited to journalists and scholars alike—a growing body of serious studies of the Jamahiriyya and of its unique political experiments has emerged in the last decade.

The works cited in this section concentrate primarily on the internal aspects of the country's political and economic development since 1969. This section lists relatively few references to the numerous journal articles, for example, that have been devoted to Libya and its leader; but it provides essential sources that can be enhanced by consulting the more detailed bibliographic reference works on Libya that have been published since 1969. In addition, historical dictionaries of Libya are now available. The most comprehensive and best until today remains Ronald Bruce St. John, *Historical Dictionary of Libya.*

The period of the Sanusi monarchy remains the least studied in recent Libyan history, in part because the Qadhafi government until the late 1980s systematically made materials relating to the period unavailable. It is therefore useful to refer to a handful of works that provide historically important insights into the political, economic, and social conditions Libya's new leaders faced both before and after the 1969 military takeover. Indeed, to understand fully the direction of the Libyan revolution and the efficacy or failure of its leaders' political directives, a good comprehension of the country's more recent social, economic, and political history is indispensable. Muhammad al-Sanusi's *Kitab al-Masa'il al-'ashr* (The Book of Ten Questions) and Muhammad Shukri's *Al-Sanusiyya Din wa Dawla* (The Sanusiyya, Religion and State) provide a good background to the religious philosophy that continued to inform the Sanusis after the creation of the monarchy in 1951. More analytical early accounts are provided in al-Ashhab's *Al-Mahdi al-Sanusi* (The Sanusi Mahdi) and his *Al-Sanusi al-Kabir* (The Great Sanusi) as well as in Dajani's *Dirasa fi al-tarikh Libiyya* (Studies of Libyan History). Rizqana's *al-Mamlaka al-Libiyya* (The Libyan Kingdom) focuses on the kingdom itself.

Anderson's *The State and Social Transformation in Tunisia and Libya, 1830–1980,* mentioned earlier, is a valuable source for understanding the impact of Libya's history on its current economic and political development. Somewhat more descriptive accounts of the same historical period are provided by Martel in his *La Libye 1835–1990: Essai de géopolitique historique.* There is, as yet, no single satisfactory source on the Sanusi monarchy. A somewhat uncritical discussion of those early years can be found in Khadduri's *Modern Libya: A Study in Political Development.* Published in 1963, *Modern Libya* is still worthwhile reading because it conveys in great detail both the zeitgeist of Libya's rulers and the perceptions that shaped the analysis of a prominent early observer. A more cautious evaluation of the prospects of the kingdom and a description of the role of the United Nations in its creation is conveyed by Adrian Pelt, the United Nations Commissioner in Libya in the period leading up to independence. His *Libyan Independence and the United Nations* contains a particularly helpful summary of interviews made at the time that reflect the attitudes of elites in the different provinces on the eve of independence.

Khadduri's and Pelt's books are extended and updated in Hasan's doctoral dissertation, "The Genesis of Political Leadership in Libya,

1952–1969." It remains an indispensable source for tracing the emergence of political elites under the monarchy. His work in retrospect also provides the contemporary researcher on Libya with a cornucopia of information on local families and tribal affiliation. This is particularly important because it provides us with information about important individuals and primordial ties. Relying on early modernization theory, Hayford in her dissertation, "The Politics of the Kingdom of Libya in Historical Perspective," argues that Libya during the monarchy made substantial progress toward nation-building. Her assertions will undoubtedly be disputed by Libya observers and Qadhafi loyalists alike. But since several pieces of legislation adopted during the monarchy—on oil exploration and arabization for example—were later claimed and became key components of Qadhafi's own search for a political community, her arguments retain a certain prescience in writing about a historical period on which no definitive study has yet been published.

The economic challenges faced by the kingdom—and later by the Qadhafi government—are recounted in two early publications. The first is a readily available study commissioned by the International Bank for Reconstruction and Development, entitled *The Economic Development of Libya.* The second is Farley's aptly titled *Planning for Development in Libya.*

For the period after 1969 the single most important publication for any Libya observer is the yearly volume of the *Annuaire de l'Afrique du Nord,* written and edited since 1963 by the staff of the Institut de Recherches et d'Etudes sur le Monde Arabe et Musulman (IREMAM) in Aix-en-Provence, and published by the Centre National de la Recherche Scientifique. Individual articles on the country's economic, political, and social developments by specialized researchers who have had continual access to the Jamahiriyya provide a wealth of data, along with references to legal documents, lists of agreements and government declarations, and a bibliography of works published inside Libya. The first eleven years of the *Annuaire*'s articles were later compiled into a separate book edited by Bleuchot titled *Chroniques et documents libyens, 1969–1980.*

The most complete descriptive account of the Qadhafi government's first decade in power remains Mattes' massive doctoral dissertation, *Die Volksrevolution in der Sozialistischen Libyschen Arabischen Volksgamahiriyya.* The best comprehensive evaluations of that decade, however, are El-Fathaly and Palmer's *Political Development and Social Change in Libya* and Fathaly, Palmer, and Chackerian's *Political Development and Bureaucracy in Libya.* Although both use as their analytical framework a now-dated body of development theory relying in part on attitudinal surveys and interviews, they remain valuable if only because the authors delineate a number of problems the country faced at the time—difficulties it would have to overcome if Qadhafi's experiments were to be successful. Two decades later, many of the authors' original questions can now be answered, and both books provide an invaluable synthesis of what had been achieved and what the potential was for Qadhafi's efforts at the time.

A first-rate analysis of the country's evolving political system and institutions is provided by Djaziri in his works *Le système politique libyen 1969–1984* and his *État et Société en Libye.* The former work expands but predates his chapter in my edited collection, *Qadhafi's Revolution 1969–1994.* Written with a sense of grudging admiration, First's *Libya: The Elusive Revolution,* when published, provided the first close look at the Qadhafi regime in office and posed important questions about the nature and the durability of the Libyan experiment. Although often dismissed as a somewhat misplaced apologia of Qadhafi and his revolution, First's questions and observations, if approached from a critical perspective, retain their importance for contemporary observers.

A special place must be reserved for Davis's highly original *Libyan Politics: Tribe and Revolution,* an anthropologist's personal observations on how the revolution affected the Zuwaya tribe. It represents one of a few books written by trained social scientists who were granted long-term access to the country, and it is probably the best account written of the Libyan people since another anthropologist, Evans-Pritchard, published his now somewhat outdated *The Sanusi of Cyrenaica* almost four decades ago. Davis's account and his conclusions bring sharply into focus the lingering split in the Jamahiriyya between the pronouncements and claims of its leader and the implementation of his directives in a society that remains in some aspects deeply traditional. *Libyan Politics* furthermore underscores how the revolutionary government tried to accommodate, despite its own rhetoric, the more traditional cultural aspects that persisted in the country.

An analysis of the economic and political liberalization attempts after 1987 can be located in the yearly articles by Burgat, Djaziri, and Monastiri in *Annuaire de l'Afrique du Nord* and in my articles "Qadhafi's 'Perestroika'" and "Qadhafi's Unfinished Revolution." Hasan's earlier observations on the country's elites are updated to the post-coup period and analyzed in Hinnebusch's "Libya: Personalistic Leadership of a Populist Revolution," in Zartman, *Political Elites in Arab North Africa.* El-Fathaly and Palmer in *Political Development and Social Change in Libya* anticipate the thesis more fully developed in this book that Qadhafi's need for support made him increasingly reliant on elements of Libyan society, whose lack of experience and abuse of power alienated growing sections of the population, and ultimately proved antithetical to building political institutions. El-Fathaly and Palmer's updated findings can be found in my work *Qadhafi's Libya, 1969–1994*. El-Kikhia's *Libya's Qaddafi* represents a more recent and partisan evaluation that nevertheless contains some valuable insights about the country's political experiments.

The economic development of Libya since 1969 has been the subject of several scholarly and professional publications. The economic counterpart to Mattes' dissertation on the political evolution of the country can be found in Yala's equally exhaustive Ph.D. dissertation, "Les hydrocarbures, facteur d'industrialisation et d'accumulation pour l'économie libyenne." In it readers can locate all the details on the Libyan oil industry, the role of the independents in the Libyan oil industry, Qadhafi's part in the nationalizations, and the Libyan contribution to the international conferences that led to the 1973 agreements. A similar but less detailed account can be found in Waddams, *The Libyan Oil Industry* and in Gazzo, *Pétrole et développement: le cas libyen.* The economic and social impact of this hydrocarbon development can be found in Allan's works *Libya: The Experience of Oil* and *Libya Since Independence.* Unfortunately there are no up-to-date accounts of the Libyan oil industry, but much of the story since the 1980s can be pieced together from quarterly and yearly accounts published by the *Economist Intelligence Unit* and from more specialized oil journals.

Several books cover other sectors of the Libyan economy and the difficulties of oil-led economic development. Unfortunately, as with other subjects, there are no recent comprehensive works available in western languages. Perhaps the best appraisal of the first decade for the agricultural sector is Hajjaji's *The Agricultural Development Plans in the Socialist People's Libyan Arab Jamahiriya and the Five-Year Agricultural Transformation Plan,* in two volumes (in Arabic). Selected sectors are discussed by Libyan and foreign contributors to Buru, Ghanem, and McLachlan, *Planning and Development in Modern Libya* and in Khader and el-Wifati's edited collection *The Economic Development of Libya.* Neither, however, provides a well-integrated analysis of economic developments in the country, but some of the individual chapters remain worth reading.

A short analysis of the impact of decreasing oil revenues after 1985 on the country's economic fortunes is provided by Allan, "Libya Accommodates to Lower Oil Revenues" and its wider ramifications in my chapter "L'économie libyenne," which can be found in Lacoste and Lacoste,

L'Etat du Maghreb, a book that provides the most recent and a very comprehensive overall assessment of Libya and other Maghrebi countries today. In addition to its discussion in this book, the phenomenon of Libya as a rentier economy—and the political consequences of this peculiar type of development—are in First's *Libya: The Elusive Revolution* and, in a more theoretical approach, in my chapter "Political Aspects of State Building in Rentier Economies" in Beblawi and Luciani's *The Rentier State.*

The broader social, cultural, and legal impact of the revolution has also been dealt with piecemeal, but several aspects are investigated by Deeb and Deeb in *Libya Since the Revolution.* Although dated by now and perhaps overly descriptive for a work aimed at a specialized audience, the authors skillfully focus on the disjunction between the rhetoric of the regime and its impact on the country's political institutions and traditional social structures. A very good early overview of the impact of the revolution can also be found in Albergoni et al., *La Libye nouvelle.*

The country's evolving legal system, as with those of all regimes with revolutionary pretensions, provides important clues to the intentions and strategies of its leadership but, surprisingly, little has been written about it in the Libyan context. In addition to her chapter in my edited book, the reader may also want to consult Mayer's earlier pieces: "Le droit musulman en Libye à l'âge du 'Livre Vert,'" "The Reinstatement of Islamic Criminal Law in Libya," and "Islamic Resurgence or New Prophethood." An interesting (albeit anecdotal) account of the changing role of women in the Jamahiriyya has been provided by Souriau, a long-time observer of North Africa, in her *Libye: l'économie des femmes.* Two excellent sources among a cornucopia of literature on opposition to Qadhafi are Anderson, "Qadhdhafi and His Opposition" and Mukhtar's "The Struggle for Libya." (Mukhtar is a pseudonym based on Libya's most prominent opposition figure to Italian colonialism.)

A good deal more has been written about Qadhafi, Islam, and the Green Book. Two earlier short articles worth consulting are Bleuchot and Monastiri's "L'Islam de M. El-Qaddhafi" and Anderson's "Qaddafi's Islam." The relevant section of Burgat's *L'islamisme au Maghreb: la voix du Sud* focuses more on Islamist opposition to Qadhafi's rule and is one of the few sources to provide information about the phenomenon. Ayoub's *Islam and the Third Universal Theory* is the most systematic and consistent analysis of the Libyan leader's interpretation of Islam, even if part of the book resembles a paean to Qadhafi more than anything else. For a study that links Qadhafi's interpretation of Islam to more direct political concerns, consult Mattes, *Islam und Staatsaufbau.*

Two excellent analyses of Qadhafi's ideology and its expression in the Green Book are St. John, "The Ideology of Mu'ammar al-Qadhdhafi" and Bleuchot, "The Green Book: Its Context and Meaning" in Allan, *Libya since Independence.* Specialists will want to consult the *Shuruh al-Kitab al-Akhdar* (Commentaries on the Green Book), of which several volumes have now been published and distributed by the Green Book Center in Tripoli, and some of the proceedings of the Green Book seminars convened in Tripoli and Benghazi. Finally, many doctoral dissertations by Libyan students have focused on social, political, and economic development in the Jamahiriyya. Although their number gradually diminished toward the end of the 1980s, they provide a rich source that can fill in some of the gaps in our knowledge about the country.

More popular accounts of Libya since 1969 have tended to focus on Qadhafi, particularly so when the Libyan leader started to confront openly the West in the 1970s. As a result, many of the books published in the 1980s provided little new information or insights and sometimes only summary descriptions of events in the country. Among those that managed to both reach a general audience and provide a more systematic appraisal I would like to single out Bearman's *Qadhafi's Libya* and Cooley's *Libyan Sandstorm.*

In addition, books are available that have relied extensively on interviews with the Libyan leader. An admiring portrait of Qadhafi and his worldview can be found in an early account by Bianco titled *Gadafi: Voice from the Desert.* The most important source, however, remains Barrada, Kravetz, and Whitaker, *Kadhafi; "Je suis un opposant à l'échelon mondial."* The result of countless hours of interviews, the book also contains a riveting transcript of the crucial July 1978 confrontation between Qadhafi and the *ulama* in the Moulay Muhammad mosque in Tripoli and takes the reader beyond the cartoonlike image of the Libyan leader often found in other accounts.

Perhaps not surprising, the amount of materials published inside the Jamahiriyya on events since 1969 is almost limitless, easily surpassing several hundred pamphlets, collections of speeches by Qadhafi and other Libyan personalities, commentaries on the Green Book and a vast supply of applications of Green Book theory to every imaginable social, economic, and political problem. Every public speech by Qadhafi is publicized in a cornucopia of publications issued primarily by the Green Book Center and the People's Establishment for Publication, Distribution and Advertising. On the occasion of the twentieth anniversary of the revolution in 1989 and again in 1994, the Libyan government issued many pamphlets and books that summarized the achievements of the

Qadhafi regime. Most of these can be ignored without peril, but there are occasionally some worthwhile materials that illuminate what often seem like incomprehensible actions or decisions.

Among the most important sources worth pursuing from a scholarly viewpoint are *As-Sijil Al-Qawmi,* the official compilation of Qadhafi's speeches that can serve as a handy reference guide to the Libyan leader's speeches. In addition to this the specialist should consult *Al-Jarida Ar-Rasmiyya,* the country's official journal, where all laws emanating from the General People's Congress and other official decrees are published. Both can be found in a few major libraries in this country, along with some Libyan newspapers. Among the latter the most important are *Al-Zahf Al-Akhdar,* the newspaper once published by the Revolutionary Committees and occasionally containing unsigned frontpage articles by Qadhafi, and *Al-Fajr Al-Jadid.*

Although their writings need to be evaluated carefully in light of the restrictive conditions they work under, it is nevertheless important to take into account works by Libyan academics, some of whom became important Revolutionary Committee members or bureaucrats. Here also the number of publications has been staggering, and I retain only a few that have risen above the hagiographic style that has marked most of them: Billal, *The Jamahiriya and the Victory of the Age of the Masses* and Abu Dabus, *Lectures on the Third Universal Theory.* Focused specifically on the Revolutionary Committees are the pamphlets by al-Hesnawi, *The Revolutionary Committees and Their Role in the Conformation and Consolidation of the People's Authority* and Ibrahim's *Revolutionary Organization.* In addition, the *majallat al-buhuth al-tarikhiya* (Journal of Historical Research) issued since 1979 by the Libyan Studies Center occasionally publishes relevant articles about the country's recent political history.

Finally, both specialists and lay audience alike can follow contemporary events in a number of journals and magazines. *The Middle East Journal, The International Journal of Middle East Studies,* and *Africa Contemporary Record* have consistently provided high-quality articles for English-only readers. Those mastering French and German will want to consult *Jeune Afrique* and *Maghreb-Machrek,* which also provide a comprehensive chronology, and *Orient,* published by the Orient Institut in Hamburg. An indispensable source is also the *Foreign Broadcast Information Service,* in which translations of local Libyan radio and television programs are made available.

Selected Bibliography

Abrahamian, Ervand. 1982. *Iran Between Two Revolutions.* Princeton, N.J.: Princeton University Press.

Abu Dabus, Rayab. 1982. *Lectures on the Third Universal Theory.* Tripoli: Green Book Center.

Abu Khzam, Ibrahim. 1987. *Al-Dasatir wa al-Zahira al-Diktaturiyya* (Constitutions and the dictatorial impulse). Tripoli: Green Book Center.

Abushawa, Malik A. 1977. "The Political System of Libya, 1951–1969." Master's thesis, Faculty of Economics and Political Science, Cairo University.

Ahmida, Ali Abdullatif. 1994. *The Making of Modern Libya: State Formation, Colonization, and Resistance, 1830–1932.* Albany: State University of New York.

Albergoni, Gianni et al. 1975. *La Libye nouvelle: rupture et continuité.* Paris: Centre National de la Recherche Scientifique.

Alexander, Nathan. 1981. "Libya: The Continuous Revolution." *Middle Eastern Studies* 17, no. 2 (April): 210–227.

Allan, John Anthony. 1983. "Libya Accommodates to Lower Oil Revenues: Economic and Political Adjustments." *International Journal of Middle East Studies* 15.

——. 1981. *Libya: The Experience of Oil.* Boulder, Colo.: Westview Press, 1981.

Allan, John Anthony, ed. 1982. *Libya Since Independence: Economic and Social Development.* New York: St. Martin's Press.

Allan, John Anthony, M. M. Buru, and Keith S. McLachlan, eds. 1989. *Libya: State and Region.* London: School of Oriental and African Studies.

Amnesty International. 1991. *Amnesty International Report.* London: Amnesty International Publications.

Anderson, Lisa. 1995. "Qadhafi's Legacy: An Evaluation of a Political Experiment." In *Qadhafi's Libya, 1969–1994,* ed. Dirk Vandevalle. New York: St. Martin's Press.

——. 1990a. "Absolutism and the Resilience of Monarchy in the Middle East." *Political Science Quarterly* (spring): 1–15.
——. 1990b. "Tribe and State: Libyan Anomalies." In *Tribes and State Formation in the Middle East,* ed. Philip S. Khoury and Joseph Kostiner. Berkeley: University of California Press.
——. 1987. "The State in the Middle East and North Africa." *Comparative Politics* 20, no. 3 (October): 1–18.
——. 1986a. *The State and Social Transformation in Tunisia and Libya, 1830–1980.* Princeton, N.J.: Princeton University Press.
——. 1986b. "Libya: The Politics of Identity." *Annals* (January).
——. 1986c. " Qadhdhafi and His Opposition." *Middle East Journal* 40, no. 2 (spring): 225–237.
——. 1983. "Qaddafi's Islam." In *Voices of Resurgent Islam,* ed. John Esposito. Cambridge: Oxford University Press.
Anderson, Perry. 1974. *Lineages of the Absolutist State.* London: Vergo.
Annuaire de l'Afrique du Nord. 30 vols. Paris: Editions du Centre National de la Recherche Scientifique.
Al-Arawi, Abd Allah. 1988. *Mafhum al-Dawlah* (The Concept of the State). Beirut: Al-Markaz al-Thaqafi al-Arabi.
——. 1984. *Mafhum-al-Huriyah* (The Concept of Freedom) Beirut: Al-Markaz al-Thaqafi al-Arabi.
Armstrong, David. 1993. *Revolution and World Order: The Revolutionary State in International Society.* Oxford: Clarendon Press.
Al-Ashhab, Muhammad. n.d. *Al-Sanusi al-Kabir* (The Great Sanusi). Cairo: Matbaat al-Qahira.
——. 1952. *Al-Mahdi al-Sanusi.* Cairo: Matbaat Maji.
Ashraf, Ahmad. 1994. "Charisma, Theocracy, and Men of Power in Postrevolutionary Iran." In *The Politics of Social Transformation in Afghanistan, Iran, and Palistan,* ed. Myron Weiner and Ali Banuazizi. Syracuse: Syracuse University Press.
Al-Assiouty, Sarwat. 1981. "Coran contre fiqh: a propos du mariage selon le livre vert de Mu'ammar Al-Qaddhafi." In *Le Maghreb Musulman en 1979,* ed. Christiane Souriau. Paris: Editions du CNRS.
Attiga, Ali Ahmed. 1973. "The Economic Impact of Oil on Libyan Agriculture." In *Libya: Agriculture and Economic Development,* ed. John Anthony Allan, Keith S. McLachlan, and Edith Penrose. London: Frank Cass.
Ayoub, Mahmoud M. 1987. *Islam and the Third Universal Theory: The Religious Thought of Mu'ammar al-Qadhdhafi.* London: KPI Limited.
Ayubi, Nazih. 1995. *Over-Stating the Arab State.* London: I. B. Tauris.
——. 1992. "Withered Socialism or Whether Socialism? The Radical Arab States as Populist-Corporatist Regimes." *Third World Quarterly* 13, no. 1: 39–105.
——. 1990. "Etatism versus Privatization: The Case of Egypt." *International Review of Administrative Sciences* 56, no. 1: 89–103.
Badri, Roswitha. 1986. *Die Entwicklung der Dritten Universaltheorie Mu'ammar al Qaddafi's in Theorie und Praxis.* Frankfurt am Main: Peter Lang.
Bakhash, Shaul. 1984. *The Reign of the Ayatollahs: Iran and the Islamic Revolution.* New York: Basic Books.

Bank of Libya. 1965. *Monthly Economy Bulletin* 5, (September): 9.

Banks, Jeffrey S., and Eric A. Hanushek. 1995. *Modern Political Economy: Old Topics, New Directions.* New York: Cambridge University Press.

Barbar, Aghil M. 1980. "The Tarabulus (Libyan) Resistance to the Italian Invasion: 1911–1920." Ph.D. diss., University of Wisconsin–Madison.

Barrada, Hamid, Mark Kravetz, and Mark Whitaker. 1984. *Kadhafi: "Je suis un opposant à l'échelon mondial."* Lausanne, France: Editions Pierre-Marcel Favre.

Bates, Robert H. 1991. "The Economics of Transitions to Democracy." *Political Science and Politics* 24, no. 1: 24–27.

——. 1989. *Beyond the Miracle of the Market: The Political Economy of Agrarian Reform in Rural Kenya.* Cambridge: Cambridge University Press.

——. 1983. *Essays on the Political Economy of Rural Africa.* Berkeley: University of California Press.

——. 1981. *Markets and States in Tropical Africa.* Berkeley: University of California Press.

Bates, Robert H., Stephan Haggard, and Joan M. Nelson. 1991. "A Critique by Political Scientists." In *Politics and Policy Making in Developing Countries: Perspectives on the New Political Economy,* ed. Gerald M. Meier. San Francisco: International Center for Economic Growth.

Bearman, Jonathan. 1986. *Qadhafi's Libya.* London: Zed Books.

Beblawi, Hazem. 1987. "The Rentier State in the Arab World." In *The Rentier State,* ed. Hazem Beblawi and Giacomo Luciani. New York: Croom Helm.

Beblawi, Hazem, and Giacomo Luciani, eds. 1987. *The Rentier State: Essays in the Political Economy of Arab Countries.* New York: Croom Helm.

Becker, David. 1987. "Bonanza Development and the New Bourgeoisie: Peru Under Military Rule." In *Postimperialism: International Capitalism and Development,* ed. David Becker, Jeff Frieden, Sayre Schatz, and Richard Sklar. Boulder, Colo.: Lynne Rienner.

Ben Achour, Yadh. 1980. *L'etat nouveau et la philosophie et juridique occidentale.* Tunis: Imprimerie de la république Tunisienne.

Bendix, Reinhard. 1978. *Kings or People.* Berkeley: University of California Press.

——. 1968. "Reflection on Charismatic Leadership." *State and Society:* 616–629.

Bensman, Joseph, and Michael Givant. 1975. "Charisma and Modernity: The Use and Abuse of a Concept." *Social Research* 2, no. 4: 570–614.

Beschorner, Natasha, and Andrew Smith. 1991. "Libya in the 1990s—Can Its Resources Be Salvaged?" Special report. London: Economist Intelligence Unit.

Bianco, Mirella. 1974. *Gadafi: Voice from the Desert.* London: Longman.

Billal, Abdallah. 1985. *The Jamahiriya and the Victory of the Age of the Masses.* Tripoli: Green Book Center.

Bleuchot, Hervé. 1983. *Chroniques et documents libyens, 1969–1980.* Paris: Editions du Centre National de la Recherche Scientifique.

Bleuchot, Hervé, and Taoufik Monastiri. 1981. "L'Islam de M. El-Qaddhafi." In *Islam et Politique au Maghreb,* ed. Ernest Gellner and Jean-Claude Vatin. Paris: Editions de Centre National de la Recherche Scientifique.

Blundy, David, and Andrew Lycett. 1987. *Qaddafi and the Libyan Revolution.* Boston: Little, Brown and Company.

Borrmans, Maurice. 1976. "Le séminaire du dialogue islamo-chrétien de Tripoli (Libye)." *Islamochristiana* 2 (February 1–6): 135–170.

Branthwaite, Alan. 1993. "The Psychological Basis of Independent Statehood." In *States in a Changing World: A Contemporary Analysis,* ed. Robert Jackson and Alan James. Oxford: Clarendon Press.

Brenner, Robert. 1976. "Agrarian Class Structure and Economic Development in Pre-Industrial Europe." *Past and Present* 20 (February): 30–75.

Brewer, John. 1989. *The Sinews of Power: War, Money and the English State, 1688–1783.* New York: Knopf.

Bromley, Simon. 1994. *Rethinking Middle East Politics.* Austin: University of Texas Press.

Bryant, Ralph. 1987. *International Financial Intermediation.* Washington, D.C.: Brookings Institution.

Buchanan, James M. 1980a. "Reform in the Rent-Seeking Society." In *Toward a Theory of a Rent-Seeking Society,* by James M. Buchanan, Robert D. Tollison, and Gordon Tullock. College Station: Texas A&M University Press.

——. 1980b. "Rent Seeking and Profit Seeking." In *Toward a Theory of a Rent-Seeking Society,* by James M. Buchanan, Robert D. Tollison, and Gordon Tullock. College Station: Texas A&M University Press.

——. 1980c. "Rent Seeking under External Diseconomies." In *Toward a Theory of a Rent-Seeking Society,* by James M. Buchanan, Robert D. Tollison, and Gordon Tullock. College Station: Texas A&M University Press.

Buchanan, James M., Robert D. Tollison, and Gordon Tullock. 1980. *Toward a Theory of a Rent-Seeking Society.* College Station: Texas A&M University Press.

Burgat, François. 1995. "Qadhafi's Ideological Framework." In *Qadhafi's Libya, 1969–1994,* ed. Dirk Vandewalle. New York: St. Martin's Press.

——. 1988. *L'islamisme au Maghreb: La voix du Sud.* Paris: Karthala.

Burgat, François, and Gilbert Beaugé. 1986. "La question des migrations en Libye." *Maghreb-Machrek* no. 112 (June).

Burgat, François, and William Dowell. 1992. *The Islamic Movement in North Africa.* Austin: University of Texas Press.

Burke, Edmund. 1955. *Reflections on the Revolution in France.* New York: Liberal Arts Press.

Buru, Mukhtar, John Anthony Allan, and Keith McLachlan, eds. 1989. *Libya: State and Region.* London: School of Oriental and African Studies.

Buru, Mukhtar, Shukri Ghanem, and Keith McLachlan. 1985. *Planning and Development in Modern Libya.* London: MENAS Press.

Bush, George. 1993. *Developments Concerning the National Emergency with Respect to Libya.* Committee on Foreign Affairs, United States House of Representatives, 103d Cong., 1st sess., Washington, D.C.: GPO.

Callaghy, Thomas M. 1984. *The State-Society Struggle: Zaire in Comparative Perspective.* New York: Columbia University Press.

Caporaso, James, ed. 1989. *The Elusive State: International and Comparative Perspectives.* London: Sage.

Caporaso, James, and David Levine. 1992. *Theories of Political Economy.* New York: Cambridge University Press.

Chase-Dunn, Christopher. 1989. *Global Formation: Structures of the World Economy.* Cambridge: Basil Blackwell.

Chatelus, Michel. 1984. "Attitudes Toward Public Sector Management and Reassertion of the Private Sector in the Arab World." Paper presented at the Middle Eastern Studies Association, San Francisco, November.

Chatelus, Michel, and Yves Schemeil. 1984. "Toward a New Political Economy of State Industrialization in the Arab Middle East." *International Journal of Middle East Studies* 16: 251–265.

Chaudhry, Kiren Aziz. 1994. "Economic Liberalization and the Lineages of the Rentier State." *Comparative Politics* 27, no. 1: 1–25.

——. 1993. "The Myths of the Market and the Common History of Late Developers." *Politics and Society* 21, no. 3: 245–274.

——. 1992. "Economic Liberalization in Oil-Exporting Countries: Iraq and Saudi Arabia." In *Privatization and Liberalization in the Middle East,* ed. Iliya Harik and Denis Sullivan. Bloomington: Indiana University Press.

——. 1989. "The Price of Wealth: Business and State in Labor Remittance and Oil Economies." *International Organization* 43, no. 1 (winter): 101–145.

Cohen, Youssef, Brian Brown, and A. F. K. Organski. 1981. "The Paradoxical Nature of State Making: The Violent Creation of Order." *American Political Science Review* 75: 901–910.

Colson, Elizabeth. 1974. *Tradition and Contract: The Problem of Order.* Chicago: Adeline Press.

Committee for Middle East Trade. 1982. *Libya: The Five-Year Development Plan, 1981–1985.* London: Committee for Middle East Trade.

Congleton, Roger. 1980. "Competitive Process, Competitive Waste, and Institutions." In *Toward a Theory of a Rent-Seeking Society,* ed. James M. Buchanan, Robert D. Tollison, and Gordon Tullock. College Station: Texas A&M University Press.

Cooley, John K. 1982. *Libyan Sandstorm: The Complete Account of Qaddafi's Revolution.* London: Sidgwick and Jackson.

Craig, Harris, and Lilian Craig. 1986. *Libya: Qadhafi's Revolution and the Modern State.* Boulder, Colo.: Westview Press.

Crystal, Jill. 1995. *Oil and Politics in the Gulf: Rulers and Merchants in Kuwait and Qatar.* New York: Cambridge University Press.

—. 1989. "Coalitions in Oil Monarchies: Kuwait and Qatar." *Comparative Politics* 21: 427–443.

Czempiel, Otto, and James Rosenau, eds. 1989. *Global Change and Theoretical Challenges.* Lexington, Mass.: D. C. Heath.

Dajani, Ahmad. 1971. *Al-Haraka al-Sanusiyya.* Cairo: al-Matba'a al-Faniyya.

—. 1968. *Dirasa fi al-Tarikh Libiyya* (Studies of Libyan history). Tripoli: al-Firjani.

Davis, Eric, and Nicolas Gavrielides, eds. 1991. *Statecraft in the Middle East.* Miami: Florida International University Press.

Davis, John. 1987. *Libyan Politics: Tribe and Revolution.* Berkeley: University of California Press.

——. 1982. "Qadhafi's Theory and Practice of Non-Representative Government." *Government and Opposition* 17: 61–79.

Dawi, Ali. 1984. *Manaht al-bahth al-qanuni* (Legal research methods). Tripoli: Al-Fatih University Press.

Deeb, Marius. 1986. "Radical Political Ideologies and Concepts of Property in Libya and South Yemen." *Middle East Journal* 40, no. 3: 445–461.

Deeb, Marius, and Mary-Jane Deeb. 1982. *Libya since the Revolution: Aspects of Social and Political Development.* New York: Praeger.

Deeb, Mary-Jane. 1991. *Libya's Foreign Policy in North Africa.* Special Studies on the Middle East. Boulder, Colo.: Westview Press.

Delacroix, Jacques. 1980. "The Distributive State in the World System." *Studies in Comparative International Development* 15, no. 3 (fall): 3–21.

Djaziri, Moncef. 1996. *État et Société en Libye.* Paris: Editions L'Harmattan.

——. 1995. "Creating a New State: Libya's Political Institutions." In *Qadhafi's Libya, 1969–1994,* ed. Dirk Vandewalle. New York: St. Martin's Press.

——. 1988. *Le système politique libyen 1969–1984.* Ph.D. diss., University of Lausanne.

Duvall, Raymond, and John Freeman. 1983. "The Techno-Bureaucratic Elite and the Entrepreneurial State in Dependent Industrialization." *American Political Science Review* 77: 569–587.

Eisenstadt, Samuel. 1978. *Revolution and Transformation of Societies.* New York: Free Press.

Ensminger, Jean. 1992. *Making a Market: The Institutional Transformation of an African Society.* Cambridge: Cambridge University Press.

Evans, Peter. 1995. *Embedded Autonomy: States and Industrial Transformation.* Princeton, N.J.: Princeton University Press.

Evans, Peter, Dietrich Rueschemeyer, and Theda Skocpol, eds. 1985. *Bringing the State Back In.* Cambridge: Cambridge University Press.

Evans-Pritchard, E.E. 1949. *The Sanusi of Cyrenaica.* Oxford: Clarendon Press.

——. 1940. *The Nuer.* Oxford: Oxford University Press.

Faluki, Muhammad Hashim. 1987. *The Concept of Education in the Green Book.* Tripoli: Green Book Center.

Farhat, Lutfi. 1983. *Ma'alim nazariya Iqtisadiya Jadida* (Landmarks of a new economic theory). Tripoli: Green Book Center.

Farley, Rawle. 1971. *Planning for Development in Libya: The Exceptional Economy in the Developing World.* New York: Praeger.

El-Fathaly, Omar, and Monte Palmer. 1995. "Institutional Development in Qadhafi's Libya." In *Qadhafi's Libya, 1969–1994,* ed. Dirk Vanderwalle. New York: St. Martin's Press.

——. 1982. "The Transformation of Mass Political Institutions in Revolutionary Libya." In *Social and Economic Development of Libya,* ed. George Joffé and Keith McLachlan. Wisbech, England: MENAS Press.

——. 1980. *Political Development and Social Change in Libya.* Lexington, Mass.: Lexington Books.

El-Fathaly, Omar, Monte Palmer, and Richard Chackerian. 1977. *Political Development and Bureaucracy in Libya.* Lexington, Mass.: Lexington Books.

Fatton, Robert. 1992. *Predatory States.* Boulder, Colo.: Westview Press.

Findlay, Ronald. 1991. "The New Political Economy: Its Explanatory Power for LDCs." In *Politics and Policy Making in Developing Countries: Perspectives on the New Political Economy,* ed. Gerald M. Meier. San Francisco: International Center for Economic Growth.

First, Ruth. 1975. *Libya: The Elusive Revolution.* New York: Homes and Meier.

Four Power Commission of Investigation, Former Italian Colonies. 1948. *Report on Libya.* London: Government Publishing Company.

Frachon, Alain. 1986. "Les défauts de l'armure du colonel." *Le Monde,* 30 April.

Furgeson, James E. 1961. *The Power of the Purse: A History of American Public Finance, 1776–1790.* Chapel Hill: University of North Carolina Press.

Gaber, Makzoum Attia. 1983. *Le mouvement du "jihad" en Libye face à la colonisation italienne de 1911 à 1919.* Ph.D. diss., University of Provence, France.

Gamson, William. 1961. "A Theory of Coalition Formation." *American Sociological Review* 26: 373–382.

Gauṣe, F. Gregory. 1994. *Oil Monarchies: Domestic and Security Challenges in the Arab Gulf States.* New York; Council on Foreign Relations Press.

Gazzo, Yves. 1980. *Pètrole et dèveloppement: le cas libyen.* Paris: Economica.

George, Alexander. 1991. *Forceful Persuasion: Coercive Diplomacy as an Alternative to War.* Washington, D.C.: United States Institute for Peace.

Gerschenkron, Alexander. 1962. *Economic Backwardness in Historical Perspective: A Book of Essays.* Cambridge, Mass.: Harvard University Press.

Ghanem, Shukri. n.d. *The Libyan Economy before Oil* (in Arabic). Tripoli: National Center for Scientific Research.

Giddens, Anthony. 1987. *The Nation-State and Violence: Volume Two of a Contemporary Critique of Historical Materialism.* Berkeley: University of California Press.

Gilpin, Robert. 1987. *The Political Economy of International Relations.* Princeton, N.J.: Princeton University Press.

Goldscheid, Rudolf. 1976. "Finanzwissenschaft und Soziologie." In *Die Finanzkrise des Steuerstaats: Beiträge zür politischen Ökonomie der Staatsfinanzen,* by Rudolf Goldscheid and Joseph Schumpeter. Frankfurt am Main: Suhrkamp Verlag.

Gourevitch, Peter. 1986. *Politics in Hard Times: Comparative Responses to International Economic Crises.* Ithaca, N.Y.: Cornell University Press.

——. 1978. "The Second Image Reversed: The International Sources of Domestic Politics." *International Organization* 32, no. 4: 881–912.

Gray, Jerry. 1996. "Foreigners Investing in Libya or in Iran Face U.S. Sanctions." *New York Times,* 24 July, A1, cont. A12.

Hablützel, Rudolf. 1981. *Development Prospects of Capital Surplus Oil-Exporting Countries: Iraq, Kuwait, Libya, Qatar, Saudi Arabia, UAE.* Washington, D.C.: World Bank.

Hajjaji, Salem. 1981. *The Agricultural Development Plans in the Socialist People's Libyan Arab Jamahiriya and the Five-Year Agricultural Transformation Plan.* (in Arabic). 2 vols. Tripoli: People's Establishment for Publishing, Advertising and Printing.

Hajjar, Sami. 1980. "The Jamahiriya Experiment in Libya: Qadhafi and Rousseau." *Journal of Modern African Studies* 18: 181–200.
Haley, Edward P. 1984. *Qaddafi and the United States since 1969.* New York: Praeger.
Hall, Peter, ed. 1986. *States in History.* New York: Basil Blackwell.
Hamilton, Adrian. 1971. "Libya Leads the Oil States." *Middle East International* (April): 30–32.
Hasan, Salaheddin Salem. 1973. "The Genesis of Political Leadership in Libya, 1952–1969." Ph.D. diss., George Washington University, Washington, D.C.
Hayford, Elizabeth. 1970. "The Politics of the Kingdom of Libya in Historical Perspective." Ph.D. diss., Tufts University, Medford, Mass.
Heikal, Mohamed. 1975. *The Road to Ramadan.* London: Longman.
Hermassi, Elbaki, and Dirk Vandewalle. 1993. "The Second Stage of State-Building in North Africa." In *State and Society in North Africa,* ed. I. William Zartman. Boulder, Colo.: Westview Press.
Herz, John. 1976. *The Nation-State and the Crisis of World Politics.* New York: David McKay.
Al-Hesnawi, Habib. 1990. "Women's Role in the Libyan Social Economic Transformation." Paper presented at the 24th Annual Meeting of the Middle East Studies Association, San Antonio, Tex., November.
——. 1987. *The Revolutionary Committees and Their Role in the Conformation and Consolidation of the People's Authority.* Tripoli: Green Book Center.
——. 1982. *Min al-Jumhuriyya Illa al-Jamahiriyya* (From republic to Jamahiriyya). Tripoli: Libyan Studies Center.
Hinnebusch, Raymond. 1984. "Charisma, Revolution and State Formation: Qaddafi and Libya." *Third World Quarterly* 6, no. 1 (January): 59–73.
——. 1982. "Libya: Personalistic Leadership of a Populist Revolution." In *Political Elites in Arab North Africa,* ed. I. William Zartman. New York: Longman.
al-Hirmasi 'Abd al-Baqi. 1987. *al-Mujtama' wa al-Dawla fi al-Maghrib* (State and society in the Maghreb). Beirut: Markaz Dirasat al-Wihda al-'Arabiyya.
Hirschman, Albert O. 1981. *Essays in Trespassing: Economics to Politics and Beyond.* New York: Cambridge University Press.
——. 1963. *Journeys toward Progress.* New York: Twentieth Century Fund.
Hoffman, Philip, and Kathryn Norberg, eds. 1994. *Fiscal Crises, Liberty, and Representative Government, 1450–1789.* Stanford, Calif.: Stanford University Press.
Huang, Yasheng. 1994. "Information, Bureaucracy, and Economic Reforms in China and the Soviet Union." *World Politics* 47, no. 1: 102–134.
Huntington, Samuel P. 1968. *Political Order in Changing Societies.* New Haven, Conn.: Yale University Press.
Hurewitz, Jacob C. 1974. *Middle East Politics: The Military Dimension.* New York: Octagon Books.
Ibrahim, Ahmad. 1983. *Revolutionary Organization.* Tripoli: Green Book Center.

Ibrahim, Saad Eddin, ed. 1987. *al-Mujtama' wa al-Dawla fi al-Watan al-Arabi* (State and society in the Arab world). Beirut: Markaz Dirasat al-Wihda al-'Arabiyya.

Ikenberry, John. 1986. "The Irony of State Strength: Comparative Responses to the Oil Shocks in the 1970s." *International Organization* 40, no. 1 (winter): 105–137.

International Bank for Reconstruction and Development. 1960. *The Economic Development of Libya.* Baltimore, Md.: Johns Hopkins Press.

International Financial Statistics. 1962–1996. Washington, D.C.: International Monetary Fund.

International Institute for Strategic Studies. 1994. *The Military Balance 1994–1995.* London: Brassey's.

International Petroleum Encyclopedia. 1982. Tulsa, Okla.: Petroleum Publishing.

International Seminar on the Green Book. 1981. International Colloquium in Benghazi. Benghazi: Foreign Liaison Office.

Jackson, Robert. 1990. *Quasi-States: Sovereignty, International Relations, and the Third World.* Cambridge: Cambridge University Press.

Jackson, Robert, and Carl Rosberg. 1982. *Personal Rule in Black Africa.* Berkeley: University of California Press.

"Al-Jaish: hashish wa taish." 1983. *Al-Zahf al Akhdar,* no. 174 (31 March).

Jefferson, Ronald L. 1991. "Institutions, Institutional Effects, and Institutionalism." In *The New Institutionalism in Organizational Analysis,* ed. Walter W. Powell and Paul J. DiMaggio. Chicago: University of Chicago Press.

Joffé, George. 1995. "Qadhafi's Islam in Local Historical Perspective." In *Qadhafi's Libya, 1969–1994,* ed. Dirk Vandewalle. New York: St. Martin's Press.

——. 1988. "Islamic Opposition in Libya." *Third World Quarterly* 10, no. 2: 615–631.

Joffé, George, and Keith McLachlan, eds. 1982. *Social and Economic Development of Libya.* Wisbech, England: MENAS Press.

Joyner, Chris C., and Wayne P. Rothbaum. 1993. "Libya and the Aerial Incident at Lockerbie: What Lessons for International Extradition Law?" *Michigan Journal of International Law* 14, no. 2: 222–261.

Kalecki, Michal. 1986. *Selected Essays in Economic Planning.* Cambridge: Cambridge University Press.

Karl, Terry Lynn. 1982a. "The Political Economy of Petrodollars: Oil and Democracy in Venezuela." Ph.D. diss., Stanford University.

——. 1982b. *Petroleum and Politics Pacts: The Transition to Democracy in Venezuela.* Working paper for the Latin American Program, no. 107. Washington, D.C.: Woodrow Wilson International Center for Scholars.

Karshenas, Massoud. 1990. *Oil, State and Industrialization in Iran.* Cambridge: Cambridge University Press.

Katouzian, Homa. 1989. "Oil and Economic Development in the Middle East." In *The Modern Economic and Social History of the Middle East in Its World Context,* ed. George Sabagh. New York: Cambridge University Press.

——. 1983. "The Aridosolatic Society: A Model of Long-Term Social and Economic Development in Iran." *International Journal of Middle Eastern Studies* 15: 259–281.

——. 1979. "The Political Economy of Oil Exporting Countries." *Peuples méditerranéens* 1: 3–22.

Khadduri, Majid. 1963. *Modern Libya: A Study in Political Development.* Baltimore, Md.: Johns Hopkins Press.

Khader, Bichara, and Bashir el-Wifati, eds. 1987. *The Economic Development of Libya.* London: Croom Helm.

Khoury, Philip, and Joseph Kostiner, eds. 1990. *Tribes and State Formation in the Middle East.* Berkeley: University of California Press.

El-Kikhia, Mansour O. 1997. *Libya's Qaddafi. The Politics of Contradiction.* Gainesville: University Press of Florida.

Kingdom of Libya, Ministry of National Economy. 1963. *Statistical Abstract* 12. Tripoli: Census and Statistical Department.

Kiser, Edgard. 1986. "The Formation of State Policy in Western European Absolutisms: A Comparison of England and France." *Politics and Society* 15, no. 3: 259–296.

Korany, Baghat. 1987. "Alien and Besieged Yet Here to Stay: The Contradictions of the Arab Territorial State." In *The Foundations of the Arab State,* ed. Ghassan Salamé. New York: Croom Helm.

Krasner, Stephen D. 1989. "Sovereignty: An Institutional Perspective." In *The Elusive State: International and Comparative Perspectives,* ed. James A. Caporaso. London: Sage.

——. 1984. "Approaches to the State: Alternative Conceptions and Historical Dynamics." *Comparative Politics* 16 (January): 223–246.

Krimly, Rayed. 1993. *The Political Economy of Rentier States: A Case Study of Saudi Arabia in the Oil Era, 1950–1990.* Ph.D. diss., George Washington University, Washington, D.C.

Krueger, Anne. 1974. "The Political Economy of the Rent-Seeking Society." *American Economic Review* 64, no. 3 (June): 291–303.

Kuznets, Simon. 1966. *Modern Economic Growth.* New Haven, Conn.: Yale University Press.

Lacoste, Camille, and Yves Lacoste. 1991. *L'État du Maghreb.* Paris: Editions La Découverte.

Lanne, Bernard. 1982. *Tchad-Libye: La querelle des frontières.* Paris: Editions Karthala.

Lemarchand, René, ed. 1988. *The Green and the Black: Qadhafi's Policies in Africa.* Bloomington: Indiana University Press.

Lenczowski, George. 1960. *Oil and State in the Middle East.* Ithaca, N.Y.: Cornell University Press.

Levi, Margaret. 1988. *Of Rule and Revenue.* Berkeley: University of California Press.

"Libya: Army versus Revolutionary Committees." 1983. *Africa Confidential,* no. 19 (21 September): 6–7.

Libyan Arab Jamahiriyya. n.d. *Al-Wathiqa al-khadra al-kubra lil-huquq al-insan fi 'asr al-jamahir* (The great green charter in the era of the masses). Tripoli: Green Book Center.

Libyan Arab Republic. 1973. *Three Year Economic and Social Development Plan in Brief, 1973–1975.* Tripoli: Ministry of Planning.

Al-Lijan ath-thawriya. 1985. Tripoli: al-Markaz al-'alami li-dirasat wa-abhath al-kitab al-akhdar.

Lindberg, John. 1952. *A General Economic Appraisal of Libya.* New York: United Nations.

Linz, Juan. 1975. "Totalitarian and Authoritarian Regimes." In *Handbook of Political Science,* ed. Fred. I. Greenstein and Nelson Polsby. Reading, Mass.: Addison-Wesley.

Little, I. M. D., Richard N. Cooper, W. Max Corden, and Sarath Rajapatirana, eds. 1993. *Boom, Crisis, and Adjustment: The Macroeconomic Experience of Developing Countries.* New York: Oxford University Press.

Loewenstein, Karl. 1966. *Max Weber: Political Ideas in the Perspective of Our Time.* Amherst: University of Massachusetts Press.

Luciani, Giacomo. 1987. "Allocation versus Production States: A Theoretical Framework." In *The Rentier State,* ed. Hazem Beblawi and Giacomo Luciani. New York: Croom Helm.

Lustick, Ian. 1993. *Unsettled States, Disputed Lands: Britain and Ireland, France and Algeria, Israel and the West Bank-Gaza.* Ithaca, N.Y.: Cornell University Press.

Al-Mahaishi, Abdelkader. 1990. "Agriculture and Development in Libya." Paper presented at the 24th Annual Meeting of the Middle East Studies Association, San Antonio, Tex., November.

Mahdavy, Hossein. 1970. "The Patterns and Problems of Economic Development in Rentier States: The Case of Iran." In *Studies in the Economic History of the Middle East from the Rise of Islam to the Present Day,* by M. A. Cook. Oxford: Oxford University Press.

Mair, Lucy. 1962. *Primitive Government.* London: Penguin.

Mammeri, Habib. 1977. "Avènement du pouvoir populaire en Libye." *Maghreb-Machrek* 76.

Marshall, Albert. 1920. *Principles of Economics.* 8th ed. London: Macmillan.

Martel, André. 1991. *La Libye 1835–1990: Essai de géopolitique historique.* Paris: Presses Universitaires de France.

Marx, Karl. 1972. *Capital.* London: Lawrence and Wishart.

Mason, John Paul. 1982. "Qadhdhafi's 'Revolution' and Change in a Libyan Oasis Community." *Middle East Journal* 36 (summer): 319–335.

——. 1978. "Petroleum Development and the Reactivation of Traditional Structure in a Libyan Oasis Community." *Economic Development and Cultural Change* 26 (July): 763–776.

Mattes, Hanspeter. 1982a. *Islam und Staatsaufbau: Das Theoretische Konzept und das Beispiel der Sozialistischen Libyschen Arabischen Volksgamahiriyya.* Masters thesis, University of Heidelberg, Germany.

——. 1982b. *Die Volksrevolution in der Sozialistischen Libyschen Arabischen Volksgamahiriyya.* Heidelberg: Kikouvou Verlag.

——. 1995a. "The Rise and Fall of the Revolutionary Committees." In *Qadhafi's Libya, 1969–1994,* ed. Dirk Vandewalle. New York: St. Martin's Press.

——. 1995b. *Qaddafi und die Islamistische Opposition in Libyen. Zum Verlauf eines Konflikts.* Hamburg: Deutsches Orient-Institut.

Mayer, Ann Elizabeth. 1995. "In Search of Sacred Law: The Meandering Course of Qadhafi's Legal Policy." In *Qadhafi's Libya, 1969–1994,* ed. Dirk Vandewalle. New York: St. Martin's Press.

——. 1990. "The Reinstatement of Islamic Criminal Law in Libya." In *Law and Islam in the Middle East,* ed. Daisy Dwyer. New York: Bergin and Garvey.

——. 1982. "Islamic Resurgence or New Prophethood: The Role of Islam in Qadhdafi's Ideology." In *Islamic Resurgence in the Arab World,* ed. Ali Hillal Dessouki. New York: Praeger.

——. 1981. "Le droit musulman en Libye à l'âge du 'Livre Vert.'" *Maghreb-Machrek* 33, no. 93 (July–August): 5–22.

——. 1977. *Islamic Law in Libya: Analyses of Selected Laws Enacted since the 1969 Revolution.* London: School of Oriental and African Studies.

Meier, Gerald M., ed. 1991. *Politics and Policy Making in Developing Countries: Perspectives on the New Political Economy.* San Francisco: International Center for Economic Growth.

Mezoughi, A. A. 1984. *Mafhum al-Idara ash-sha'biya* (The principles of administration). Tripoli: Green Book Center.

Migdal, Joel. 1994. "The State in Society: An Approach to Struggles for Domination." In *State Power and Social Forces: Domination and Transformation in the Third World,* ed. Joel Migdal, Atul Kohli, and Vivienne Shue. Cambridge: Cambridge University Press.

——. 1988. *Strong Societies and Weak States: State-Society Relations and State Capabilities in the Third World.* Princeton, N.J.: Princeton University Press.

Migdal, Joel, Atul Kohli, and Vivienne Shue, eds. 1994. *State Power and Social Forces. Domination and Transformation in the Third World.* New York: Cambridge University Press.

Mitchell, Timothy. 1991. "The Limits of the State: Beyond Statist Approaches and Their Critics." *American Political Science Review* 85 (March): 77–96.

Moe, Terry M. 1990. "Political Institutions: The Neglected Side of the Story." *Journal of Law, Economics, and Organization* 6: 213–254.

——. 1989. "The Politics of Bureaucratic Structure." In *Can the Government Govern?* eds. John E. Chubb and Paul E. Peterson. Washington, D.C.: Brookings Institution.

Moe, Terry M., and Michael Caldwell. 1994. "The Institutional Foundations of Democratic Government: A Comparison of Presidential and Parliamentary Systems." *Journal of Institutional and Theoretical Economics* 150, no. 1: 171–195.

el-Mogherbi, Mohamed Zahi. 1978. "The Socialization of School Children in the Socialist People's Libyan Arab Jamahiriya." Ph.D. diss., University of Missouri.

Monastiri, Taoufik. 1995. "Teaching the Revolution: Libyan Education since 1969." In *Qadhafi's Libya, 1969–1994,* ed. Dirk Vandewalle. New York: St. Martin's Press.

Moore, Mich. 1991. "Rent-Seeking and Market Surrogates: The Case of Irrigation Policy." In *States or Markets? Neo-Liberalism and the Development*

Policy Debate, ed. Christopher Colclough and James Manor. Oxford: Clarendon Press.

Mukhtar, Omar. 1984. "The Struggle for Libya." *Arabia* (June).

Najmabadi, Afsaneh. 1987. "Depoliticization of a Rentier State: The Case of Pahlavi Iran." In *The Rentier State,* ed. Hazem Beblawi and Giacomo Luciani. New York: Croom Helm.

Al-Naqib, Khaldun. 1989. *al-Mujtama' wa al-Dawla fi al-Khalij wa al-Jazira al-'Arabiyya Min Manzur Mukhtalif* (State and society in the Gulf and the Arabian Peninsula from a different perspective). Beirut: Markaz Dirasat al-Wihda al-'Arabiyya.

Nasser, Gamal Abdul. 1970. *Falsafat ath-Thawra wa al-Mithaq* (Philosophy of the Revolution). Beirut: Dar al-Qalam.

National Front for the Salvation of Libya. 1992. *Libya under Gaddafi and the NFSL Challenge.* Chicago: National Front for the Salvation of Libya.

Nettl, J.P. 1968. "The State as a Conceptual Variable." *World Politics* 20: 559–562.

Neuberger, Benjamin. 1982. *Involvement, Invasion and Withdrawal: Qadhdhafi's Libya and Chad 1969–1981.* Syracuse, N.Y.: Syracuse University Press.

North, Douglass C. 1990. *Institutions, Institutional Change and Economic Performance.* New York: Cambridge University Press.

——. 1981. *Structure and Change in Economic History.* New York: Norton.

North, Douglass C., and Barry R. Weingast. 1989. "Constitutions and Commitment: The Evolution of Institutions Governing Public Choice in Seventeenth-Century England." *Journal of Economic History* 49, no. 4 (December): 803–832.

Norton, Augustus Richard. 1995. *Civil Society in the Middle East.* New York: Brill.

Otayek, René. 1987. *La politique africaine de la Libye.* Paris: Karthala.

Owen, Roger. 1992. *State, Power and Politics: The Modern Middle East.* New York: Routledge.

Parsa, Misagh. 1989. *Social Origins of the Iranian Revolution.* New Brunswick, N.J.: Rutgers University Press.

Pelt, Adrian. 1970. *Libyan Independence and the United Nations: A Case of Planned Decolonization.* New Haven, Conn.: Yale University Press.

Perkins, Dwight, and Mike Roemer, eds. 1991. *Reforming Economic Systems in Developing Countries.* Cambridge: Harvard Institute for International Development.

Poggi, Gianfranco. 1978. *The Development of the Modern State: A Sociological Introduction.* Stanford, Calif.: Stanford University Press.

Polanyi, Karl. 1944. *The Great Transformation.* New York: Farrar and Rinehart.

Powell, Walter W., and Paul J. DiMaggio, eds. 1991. *The New Institutionalism in Organizational Analysis.* Chicago: University of Chicago Press.

al-Qadhafi, Mu'ammar. n.d. "Intervention at the First World Symposium on the Green Book." In *International Colloquium in Benghazi: The Green Book.* Tripoli: Foreign Liaison Office.

——. 1980. *The Green Book,* vols. 1–3. Tripoli: Green Book Center.

——. 1978. *The Revolutionary Declaration of Brother Col. M. al-Qadhafi, September 1, 1978.* Tripoli: Secretariat of Foreign Affairs.

——. 1969–1995. *As-Sijil al-Qawmi Bayanat wa Ahadith al-Aqid Mu'ammar al-Qadhafi* (The national register: declarations and speeches of Mu'ammar al-Qadhafi). Tripoli: Marakiz ath-thaqafiya al-qawmiya.

Quarterly Economic Review of Libya. London: Economist Intelligence Unit.

Rennell, Francis Rodd. 1948. *British Military Administration of Occupied Territories in Africa during the Years 1941–1947.* London: Her Majesty's Stationery Office.

Repetto, R. 1986. *Paying the Price: Rent-Seeking and the Performance of Public Irrigation Systems.* Washington, D.C.: World Resources Institute.

Revolutionary Committees n.d. membership card Tripoli: n.p.

Ricardo, David. 1953. "On the Principle of Political Economy and Taxation." In *The Works and Correspondence of David Ricardo,* by David Ricardo. Cambridge: Cambridge University Press.

Riker, William H. 1962. *The Theory of Political Coalitions.* New Haven, Conn.: Yale University Press.

Riker, William H., and David L. Weimer. 1995. "The Political Economy of Transformation: Liberalization and Property Rights." In *Modern Political Economy: Old Topics, New Directions,* ed. Jeffrey S. Banks and Eric A. Hanushek. New York: Cambridge University Press.

Riordan, E. Mick, et al., n.d. *The World Economy and Implications for the MENA Region, 1995–2010.* Working Paper Series, no. 9519. Cairo: Economic Research Forum.

Rizqana, Ibrahim. 1964. *al-Mamlaka al-Libiyya.* Cairo: Dar al-Nahda al-'Arabiyya.

Roemer, Michael. 1983. *Dutch Disease in Developing Countries.* Paper no. 156. Cambridge: Harvard Institute for International Development.

Rosecrance, Richard. 1986. *The Rise of the Trading State: Commerce and Conquest in the Modern World.* New York: Basic Books.

Roumani, Jacques. 1983. "From Republic to Jamahiriya: Libya's Search for Political Community." *Middle East Journal* 37, no. 2 (spring): 151–168.

——. 1973. "Libya and the Military Revolution." In *Man, State and Society in the Contemporary Maghrib,* ed. I. William Zartman. New York: Praeger.

Rubin, Barnett. 1995. *The Fragmentation of Afghanistan: State Formation and Collapse in the International System.* New Haven, Conn.: Yale University Press.

——. 1992. "Political Elites in Afghanistan: Rentier State Building, Rentier State Wrecking." *International Journal of Middle East Studies* 24: 77–99.

Rudolph, Susanne. 1987. "Presidential Address: State Formation in Asia—Prolegomenon to a Comparative Study." *Journal of Asian Studies* 46, no. 4: 731–746.

Salamé, Ghassan. 1987a. *al-Mujtama' wa al-Dawla fi al-Mashriq al-'Arabi* (State and society in the Arab East). Beirut: Markaz Dirasat al-Wihda al-'Arabiyya.

Salamé, Ghassan, ed. 1987b. *The Foundations of the Arab State.* New York: Croom Helm.

Al-Sanusi, Muhammad. 1947. *Kitab al-Masa'il al-'ashr* (The book of ten questions). Cairo: Matba'at al-I'timad.

Schumpeter, Joseph A. 1918. "The Crisis of the Tax State." In *Joseph R. Schumpeter: The Economics and Sociology of Capitalism,* ed. R. Swedberg. Princeton, N.J.: Princeton University Press, 1991.

Scott, W. Richard. 1991. "Unpacking Institutional Arrangements." In *The New Institutionalism in Organizational Analysis,* ed. Walter W. Powell and Paul J. DiMaggio. Chicago: University of Chicago Press.

Segrè, Claudio G. 1974. *Fourth Shore: The Italian Colonization of Libya.* Chicago: University of Chicago Press.

Sharabi, Hisham. 1988. *Neopatriarchy: A Theory of Distorted Change in Arab Society.* New York: Oxford University Press.

Sharabi, Hisham, ed. 1990. *Theory, Politics and the Arab World.* London: Routledge.

Shukri, Muhammad. 1948. *Al-Sanusiyya Din wa Dawla* (The Sanusiyya, religion and state). Cairo: Matba'at al-I'timad.

Shuruh Kitab al-Akhdar (Commentaries on the Green Book). 1984–1995. Tripoli: Green Book Center.

As-Sijil Al-Qawmi bayanat wa ahadith al-aqid Mu'ammar al-Qadhafi (The national register: declarations and speeches of Mu'ammar al-Qadhafi. 1969–1995. 26 vols. Tripoli: Marakiz ath-thaqafiya al-qawmiya.

Simons, Geoff. 1993. *Libya: The Struggle for Survival.* New York: St. Martin's Press.

Sirageldin, Ismail, and Motaz Khorshid. n.d. *Human Resource Development and the Structure of Oil Economies: Critical Issues with Illustrations from Kuwait.* Working Paper Series, no. 9518. Cairo: Economic Research Forum.

Skocpol, Theda. 1994. *Social Revolutions in the Modern World.* 2d ed. Cambridge: Harvard University Press.

——. 1985. "Bringing the State Back In: Strategies of Analysis in Current Research." In *Bringing the State Back In,* ed. Peter Evans, Dietrich Rueschemeyer, and Theda Skocpol. New York: Cambridge University Press.

——. 1982. "Rentier State and Shi'a Islam in the Iranian Revolution." *Theory and Society* 11, no. 3.

——. 1979. *States and Social Revolutions: A Comparative Analysis of France, Russia, and China.* New York: Cambridge University Press.

Skowronek, Stephen. 1982. *Building a New American State: The Expansion of National Administrative Capacities.* New York: Cambridge University Press.

Smith, Adam. 1884. *An Inquiry into the Nature and Causes of the Wealth of Nations.* London: Nelson and Sons.

Snider, Lewis. 1988. "Comparing the Strength of Nations: The Arab Gulf States and Political Change." *Comparative Politics* 20, no. 4: 461–484.

Souriau, Christiane. 1986. *Libye: l'économie des femmes.* Paris: L'Harmattan.

Spruyt, Hendrik. 1994. *The Sovereign State and Its Competitors: An Analysis of Systems Change.* Princeton, N.J.: Princeton University Press.

Steinmo, Sven. 1993. *Taxation and Democracy.* New Haven, Conn.: Yale University Press.

Stepan, Alfred. 1978. *The State and Society: Peru in Comparative Perspective.* Princeton, N.J.: Princeton University Press.

St. John, Ronald Bruce. 1991. *Historical Dictionary of Libya.* 2d ed. Methuchen, N.J.: Scarecrow Press.

——. 1983. "The Ideology of Mu'ammar al-Qadhdhafi: Theory and Practice." *International Journal of Middle East Studies* 15, no. 4 (November): 471–490.

——. 1987. *Qaddafi's World Design: Libyan Foreign Policy 1969–1987.* London: Saqi Books.

Strayer, John. 1970. *On the Medieval Origin of the Modern State.* Princeton, N.J.: Princeton University Press.

Tapper, Richard. 1990. "Anthropologists, Historians and Tribespeople on Tribe and State Formation in the Middle East." In *Tribes and State Formation,* ed. Philip S. Khoury and Joseph Kostiner. Berkeley: University of California Press.

Taylor, Michael. 1982. *Community, Anarchy and Liberty.* Cambridge: Cambridge University Press.

Thomas, Frederic C. 1973. "The Libyan Oil Worker." In *Man, State and Society in the Contemporary Maghrib,* ed. I. William Zartman. New York: Praeger.

Tilly, Charles. 1990. *Coercion, Capital, and European States, A.D. 990–1990.* Oxford: Basil Blackwell.

——. 1985. "War Making and State Making as Organized Crime." In *Bringing the State Back In,* ed. Peter Evans, Dietrich Rueschmeyer and Theda Skocpol. Cambridge: Cambridge University Press.

——, ed. 1975. *The Formation of Nation-States in Western Europe.* Princeton, N.J.: Princeton University Press.

Tollison, Robert. 1982. "Rent Seeking: A Survey." *Kyklos* 35: 28–47.

Trimberger, Ellen Kay. 1978. *Revolution from Above: Military Bureaucrats and Development in Japan, Turkey, Egypt, and Peru.* New Brunswick, N.J.: Transaction Books.

Tullock, Gordon. 1980. "Rent-Seeking as a Negative-Sum Game." In *Toward a Theory of a Rent-seeking Society,* ed. James M. Buchanan, Robert D. Tollison and Gordon Tullock. College Station: Texas A&M University Press.

——. 1974. *The Social Dilemma.* Blacksburg, Va.: University Publications.

United Nations. 1989. *National Accounts Statistics: Analysis of Main Aggregates 1988–1989.* New York: Author.

——. 1952. *A General Economic Appraisal of Libya.* New York: United Nations Technical Assistance Administration.

Vandewalle, Dirk. 1995a. "The Failure of Liberalization in the Jamahiriyya." In *Qadhafi's Libya, 1969–1994,* ed. Dirk Vandewalle. New York: St. Martin's Press.

——. 1995b. "The Libyan Jamahiriyya since 1969." In *Qadhafi's Libya, 1969–1994,* ed. Dirk Vandewalle. New York: St. Martin's Press.

——. 1994. "Research Facilities and Document Collections in the Socialist People's Libyan Arab Jamahiriyah." *Middle East Studies Association Bulletin* 28, no. 1 (July): 9–13.

——. 1991a. "L'economie libyenne: un développement très lent malgré des revenus pétroliers considérables." In *L'Etat du Maghreb,* ed. Camille Lacoste and Yves Lacoste. Paris: Editions La Découverte.

——. 1991b. "Qadhafi's 'Perestroika': Economic and Political Liberalization in Libya." *The Middle East Journal* 45, no. 2: 216–231.

——. 1991c. "The Libyan Revolution after Twenty Years, Part 1: Evaluating the Jamahiriyah." *Universities Field Staff International,* Africa/Middle East, no. 2.

——. 1991d. "The Libyan Revolution after Twenty Years, Part 2: A Libyan 'Perestroika'?" *Universities Field Staff International,* Africa/Middle East, no. 8.

——. 1990. "Qadhafi's Unfinished Revolution. *Mediterranean Quarterly* (winter.)

——. 1987. "Political Aspects of State Building in Rentier Economies: Algeria and Libya Compared." In *The Rentier State,* ed. Hazem Beblawi and Giacomo Luciani. London: Croom Helm.

——. 1986. "Libya's Revolution Revisited." *Middle East Report* 16, no. 6 (December): 30–35.

Vandewalle, Dirk, ed. 1996. *North Africa: Development and Reform in a Changing Global Economy.* New York: St. Martin's Press.

——. 1995. *Qadhafi's Revolution 1969–1994.* New York: St. Martin's Press.

van Wijnbergen, Sweder, and J. Peter Neary. 1986. *Natural Resources and the Macroeconomy.* Cambridge, Mass.: MIT Press.

Verba, Sidney. 1971. "Sequences and Development." In *Crisis and Sequences in Political Development,* by Leonard Binder et al. Princeton, N.J.: Princeton University Press.

Villard, Henry Serrano. 1956. *Libya: The New Arab Kingdom of North Africa.* Ithaca, N.Y.: Cornell University Press.

Waddams, Frank. 1980. *The Libyan Oil Industry.* Baltimore, Md.: Johns Hopkins University Press.

Wade, Robert. 1990. *Governing the Market. Economic Theory and the Role of Government in East Asian Industrialization.* Princeton, N.J.: Princeton University Press.

El-Warfally, Mahmoud. 1998. *Imagery and Ideology in U.S. Policy Toward Libya, 1969–1982.* Pittsburgh, Pa.: University of Pittsburgh.

Webber, Carolyn, and Aaron Wildavsky. 1986. *A History of Taxation and Expenditure in the Western World.* New York: Simon and Schuster.

Weber, Max. 1968. *Economy and Society.* New York: Bedminster Press.

——. 1947. *The Theory of Social and Economic Organization.* New York: Free Press.

Weiner, Myron, and Ali Banuazizi, eds. 1994. *The Politics of Social Transformation in Afghanistan, Iran, and Palistan.* Syracuse, N.Y.: Syracuse University Press.

Weingast, Barry R. 1994. "Institutional Foundations of the 'Sinews of Power': British Financial and Military Success Following the Glorious Revolution." In *Fiscal Crises, Liberty, and Representative Government, 1450–1789,* ed. Philip Hoffman and Kathryn Norberg. Stanford, Calif.: Stanford University Press.

World Bank. 1991. *Accelerated Development in Sub-Saharan Africa.* Washington, D.C.: International Bank for Reconstruction and Development.

——. 1992. *World Tables 1992.* Baltimore, Md.: Johns Hopkins University Press.

Wright, John. 1982. *Libya: A Modern History.* Baltimore, Md.: Johns Hopkins University Press.

Yala, Haji. 1981. "Les hydrocarbures, facteur d'industrialisation et d'accumulation pour l'économie libyenne." Ph.D. diss., University of Marseilles III.

Young, Crawford. 1982. *Ideology and Development in Africa.* New Haven, Conn.: Yale University Press.

Young, Oran. 1986. "International Regimes: Toward a New Theory of Institutions." *World Politics* 39, no. 1: 104–122.

INDEX